o EXTREMELY LOW for CASH.
July 20th, 1829. 270-Y.

BRITISH AND INDIA GOODS.

R. A. PARKER,

just received a general assortment of Fancy and aple DRY GOODS, suitable for the season; to-ith a Choice assortment of GROCERIES, WINES RITUOUS LIQUORS, CROCKERY, China and are; AMERICAN GOODS, Looking Glasses, Dye ad Dye Stuffs, Oil and Paints; Window Glass, owder & Shot; Iron, Steel, Nails, Shovels, Spades, erm Candles; Tobacco, Sperm Oil, Rosin, Pitch, , and a variety of other Goods, all of which will HOLESALE OR RETAIL at LOW PRICES.
Street, York, July 23rd, 1829. 270-Y.

New HAT STORE YORK.

JOHN BENNETT, wishes respectfully to inform his friends and the pub-e has commenced the Hatting business, on Yonge between Montgomery's and Wilmot's taverns, e has and intends keeping on hand a general as-of Hats and Bonnets, which he flatters himself as good quality and as cheap as can be had else-

All orders received with thankfulness and atten-th punctuality.
anted.
th, 1829. 265z.

EAM BOAT HOTEL.

THE subscriber begs leave to inform the Public in general, that he has taken the Steamboat Hotel, lately occupied by Mr. Ulick Howard, the elegant and extensive accommodations of which are so well known. He also begs leave to acquaint them that he has engaged Mr. ok, and his other servants are of the best des-His house will be at all times found supplied with ovisions, Wines, and all other sorts of Liquors; pains nor expense will be spared to render his at worthy the patronage it has so long enjoyed.
JOHN BRADLEY.
March, 1829.
Dixon is well known to be a first rate Cook, ha-with the Governor for three years, and also with emen of the first respectability in the province.
252-z.

York Hotel.

SUBSCRIBER respectfully begs leave to rm his Friends and the Public in gene-he has opened a TAVERN, in that old d House, formerly occupied by Mrs. JANE and known by the name of the

"YORK HOTEL,"

e is constantly supplied with Liquors, c. &c. of the first quality. Gentlemen Country will find it to their advantage to this HOTEL, the charges being mode-the accommodations not excelled by any Being in a retired part of the Town, it ably suited to those resident gentlemen, d prefer a House of Entertainment, secure noise and bustle usually attendant on the uented parts of this City.
JOHN MARTIN.
July 8th, 1829 268-z.

E LOVERS OF GOOD EATING!

JAMES BELL respectfully informs the public, that he has commenced Innkeeping at the House formerly occupied by Mr. Wilmot, SIGN OF THE HALF MOON, in New-Street, near the Market square, York. mmodation for Travellers and Boarders, on the nable terms; and the best of Beer, Wine, and Liquors, always on hand; and good lodging; accommodation for horses. With these assu-olicits a share of public patronage.
ept. 10, 1829. 277z

PERRY, BLACKSMITH, Respect-informs his friends and the public, that complete operation a large TURNING capable of turning nine feet long and nches in diameter, & a GRIND STONE the same machine, for his AXES; also SCREW-PLATES for mill work, and WORK or carriages. HORSE SHOE and other repairs on a short notice.

Sauces, Pickles, East India Preserves, Candied Lemons, Citron, and Orange Peel.
Anchovy Paste and Fresh Curry.
Codfish of various kinds.
Digby and Lochfine Herrings.
English Cheese—Dolphin, King's Arms, Berkley, Pine Apple, Truckle, and Double Glocester.
English Wax and Sperm Candles.
Window Glass of all sizes.
Decanters, Tumblers, Wine Glasses, and English Jars.
Tobacco, Snuff, Havanna Cigars, and Pipes.
Paper—Fools, Pot, and Wrapping.
Brushes, Blacking, &c. &c. &c.
JAMES F. SMITH,
Corner of Church and Palace Streets.
November 15th, 1829.
☞ He daily expects Oysters, (in shell,) Lobsters, Mackarel, North Shore Herring, and Salmon pickled and smoked. 2879.

NOTICE.

THE Subscriber, Eldest son and heir of the late Captain James Fulton, of Markham, in the county of York, in the Home District, requests all persons who have claims against his father's estate to forward them to him without delay, properly authenticated, for payment; and those who are indebted to the said estate are requested to make immediate payment of their several debts to the Subscriber.
JAMES FULTON.
Richmond Hill, Markham, Nov. 13th, 1829. 2873

Stray Ox and Steer.

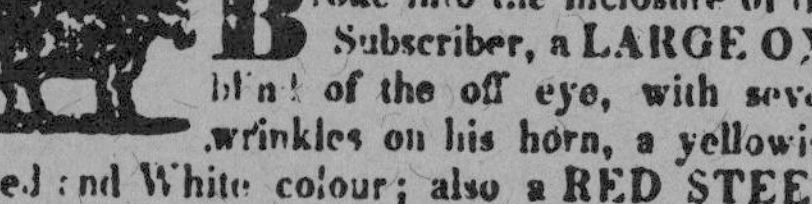

Broke into the inclosure of the Subscriber, a LARGE OX, blind of the off eye, with seven wrinkles on his horn, a yellowish Red and White colour; also a RED STEER with him, nearly three years old; with a brindle face, and part white under his breast. The owner or owners are requested to prove property, pay charges, and take the animals away.
THOMAS BURRELL.
Lot No. 10, of the 4th Concession, East of the centre-road, Toronto.
Nov. 19 1829. 2874.

Strayed Cow.

STRAYED from a Field, near the Don Bridge, a Black Cow, with a small Streak of White under her belly, her horns on the top are cut off. Whoever has found the same, and will bring her to the Subscriber, shall be handsomely rewarded for their trouble.
J. C. GODWIN.
York 17th Nov. 1829. 2873.

HOTEL AND LANDS IN TORONTO FOR SALE.

THE subscriber offers for sale, by private bargain, that valuable freehold property, on Dundas Street, Toronto, known by the name of "CODY'S TAVERN;" comprising the Inn itself, which has been long and well established as a stopping place for Travellers, on the great western thoroughfare; and one, or five, or one hundred acres of land immediately adjoining, as might be found most suitable for a purchaser; also the stables, out-houses, Gardens, yard, &c. thereto annexed.

*** The property will be sold very low indeed for cash, or if one half or one third of the purchase money is paid down. Immediate possession can be given, and, for further particulars appply to
PHILIP CODY.
Toronto, Nov. 16th, 1829. 287z.

WHERE IS WILLIAM SUTHERLAND?

THE Subscriber is desirous of ascertaining the place of abode of Mr. William Sutherland and family. They lived in or near Glengarry, about the time of the last war, and were originally from the parish of Kindonan, Sutherlandshire. Address a letter to the Subscriber, at Niagara, care of Messrs. Chrysler, Merchants.
N. B. Mrs. Sutherland's maiden name was Catharine Macpherson.
DANIEL MACPHERSON.
Niagara, 17th Nov. 1829. 2873.

e well delivered at his mills, at Springfield, River Credit, Toronto.
JOHN McGILL.
November 12th, 1829. 268

Grist Mill, ... Mill, ... Dwel... Sale; ... LET.

...perty in the Village of Stony Creek and its vicinity, consisting of a NEW GRIST and SAW-MILL, and several MILL SCITES, on the same stream; Seventy acres of Land, with quantity of excellent Pine Timber; a very COMMODIOUS HOUSE, and OUT-HOUSES, &c. well situated for kind of public business.
The above Property extends from the Village to the of the Mountain; is very beautiful, and affords an extensive prospect of Lake Ontario, the Burlington Canal, surrounding country. All of which property will be s on the most advantageous terms to purchasers.
Also; TO LET, for one or more years, the SA WORKS of the Subscriber.
For further particulars, apply to the subscriber, on premises.
Stoney Creek, Nov. 13, 1829. WILLIAM KENT. 87z

THE SUBSCRIBERS have just received direct fr London, a general assortment of
Hosiery,
Black and Colored Gros-de-Naples,
Figured Norwich Crapes,
Black Silk and Cotton Velvets,
Sewing Silks,
Lace Thread Edgings,
Worked Insertions, and Scollop Muslins,
Reed and Bell Cotton,
Geo. the 4th Regulation Swords, Belts, a Sashes,
Hardware and Cutlery,
With a general Stock of Saddlery: also an extensive ortment of West of England Cloths, &c. &c.
J. C. GODWIN & Co.
York, 14th Oct. 1829. 282z.

FOR SALE, by the Subscribers, either wholesale retail,

20 Jars Superfine Mustard

Families will find it to their advantage to purchase it b the pound instead of in bottles, as it is commonly sold.
ALSO, FOR SALE, 50 Barrels of
SUPERIOR OLD WHISKEY.
J. C. GODWIN & Co.
York, 14th Oct. 1829. 282z

MIDWIFERY.

MRS. SARAH TEBBUTT respectfully informs the inhabitants of York and its vicinity, that she practised for several years as a Midwife in England, and will be ready to attend families in that capacity, either in the Town or neighborhood of York.
☞ Refers to Dr. WIDMER.
Newgate-Street, Oct. 6th, 1829. 281z

NEWMARKET MAIL STAGE.

WILLIAM GARBUTT, having taken the contract for carrying His Majesty's Mails between York and Newmarket, for the next four years, respectfully informs the public that THE MAIL STAGE will start from Joseph Bloor's Hotel, York, on Mondays and Thursdays, at 12 o'clock, noon, and arrive at nine o'clock, the same evening in Newmarket;—and will leave Mr. Barber's Tavern Newmarket, for York, on Wednesdays and Saturdays, at in the morning, and arrive in York at 2 P. M. on the same days.
Price for passengers conveyed between York and Newmarket, six shillings and three pence currency, and in proportion for shorter distances. Packages carried on the route at moderate rates.
Mr. BARBER will accommodate passengers arriving with the Mail Stage at Newmarket; and they may be comfortably conveyed to the Holland Landing, or in other directions if required.
York, March 30th, 1829. 254z.

TOMB STONES.—The advertisers offer for sale, at their yard, back of Sprage's Central School, Tomb Stones, Polished Hearths, and Stove Pipe Stones, Jaumbs, Lentils, &

Tavern in the Town

Margaret McBurney

Mary Byers.

Margaret McBurney and Mary Byers

Early Inns and Taverns of Ontario

PHOTOGRAPHY BY HUGH ROBERTSON

UNIVERSITY OF TORONTO PRESS
Toronto Buffalo London

Toronto Buffalo London
Printed in Canada
ISBN 0-8020-5732-2

Canadian Cataloguing in Publication Data

McBurney, Margaret, 1931–
Tavern in the town

Bibliography
Includes index.
ISBN 0-8020-5732-2

1. Hotels, taverns, etc. – Ontario – History.
2. Historic buildings – Ontario. 3. Ontario –
Social life and customs. I. Byers, Mary, 1933-
II. Title.

TX950.59.C3M22 1987 647′.9471301 C87-094666-8

This book has been published with the assistance of the Canada Council and the Ontario Arts Council under their block grant programs.

Contents

Lake
Nipigon

HIGHWAY 11

Thunder Bay

LAKE SUPERIOR

ONTA

Sault Ste Marie

St Mary's River

LAK
HUR

LAKE MICHIGAN

UNITED
STATES

Detroit

Detroit R.

Windsor

Amherstburg

Leami

TAL

Tavern in the Town

JAMES FULTON.

Richmond Hill, Markham, Nov. 13th, 1829. 2873

Stray Ox and Steer.

Broke into the inclosure of the Subscriber, a LARGE OX, blind of the off eye, with seven wrinkles on his horn, a yellowish Red and White colour; also a RED STEER with him, nearly three years old; with a brindle face, and part white under his breast. The owner or owners are requested to prove property, pay charges, and take the animals away.

... deed for cash, or if one half or one third of the purchase money is paid down. Immediate possession can be given, and, for further particulars apply to PHILIP CODY.

Toronto, Nov. 16th, 1829. 287z.

WHERE IS WILLIAM SUTHERLAND?

THE Subscriber is desirous of ascertaining the place of abode of Mr. William Sutherland and family. They lived in or near Glengarry, about the time of the last war, and were originally from the parish of Kindonan, Sutherlandshire. Address a letter to the Subscriber, at Niagara, care of Messrs. Chrysler, Merchants.

N. B. Mrs. Sutherland's maiden name was Catharine Macpherson.

DANIEL MACPHERSON.

Niagara, 17th Nov. 1829. 2873.

Boarding.

THE Subscriber can furnish Boarding, Lodging, &c. for six steady mechanics, reasonable, on Dundas Street, between Mr. Willmot's Tavern and four doors from Mr. Bird's Tavern, in the house lately occupied by Mr. George Hutchison, Plaisterer.

JAMES PARKER.

Nov. 18. 87.

STRAYED, on the 10th October last, into the premises of ANDREW BIGHAM, on lot No. 12, in the first concession of ETOBICOKE, A LIGHT IRON-GREY HORSE, rising five or six years of age.—The owner is requested to prove property, pay charges, and take him away.

Nov. 17. 873.

SAWYER & LABOURERS WANTED.

WANTED by the subscriber, a Sawyer who understands his business, and two men who understand Chopping; to whom liberal encouragement will be given. Apply to JAMES STEPHENS.

WORKS of the Subscriber. For further particulars, apply to the subscriber, on premises.

WILLIAM KENT

Stoney Creek, Nov. 13, 1829. 87z

THE SUBSCRIBERS have just received direct from London, a general assortment of Hosiery, Black and Colored Gros-de-Naples, Figured Norwich Crapes, Black Silk and Cotton Velvets, Sewing Silks, Lace Thread Edgings, Worked Insertions, and Scollop Muslins, Reel and Ball Cotton, Geo. the 4th Regulation Swords, Belts, Sashes, ... ware and Cutlery, ... eral Stock of Saddlery: also an extensive ... of England Cloths, &c. &c.

J. C. GODWIN & Co.

NEWMARKET MAIL STAGE.

WILLIAM GARBUTT, having taken the contract for carrying His Majesty's Mails between York and Newmarket, for the next four years, respectfully informs the public that THE MAIL STAGE will start from Joseph Bloor's Hotel, York, on Mondays and Thursdays, 12 o'clock, noon, and arrive at nine o'clock, the same evening in Newmarket;—and will leave Mr. Barber's Tavern, Newmarket, for York, on Wednesdays and Saturdays, in the morning, and arrive in York at 2 P. M. on the same days.

Price for passengers conveyed between York and Newmarket, six shillings and three pence currency, and in proportion for shorter distances. Packages carried on the route at moderate rates.

Mr. BARBER will accommodate passengers arriving with the Mail Stage at Newmarket; and they may be comfortably conveyed to the Holland Landing, or in other directions if required.

York, March 30th, 1829. 254z

NEW ARRANGEMENT OF STAGES

Between York and the Carrying Place at the head of the Bay of Quintie.

THE Public are respectfully informed that a Mail Stage will run regularly twice a week between York and the Carrying Place; leaving York every Monday and Thursday at 12 o'clock, noon, and arriving at the Carrying Place on Tuesdays and Fridays at 2 o'clock, P. M. Will leave the Carrying Place every Tuesday and Friday at ... o'clock A. M. and arrive at York on Wednesdays and Saturdays, at 12 o'clock noon. There will also a Stage leave Cobourg every Monday at 10 o'clock, A. M. and arrive at the Carrying Place the same day, and leave the Carrying Place every Saturday at 9 o'clock, A. M. and arrive at Cobourg the same day.

The above arrangements are in connexion with the Steam Boats *Sir James Kempt* and *Toronto*, so that Travellers going the route will find a pleasant and speedy conveyance between Kingston and York, as the line is now fitted up in good order with good carriages, good horses and careful drivers.

Every attention will be given to render passengers comfortable while on the line, and the drivers instructed to stop at the best hotels on the route.

All baggage at the risk of the owners.

Extras furnished to any part of the country.

The Stage Books will be kept at Mr. Bradley's Steamboat Hotel.

The roads between Kingston and York are of late much improved.

SALT RHEUM.—This inveterate disease, which has long baffled the art of the most experienced physicians, has, at length, found a sovereign remedy in Dr. La Grange's genuine ointment. ...

PETER PATERSON, *Agent.*

SWEDES IRON.

Landing from the Ship *General Wolfe*, direct from GOTTENBURGH, ... ASSORTED SWEDES IRON. Apply to WILLIAM BUDDEN, *Point a' Callier.*

Montreal, August 18, 1829. 274z

LOOKING GLASSES.

Just received by the subscriber, a large and elegant assortment of Looking Glasses; German Plate; ... sizes, and the prices remarkably low.

J. R. ARMSTRONG.

Sept. 16th, 1829.

YORK FURNACE.

F. R. DUTCHER continues his FURNACE in complete operation, where can be had, at short notice,

Castings of any description from one to thirty cwt:

Also on hand a general assortment of STOVES, HOLLOW WARE, PLOUGH CASTINGS and PLOUGHS.

F. R. D. having erected a first rate Lathe for Iron, is ready to complete any order at short notice.

Sept. 22.

THEODORE BURLEY,

SMITH AND *Brass Founder:*

Yonge Street, next door to Judge Macaulay.

BRASS CASTINGS for Mill work, &c. &c. done on the shortest notice. ... White and Blacksmith's work done to order. The highest prices, in CASH, will be paid for old copper and tin.

Sept. 24th, 1829.

Introduction

'No tippling.' That restriction, found on virtually every list of tavern regulations in nineteenth-century Upper Canada, seems contradictory. If tippling couldn't take place in a tavern, then where could it? But the ancient meaning of the word, 'to drip slowly,' says it all. Tippling originally meant 'slow and continuous drinking' – and when the product of the local still dripped slowly down a customer's throat for too many hours, the result was predictable. Innkeepers who allowed tippling could be fined or could lose their licences. Sometimes they landed in the stocks.

If an innkeeper's lot was not always an easy one, innkeeping nevertheless offered considerable scope to those with energy and imagination. Of necessity the innkeeper was a jack-of-all-trades, functioning as everything from banker to businessman to judge. The local tavern became all things to all settlers, and its incumbent was the linchpin of every pioneer settlement.

It is not surprising, then, that innkeepers were among the province's first successful entrepreneurs. Opportunities were available in abundance. Because innkeeping and travel were so closely linked, involvement in the stage-coach, ferry, and steamship businesses could make a talented innkeeper a wealthy man. He could, and often did, serve as travel agent, banker, realtor, theatrical producer, and officer of the court, as well as host to the banquets and balls that took place within the inn's sheltering walls. He was often one of the pioneer community's most respected and influential citizens. Take, for instance, John Dynes, long-time host in Burlington. When his hostelry burned to the ground his loyal patrons rebuilt it for him, with donations handled through the office of the Hamilton *Spectator.* (Not all innkeepers, of course, were pillars of the community – many a shifty host presented bills that were as full of 'extras' as his beds were full of fleas.)

As soon as there were roads, even narrow trails through the bush, there were inns and taverns. Their presence was essential to the settlers travelling the stump-strewn, hazardous length of these routes. In fact when the Huron Tract was being cut into western Ontario the government paid innkeepers to establish inns along the road from Guelph to Goderich. These early establishments were as primitive as the trails they bordered, but they served so many diverse purposes that a fledgling community could hardly develop without them.

Inns were much more than drinking and lodging places. Until town halls were built later in the century the inn was often a community's only public building. Every imaginable activity took place there – political meetings, sales of Crown lands, distribution of lots, church services, Sunday school, court sessions, township-council sessions, and all public entertainments. The Legislative Assembly of Upper Canada met in a Toronto tavern and, some years later, plans for the Mackenzie Rebellion were hatched within tavern walls in the same town. After mid-century, travelling salesmen appeared on the scene. They set up their wares at inns in every town they visited, their showmanship providing local patrons with entertainment that was a change from the usual political wrangling and the occasional brawl. Doctors, dentists, photographers, and travelling artisans frequently met their public in the local hostelry.

During the stage-coach era the inn was the place to go for news of the day. Because newspapers arrived erratically, it was often travellers and stage drivers who spread the news from village inn to village inn. Trials took place in these inns, with punishment meted out conveniently in the inn courtyard. The first man sentenced to death in Upper Canada was convicted and hanged at a tavern near Kingston. In an old hostelry off the Pelham Road near St Catharines, local legend holds, prisoners were tried, convicted, and hanged in the yard outside the door.

In early days, it could be said that everyone's house served as an inn at one time or another. When settlement was sparse there were stretches of road where, in the absence of a regular inn, a hospitable settler (even with his house brimful of children) would offer the weary traveller a place to sleep, if only on the floor. Travellers learned to be grateful for any shelter, however meagre.

At the heart of the system was the intrepid traveller. We have made extensive use of the original journals of travellers, and those who took the time to vent their feelings in their diaries each night are fellow authors of this work. Their words have an immediacy that no present-day descriptions can provide. The sights, sounds, and smells of the halfway houses come to life in such chilling descriptions as 'beefsteak ... cold and stiff, entombed under a coating of congealed grease and butter,' and 'certain little vampyres, the terror and torment of weary travellers.' These diaries suggest that masochism – or at least stoicism – might have been an essential part of a traveller's character; certainly few could endure the vicissitudes of travel without one or the other. One also senses, however, that many writers, with an eye on future publication, didn't hesitate to heap scorn on everything new or different in order to impress gullible readers with their worldliness.

One frustration prompted more emotional outpourings than either the state of the roads or the quality of the accommodation – and resulted in clashes of memorable proportions. British travellers frequently found themselves sharing a table, a fireside, and even a bed with someone from a lower social class. They were shocked to the marrow of their aristocratic bones. The problem was even worse when the 'inferior' individual happened to be an upstart Yankee who, with his egalitarian views, was likely to consider himself the equal of anyone, aristocrat or no. Collisions occurred with some regularity, for most innkeepers were either American or Irish. As one anguished diarist recorded: 'I felt my English blood almost boil in my veins when I found myself sitting in company with two servant women at the table d'hote,' or 'neither man, woman nor child in the British Isles now troubled themselves about the war of American Independence, except to think their ancestors unwise for having fought about it.' A British traveller might refer condescendingly to a settler of American descent either as a Yankee or as 'brother Jonathan' (after Connecticut Governor Jonathan Trumbull [1710–85] who rendered great service to the rebel cause during the American Revolution and who, according to tradition, was so called by George Washington).

Once settlement began, it didn't take long for the government to draw up a list of regulations for taverns and inns – regulations that governments have been revising and extending ever since. Then as now the purpose was two-fold: to set minimum standards and to raise money for the government. As early as 1774 the British Parliament passed a law introducing a tavern licensing system into what was then the Province of Quebec, which, in 1791, was divided into Upper and Lower Canada. The act established pragmatically 'a fund towards further defraying the charges of the administration of justice, and support of the civil government within the Province of Quebec in America.' This umbrella was later expanded by a Statute of Upper Canada, which noted that the salaries of the Legislative Council and House of Assembly would be paid from tavern, shop, and still

London District,

TO WIT;

In General Quarter Sessions of the Peace, held at London, this Sixteenth day of April,
1832;

IT IS ORDERED,

That as Inns and Houses of Public Entertainment are established and authorised for the convenience and accommodation of Travellers, and not for the encouragement of Tippling and Drinking :---

No Inn-keeper shall suffer or allow any person whatever, to be Tippling, or unnecessarily Drinking, in or about the Inn or Premises.

No Inn-keeper shall allow or suffer profane language or obscene conversation in his House.

No Inn-keeper shall allow or suffer any Gaming at Dice, Cards, or otherwise, in his House, or in any place adjoining thereto.

That every Inn-keeper shall keep good and sufficient Sheds, Stable, and Barn, for the safe keeping of Horses, Carriages, and Wagons; and shall have some person at all times in attendance to take charge of the same.

That every Inn-keeper shall provide and keep at least Four good Beds, for the use of Travellers, besides those required for the use of his Family.

J. B. Askin,

Clerk of the Peace, London District.

The Patriot Office, London.

Tavern regulations

licences. The authority to issue these licences rested initially in the hands of the governor of the colony, then, from 1818 to 1849, with provincial magistrates; from 1849 to 1876 with municipal governments; and since that time with the provincial government.

Every few years another statute appeared on the books, as succeeding governments tackled the ever-present difficulties created by the vagaries of human nature and the growing demand for well-run, comfortable accommodation. The authorities recognized that a sufficient number of inns to serve the pioneer communities was necessary for the settlement of the province. However, the innkeeper was a person of sufficient importance that he must be carefully selected; and though a judicious use of alcohol might be considered beneficial, alcohol abuse was a growing threat to the pioneer community.

For these reasons, controls were aimed at limiting the number of houses that merely dispensed spirits and encouraging those that offered accommodation. In order to ensure minimum standards it was decreed that three or four beds must be available for travellers, plus stabling and other facilities. In an effort to ensure that there were enough inns operating, the government accepted petitions from persons who felt there was inadequate provision in their area. In order to obtain a licence to dispense 'spiritous liquors' a candidate needed character endorsements that vouched for his sobriety, honesty, and diligence. Numerous acts were passed to control drunkenness, and heavy fines were levied on any innkeeper who allowed excessive drinking, in particular drinking that led to death by accident or suicide.

Breaches of regulations were to be reported by government-appointed inspectors. The position of Inspector of Taverns, Shops, and Stills was a plum because the inspector was paid and also got a percentage of the fees he collected. The first inspectors were appointed in 1803, one for each of the eight districts that then comprised Upper Canada. When John Cumming, inspector of the Midland District, died in 1829, fifteen eager applicants scrambled for his job. The applications, which were made to Lieutenant-Governor Sir John Colborne, were all endorsed by every prominent clergyman and magistrate the candidates could enlist. Coveted though it seems to have been, the position was not without hazards. Cumming reported that when he had sent out Constable Robert Young several times to seize an unlicensed still, the constable was 'in many instances threatened with the loss of his life.' Some things, of course, never change. One hopeful candidate in Walkerton was told that the stumbling block in the way of his getting a tavern licence was politics. He was a Grit, and therefore, 'If he would change his politics, the licence would be all right.' By another wrinkle in the regulations, those who reported violations received half of the fine imposed, a situation that begged for abuse.

Licensed or unlicensed, the local stills produced the liquid that made pioneer life endurable. And what was it like? Often foul. Most operators claimed that their whisky was made from the best grain and the purest water, but some of their customers disagreed. One speculated that the ingredients were most likely 'frosty potatoes, hemlock, pumpkins and black mouldy rye.' As the product of the stills was usually sold the day after the distilling process was completed, the word 'mellow' was hardly applicable to its taste. Whisky advertised as 'old' had been sitting for a month.

Quality improved when the large distillers (Henry Corby, Hiram Walker, J.P. Wiser, James Worts, William Gooderham, and Joseph Emm Seagram) became established in mid-century. The big distilling operations were allied to milling and cattle raising. When a farmer brought his grain to the mill the surplus was distilled for him, with the owner of the mill receiving a portion of the product in return. Some millers soon found that distilling was a more lucrative enterprise than milling. A fifty-six-pound bushel of grain yielded about three gallons of spirits and sold for twenty cents. There was a link to the livestock business. The garbage of the distilling process was a liquid waste or 'mash' that was excellent for fattening cattle and pigs. This sort of feed caused the animals' teeth to fall out, but they met their end in a good frame of mind.

There were a variety of ways in which the taste of raw spirits could be disguised. We have included on page 241, for interest's sake only, a number of recipes that were popular in pioneer days. Some of the ingredients, however, are either suspect or no longer available. These concoctions are not recommended for current use.

Early barns, mills, churches, houses, and public buildings have all been the subject of serious research. The lowly tavern, by contrast, has been somewhat neglected by scholars. This reticence was in part the result of Victorian sensibilities – early historians sometimes chose to ignore the presence of the local hostelry, which, sad to say, was at times the scene of gambling, drunkenness, and prostitution – in spite of valiant attempts by the authorities to curtail these timeless human vices. The exception to the general scholarly neglect is a major one – the extensive work of E.C. Guillet in the 1950s for his five-volume *Pioneer Inns and Taverns,* the definitive study of the subject. To him we owe an enormous debt.

Most of the inns discussed in this book were built during the stage-coach era, before the coming of the railroad changed the face of the province. They were selected because they were built as inns and because their appearance has changed little over the years. Some few still offer accommodation; others meals only. However many are now private homes.

We have not discussed the architecture of these buildings extensively, but have left many such details to be communicated directly through the photographs of Hugh Robertson. As these photographs indicate, the hostelry with a two-storey verandah well endowed with bargeboard is the

ST. ANDREW'S SOCIETY!

Scotchmen and their descendants

are requested to meet at the

Albion Hotel, Court-house Avenue

— ON —

THURSDAY NEXT, THE 30TH INST.,

AT 9:30 O'CLOCK, A.M.,

To Walk in Procession to St. Andrew's Church,

Where a SERMON will be preached by the Rev. H. J. Borthwick, M.A.

THE ANNUAL DINNER

Will take place in the evening, at 8 o'clock when some eloquent Addresses will be delivered by strangers as well as citizens.

☞ Good Vocal and Instrumental Music will also enliven the proceedings

Tickets $1.50 Each.

Can be had at McGillivray's, Upper Town; Scott's, Centre Town, Miles' Hair-Dressing Saloon, and Nicholson's Confectionery, Rideau Street; and of the members of Committee.

J. P. ROBERTSON,
Hon. Secretary.

Ottawa, Nov. 25th, 1865. 428-4in

Daily Union, Ottawa

hallmark of the breed, though many such buildings have lost their verandahs over the years, and other styles certainly existed. One tell-tale mark of an inn was the presence of two doors, one on the side of the building leading to the taproom; ladies could avoid the rowdier elements by using the main entrance.

We could not have found many of the inns without the help of historical societies and a host of co-operative individuals throughout the province. We began our search by writing to every historical society in Ontario and many Local Architectural Conservation Advisory Committees (LACACs) as well. Thanks to an enthusiastic response we were given many leads to follow and, in the process of doing so, we found many more. Over the past four years we have tracked down more than two hundred early inns, and have selected those with the fewest architectural changes for current photographs.

In choosing the buildings, we assessed the information available about the past history of particular inns so we could present a picture of important events that took place in them. We have included several inns that are now part of pioneer villages. These seemed important because their interiors have been restored to give a feeling for the way in which an early inn was furnished. Such furnishings were usually a far cry from what is found in old inns that have been refurbished to serve the public today. The present amenities are delightful. The early ones were rarely more than primitive.

As we marked the inns on a map of the province, old stage-coach routes sprang into outline, much as a child's join-the-numbers puzzle produces a picture when the numbers are connected. Each chapter therefore covers one of these old roads – which fan out like the spokes of a wheel, with Toronto as the hub. There were, as well, themes that naturally associated themselves with a study of inns, and we have covered one in each chapter. In the case of

Toronto, we have included a number of inns that are no longer standing and have used old drawings to represent them. Since the face of Toronto has changed so dramatically, there are few old hostelries left, but they were exceedingly important at one time.

We found a universal interest in the subject. People to whom we spoke casually about our work often commented that they knew of an old inn near them or had always been curious about one they regularly passed in their travels. We hope that this book will encourage some recognition of these important buildings and their role in the settlement of the province. We also 'met' some of the unforgettable characters who played a leading role in the history of Ontario. Among these are 'The Laird' MacNab of the Ottawa Valley, 'Tiger' Dunlop, and Thomas Talbot – eccentrics and, in a figurative sense, giants whose exploits dispel forever the belief that our history is dull.

Too often books that purport to be architectural and social histories of Ontario ignore the vast northern part of the province. We have therefore included two inns in northern Ontario. Clearly two hostelries cannot fully represent the many that served the area, but the two inns we have included, in Sault Ste Marie and Swastika, indicate, respectively, the role of inns in the fur trade and in the period of gold and silver mining. Hotels in northern Ontario chiefly came with the advent of the railroad; thus most date after 1900. They nevertheless served the same crucial purpose as earlier inns in facilitating settlement.

There are many different words applied to buildings that offered accommodation, food, and drink to the public. The term 'tavern' is usually associated with establishments that offered only food and drink, whereas 'inn' suggests an establishment that also offered accommodation. Also used are 'house of entertainment' and 'hostelry.' In fact all these terms were practically synonymous at the time, since many buildings called 'taverns' also offered rooms. Another term for an inn was 'halfway house.' We were told time after time that a certain inn was called a halfway house because it was halfway between two local points. It may well be true that such inns were approximately halfway between two locations, but the term was actually used interchangeably with inn and tavern.

As is always the case in dealing with surnames in historical documents there is little consistency in spelling. We have used the earliest spelling available from a reliable original source, recognizing that it may differ from the spelling in current use. The question of spelling occurs with one word that, given the subject of our study, occurs with some frequency. We have used the Canadian and Scottish spelling for whisky (Irish and American spelling being whiskey).

Only the words of a traveller of the period can convey the pleasure of a warm welcome after the rigours of travel on the bad roads of the time. W.H.G. Kingston, travelling in the bush near Barrie in 1853, feared the worst as he approached a backwoods tavern. He expressed in his journal that night what so many felt when they entered the door of good simple inn.

> At about eight o'clock we came bumping up to Mrs Barr's clearing and inn. It was a regular log-hut, or rather house composed of huge trunks of trees, grooves being chopped in their ends so as to allow of one fitting into the other. It had several rooms. The entrance had a noble, wide chimney and fireplace, worthy of the mediaeval age, full of blazing logs, in front of which sat a number of rough backwoodsmen, regular pioneers of civilisation, smoking short black pipes. Upstairs were six little rooms lined with plank, and in each was a clean bed, a table, and chair, so neat and comfortable that we were well content at the thoughts of resting there. In a good-sized inner room, neatly lined and roofed with the ruddy pine-boards, on a long table, with a clean white cloth, was laid out a capital supper and tea – consisting of wild-pigeon pies, cold lamb [and] excellent hot potatoes.

Inns along the St Lawrence River

CHAPTER ONE

Inns along the St Lawrence River

THE INNKEEPER

'John Chitty is a favourite name,
His old hotel was known to fame,
And travellers, from far and near,
Called at his temple of good cheer.

And there in whitewashed shanty grand,
With kegs and bottles on each hand,
Her face decked with a winning smile,
Her head with cap of ancient style,
Crowned arbiter of frolic's fate,
Mother McGinty sat in state,
And measured out the mountain dew
To those whom strong attraction drew
Within the circle of her power
To while away a leisure hour.
She was the hostess and the host,
She kept the reckoning, ruled the roast,
And swung an arm of potent might
That few would dare to brave in fight.'

W.P. Lett, *Recollections of Bytown and Its Old Inhabitants*, Ottawa, 1874

GILLES BOURBONNAIS was the owner of a stage-coach inn in Lancaster Township, Glengarry County. His hostelry, a low frame structure, straddled the border between Upper and Lower Canada with nine feet to the west of the border and twenty-three feet to the east. Bourbonnais, a pragmatic man, equipped his establishment with a portable bar. When revenue officers from one side of the border arrived on the scene, the bar was sure to be located on the other side.

The agile Gilles Bourbonnais was demonstrating a certain native inventiveness he shared with his peers behind the bar of the nineteenth-century inn. Others were equally devious: the genial host who, after each snowfall, fetched his wheelbarrow to make double tracks in the snow to his barroom door indicating a heavy and inviting trade at his tavern; the Etobicoke proprietor who blazed a short-cut – within a foot of his tavern door – leading to the local mill; the magistrate who, as innkeeper, stopped brawls on his premises by charging the culprits, trying them, fining them on the spot, and then insisting they 'treat' at his bar.

The innkeeper was the linchpin of his budding settlement. As his hostelry was a landmark on the road, its name often became the first name of the community (Keeler's Tavern, Steele's Tavern, Finch's Tavern, etc.). He was the last resource for the settler going into the bush – sometimes staking a pioneer to his first necessary supplies. He was a walking newspaper, employment agency, pawnbroker, and post office. Within his walls bills were paid and deals were made. Nineteenth-century hostelries were, for the most part, the only public places in which men could meet in comfort. As banker at the bar the master of the house was often directly involved in facilitating transactions and advertising job opportunities. The news of the market and the world arrived at the innkeeper's door – as did the mail, heralded by the horn of the stage-coach.

By turns an innkeeper might be theatrical manager, parson, and librarian. Before the era of town halls every production from circuses to Shakespearian plays took place in the local inn, with the host as resident stage manager. In a quick change of pace the innkeeper might put on his clerical demeanour and conduct church services in his hostelry. Mary Lundie-Duncan, travelling in America in 1852, noted:

> It is very pleasant to meet three or four score of travellers in the saloon by seven in the morning and nine at night to join in a hymn, led perhaps by a son or daughter of the house accompanied by an organ-toned pianoforte. Then to hear a passage of Holy Writ, read perhaps by the master of the hotel, and to join in a prayer by him ...

As he often collected the available foreign and local newspapers and other publications of current interest, the innkeeper operated as community librarian. A sign in one early tavern indicated the problems inherent in too many budding readers: 'Would those patrons learning to read please use yesterday's newspaper.'

The political bent of an innkeeper drew men of like mind to his tavern. Reform movements were planned and pamphlets drafted and sometimes printed in his establishment. By offering hospitality to individuals or groups he could be a catalyst for action. Because he operated under strict tavern regulations, he was part of the system of law and order, sometimes with official office, such as magistrate or justice of the peace. As the law courts were frequently held in taverns, the tavern-keeper acted as a sort of clerk for their sessions. His name was frequently found on the list of appointments for fence-viewer and pound-keeper. Even that symbol of an omnipotent government, the tavern inspector, could be in only one pub at a time, so the onus was on innkeepers to keep the peace. In order to obtain a licence to keep tavern the applicant needed character references attesting to the fact that he was 'a person of sober habits, good fame and conversation and a good and loyal subject of Her Majesty.' But in an age when intemperance was the norm, no amount of character endorsements could stand the host in as good stead as a fearsome girth. Big Anthony Allen kept tavern near Goderich. He was six foot six and weighed three hundred pounds. His trick with unruly customers was to grab two by the collar, hold them out at arm's length, and crack their heads together.

But of course the prime function of the innkeeper was to preside over the workings of his inn, that oasis for weary travellers longing for the next tavern to appear, with the possibility of a brief respite from their punishing journey.

Women were among the most successful innkeepers; widows for the most part, their years of experience in the business gave them the confidence to meet their male customers as equals. In fact female innkeepers were seldom criticized. They were no-nonsense women with wide expertise gained from the kitchen up. Mrs Sovereign, a widow who kept a tavern in the Long Point area, enjoyed conversing with her patrons, one of whom, Joseph Pickering, recalled that she was 'seldom without a beloved pipe.'

Many innkeepers were involved in a web of activities of which the inn, though central, was only a part. The obvious connection was to the stage-coaching business. Some innkeepers farmed, some owned stage lines, some drove their own coaches and delivered mail. The shipping and ferry businesses were natural offshoots for an entrepreneurial innkeeper, but there were some who owned mills, stores, or any number of other enterprises. In London, innkeeper McGregor ran the jail. Since he had to feed the prisoners, it seemed logical that he would do so in his hostelry – an arrangement that failed to amuse the judges and court officials who lodged there. Not only were they forced to share their board with the prisoners but, making matters worse, they had to wait their turn for meals, since McGregor liked to serve his charges first.

Of course too many involvements meant that the host could not be behind the bar all the time. The enterprising owner of a rural inn on the Huron Road found a simple solution to that problem. When he was out he left a pail of whisky, a cup, and a box for cash by his door.

Census records show that 'Yankees' far outnumbered all others as innkeepers for most of the nineteenth century. In second place came the Irish. Class lines were non-existent in a Yankee tavern, and thus men and women as disparate as the unwashed backwoods settler and the aristocratic British traveller were forced to keep company. The host to this menage put them all at the same table and coped with the flying sparks.

Many a stoic wayfarer penned a nightly journal, partly as an emotional release and as a warning to those who held too romantic a view of travel in the wilderness. Most of the extant journals were written by British travellers who displayed an unshakeable belief in a rigid class system and the correctness of all things British. Anything done differently from 'at home' was, by definition, wrong. It was an attitude that failed to endear them to a people struggling to survive in a harsh new land. In general, an ill-mannered innkeeper was assumed by the British to be an American. British novelist Anthony Trollope, in his book *North America* (1862), bemoaned American manners, stating pathetically that 'the heart is sickened, and the English traveller pines for the civility ... of a well-ordered servant.'

American-born innkeepers found this patronizing approach particularly offensive and frequently delighted in flaunting their democratic views – to the horror of visiting Britishers. Americans felt themselves to be (and did not hesitate to say so) on an equal footing with anyone from Britain – and woe betide the aristocratic traveller who demanded to be treated with the respect he felt was his due. Slim indeed were his chances of finding a warm welcome.

The surprise of the British at encountering such egalitarian attitudes runs as a common thread through their journals. Thomas Duncumb, travelling in Upper Canada in 1837, knew why servants tended to forget their station. It was partly the result of the way inns were built, with those unpleasant, large, all-purpose rooms in which one had to associate with the great unwashed. There was also something in the air 'arising wholly from the daily lessons on liberty and equality, which are foolishly and practically taught by others, and which the newly-arrived menial attentively attends to, and readily imbibes.'

Duncumb shared the view espoused by the stern William Bell, a clergyman who had taken the same trip in 1824. Bell remarked with asperity that, 'The tavern-keepers in Canada are mostly from the United States, and they seldom fail to resent the least appearance of superiority shown by travellers.' He recounted that, at a tavern near Perth, he had not deigned to join his landlady at her breakfast table. Sitting with her were 'three or four savage-looking fellows, who appeared to be farm servants.' Joining this motley crew was, of course, unthinkable to the good gentleman. The landlady, however, retaliated by making Bell cool his heels for half an hour while she finished her meal. His breakfast, when it finally arrived, consisted of 'rye bread, rancid butter, [and] a stinking mutton chop.'

Thomas Need, an Oxford graduate and author of *Six Years in the Bush,* encountered the quintessential Yankee innkeeper while travelling in the Brantford area in 1838:

> On arriving at the door of the inn, we had bitter proof that we were in the land of independence: – no ready waiter answered our summons – no careful ostler appeared to take

charge of our jaded steed – no bustling landlady, with anxious enquiries after our safety and condition; but every thing silent as death: our plight did not admit of ceremony however, so on the faith of a written assurance over the door, that Captain ——, late of the U.S. Militia, and now of the 'Washington's Head' did profess to entertain travellers, we groped our way to the bar, where we found the redoubtable Captain occupying all the chairs in the apartment, (one of which supported his legs on a higher elevation than his head), and smoking a cigar: after a cool survey of our persons, which he contrived to effect without moving himself, or removing his hat, he calculated that 'we must be tarnation wet, for it did rain almighty' and then continued pulling away as composedly as before; this we supposed was to impress 'us Englishers,' as he immediately discerned us to be, with a due notion of his independence.

Sir Richard Bonnycastle, traveller and author of three books, including *Canada and the Canadians*, summed up the prevailing British viewpoint:

If you find neatness at an hostel it is kept by old-country people. If you meet with indifference and greasy meats they are Americans. If you see the best parlour hung round with bad prints of presidents looking like Mormon preachers, they are radicals of the worst leaven.

No dour pictures of American presidents hung in the parlour of Michael Cook's inn on the shore of the St Lawrence River. Cook had served in the British army during the American Revolution. As a United Empire Loyalist he received three hundred acres of land in Williamsburgh Township, Dundas County. As soon as he got his first tavern licence in 1804, Cook quickly purchased more land, including lot 7, concession 1, Williamsburgh Township, on which stood a small log house. This was his first tavern.

The same year that Cook became a licensed tavern-keeper, W. Henderson, a British tourist struggling through the river front of Williamsburgh Township, noted in his journal that the settlers' dwellings were little more than log hovels 'erected after the first trees were chopped down, and almost every second one a tavern or house of entertainment, where the opulent master, his wife, children and farm labourers and rum-imbibing customers are all mixed up together higgelty-piggelty in the one small room.' Cook's bent for the business of innkeeping took him from a log hovel such as Henderson described to a handsome brick tavern. Today Cook's Tavern stands, restored to the 1835 period, at Upper Canada Village, moved there from its original location on the river front about a mile away.

Cook's log tavern had been operating for some years when, during the War of 1812–14, it was commandeered by the advancing American troops and for a few days served as headquarters for General James A. Wilkinson, commander-in-chief of the US North-Eastern Army, 1813–14, during the battle at Crysler's Farm. Michael Cook's wife was forced to hide with their children in the basement when the building was bombarded by defending British forces. The family suffered heavy losses and later claimed for such diverse items as one hundred bushels of wheat, twenty-five sheep, eighteen white blankets, three silk shawls, ten calico gowns, one set of calico bed curtains, one string of gold beads, and half a bushel of salted sausage – a strange assortment of necessities to sustain an army living off the land.

The looting of Cook's Tavern may, in part, be explained by the unsavoury character of the infamous General Wilkinson. As described by one biographer, Wilkinson was 'As utterly destitute of all real honour, as venal, as dishonest, as faithless as any man whoever lived.' When he and his troops took over Cook's Tavern during the war the general was sick and confined to bed perhaps as a result of his propensity for 'over-indulgence in spirits and possibly opium.' At the war's end he faced a court

One of the best: Michael Cook's tavern (1822), Upper Canada Village, Morrisburg

martial. Its verdict was severe censure and dismissal from the service.

Michael Cook's inn was prospering, so, in spite of his losses, he was able to keep investing in land after the war. By 1820 he had 750 acres. Two years later he was building the present splendid brick tavern, with outbuildings, including an open drive shed that held five buggies with horses. Architect Anthony Adamson, in his assessment of Cook's Tavern for Upper Canada Village, concluded that the family could have lived on the second floor of the tavern at first, partitioning rooms for themselves and leaving the rest as an open ballroom. Later Michael Cook would certainly have used his other farms and farmhouses to accommodate his wife and their six boys and four girls. These eleven resident helpers and the fortuitous location of his inn on the Cornwall-to-Prescott stage route no doubt contributed to Cook's success. He stayed in business until the coming of the railroad.

Innkeepers like Cook who kept tavern in one place for many years were the exception. The majority were of somewhat fly-by-night habits, always with an eye open for greener fields. In many instances a new proprietor was behind the bar every year or two. Willard's Hotel, the other hostelry in Upper Canada Village, had three owners. Built in the late 1790s, the hotel was purchased in 1821 by Alexander Wilkinson, who ran it for nine years and then sold it to John W. Willard in 1830. Willard had been operating the hotel for a while before he purchased it and thus knew that he was buying a thriving business. His records show that for the month of February 1830

Interior: Cook's Tavern

Interior: Cook's Tavern

Innkeeper John Willard's thriving establishment, Upper Canada Village, Morrisburg

– only a few weeks after he became owner – he served nearly five hundred people with food, or lodging, or both.

In the Willard House Day Book, now in the Provincial Archives of Ontario, John Willard recorded in precise detail the names of his patrons, the amount they were charged, and what was provided. On a typical day (17 February 1830) he served a remarkably large number of people:

Mr Walker – 2 horses and lodging – 0.3.6
Mr Gass – 1 horse
Joseph Brick – 3 days, lodging and meals – 14 shillings.
Jacob Backers – 2 horses, breakfast – 4 shillings
Peter Backers – horses and breakfast – 2 shillings 9 p.
Benjamin Howver [?] – 2 horses and breakfast – 0.2.7.
Capt. Horr – 2 days board with horses – 0.11.10
Phillip Wood – 2 horses, 2 meals & lodging – 0.6.0.
John Church – 4 horses
Geo. Briggs – 2 horses, 3 meals & lodging – 0.7.9.
Chas Blinn – 2 horses – 0.4.2.
Mr Torrence – horses, bushel of oats – 0.12.10
Christopher Morey & Son – 2 horses, 1 meal & lodging – 0.4.11
Christopher Herrington – 0.5.2
Jude Bartlet – 4 days of lodging – 0.11.3
Mr Dennison – Super, 3 meals and lodging – 0.69.0
Mr Clements – 1 horse, 3 meals & lodging – 0.11.0
Mr Denny – 1 dinner, two days room and board – 0.8.1.
Mr Hubbard – 2 horses, 7 meals – 0.17.3.
Mr Colesworth – 2 horses, 2 meals – 0.6.0.
Anson Buck – 2 horses, 4 meals, 2 lodgings – 0.8.0
Mr Ballard – 2 horses, lodging – 0.5.3.

Mr Jones – 2 horses, lodging – 0.3.2.
Mr Paine – 2 horses, 5 meals & 2 lodgings – 0.12.0.
Mr Sherman – 5 meals, 2 lodgings – 0.69.0
Mr Northrup – 2 horses, 5 meals – 0.12
Mr Gregory – 2 horses, 3 lodgings, supper – 0.3.3.
Mr Barker – 2 horses, 3 cider – 0.5.0
Mr Gallup – 2 horses, 2 meals – 0.11.10.
Mr Barker – 2 horses, 2 lodgings – 0.6.0.
Mr Ballard – 2 horses – 0.3.0.
Mr Wilkey – 2 horses, 2 lodgings – 0.57
Nathan Gallup – 2 horses, 2 lodgings – 0.9.0.
Benjamin Gallup – 2 horses, 2 lodgings – 0.7.7.
Mr Kinney – 2 horses, 5 meals, 2 lodgings – 0.12
George Shufelt – 1 horse, breakfast – 0.4.3.
Robin Nultin – 2 horses, lodgings – 0.3.6.
John Parsons – 3 days board, supper – 0.10.3.
George Shufelt – 3 meals, lodging – 0.4.3.

The list raises some questions. Why for instance did the thirsty Mr Barker pay only one shilling less for '2 horses, 3 cider' than did Phillip Wood for '2 horses, 2 meals & lodging'? Perhaps the cider was particularly expensive or dispensed in large measures. In any event, his day book makes clear that Willard was indeed a busy man.

In spite of his apparent success, however, Willard had financial problems. His day book contains dunning letters from creditors and one pathetic note, dated 9 January 1837, from a certain John Pickel, possibly a brother-in-law. He too wanted money: 'I stand in most need of it for my health ... I hope you will all remember me if I never see you in this world. I expect to meet you all in another ... the Doctors have all given me over and think I have the consumption. Your dear brother, John Pickel.'

Willard, his wife, Elizabeth, and their son, Mathew, appear on the 1851 census as 'living in a 2-storey frame house,' no doubt the hotel. Four years later the property was registered in Mathew's name. Presumably John Willard had died. Mathew soon sold the hotel. It has been restored to the 1850 period, the time of its greatest prosperity. Within a few years the arrival of the railroad brought that prosperity to an end, as it did in the case of Michael Cook and scores of other innkeepers, when rail travel gradually replaced travel by boat, stagecoach, and sleigh.

A star atop a pole has announced the hospitality of the Star Inn in Dunvegan (lot 24, concession 9, Kenyon Township) since Donald MacMillan opened its doors to travellers in 1865. Until that time the log building had been Angus McIntosh's general store. The presence of a second door on the main floor announced the way to MacMillan's taproom. Today his bar is still in place, but the genial host has been replaced by a tour guide, for the Star Inn, carefully restored, now houses the Glengarry County Museum. The building, typical of so many small, spare country taverns, was a gift to the county by a MacMillan descendant. Outbuildings and a livery shed and barn moved to the location complete the group.

The layout of the Star Inn was basic – three rooms above and three below. Bedrooms on the second floor were something of a luxury in such a small inn – normally one dormitory served all. A rural inn usually had little more than three rooms all told – a kitchen, a sleeping compartment, and a taproom. Meals were prepared and served in the kitchen; the taproom was office, lounge, and dram shop; the bedroom accommodated all and sundry and doubled as a store-room and wardrobe. Washing was accomplished at an outdoor trough or pump, or in a basin in the taproom.

On St Andrew's Day, 30 November 1865, six or seven hundred lads and lasses danced Scottish reels in the streets of St Andrews, a village north-east of Cornwall. They were guests at a party given for this whole community of Roman Catholic Highlanders by the owner of the partially completed two-storey stone inn in the centre of the village. The owner of the inn and host of the party was a popular politician, John Sandfield Macdonald.

Hospitality in the backwoods: Donald MacMillan's primitive hostelry, Dunvegan

Sandfield Macdonald's father, Alexander Sandfield Macdonald, emigrated in 1786 as one of a group of five hundred people from his Highland parish who came to settle in Glengarry County. The son, a lawyer, held the Glengarry seat for all eight sessions of the United Province of Canada. At Confederation, to which he was initially opposed, Sandfield Macdonald became the first premier of Ontario, an office he held for four years.

A year before he ran for political office Macdonald had eloped with Marie Christine Waggaman, whose father, a former American senator, had done all he could to discourage the romance. In Sandfield Macdonald's will, dated 31 May 1872, the day before his death, he left Marie their house in Cornwall, silver, furnishings, and, considerately, all the wine in the wine cellar. There were bequests to his son and daughters and, lastly, mention of his substantial stone tavern in St Andrews:

> I charge and direct that the basement storey of the stone tavern at Saint Andrews ... shall for the period of twenty years after my decease be reserved for the use of the Catholic inhabitants of the Parish of Saint Andrews upon all Sundays, holidays and all days upon which any funeral takes place and the lessee, purchaser or other person occupying the same shall be bound on the days hereinbefore prescribed during the said period of twenty years.

John Sandfield Macdonald was buried in St Andrews beside the explorer Simon Fraser, who had died there ten years earlier. Their graves lie a stone's throw from Macdonald's tavern, the focal point for so many years of every community activity, secular and religious, in that village of doughty Highland Scots. Through his will Macdonald had managed to prolong his role as host to the village.

Even travel by rail, when it arrived, meant intermittent stops for those who hoped for a good night's sleep. After mid-century when the country was becoming more 'civilized,' finding clean and comfortable accommodation was still an uncertain business. The town of Prescott appeared to present particular difficulties in this regard, and it was frequently mentioned by travellers, few of whom had anything good to say about it. Anthony Trollope called this rough-and-tumble community 'one of the most wretched little places to be found in any country.' In his own inimitable fashion, Trollope managed to find fault with both the town and its citizens, for he was 'much struck at Prescott – and indeed all through Canada ... by the sturdy roughness, some would call it insolence, of those of the lower classes of the people with whom I was brought into contact.'

Another British traveller, Charles Mackay, journeying by rail in 1857–8, called Prescott 'a miserable town at the eastern extremity of Lake Ontario where it narrows into the St. Lawrence ... I passed the night in a fourth-rate inn.'

Horton Rhys, an English actor who toured Upper Canada in 1860 with his actress / companion, Lucille, shared to a degree the British disdain for all things un-British; but, unlike many of his countrymen, Rhys was blessed with a sense of humour and a *joie de vivre* that shines through in his delightful memoirs. In Prescott, his stay at a hotel run by an 'enormous' Irishman proved educational:

> Unpromising as the 'house of call' was externally, its interior arrangements were even more unprepossessing ... Beds there were, and a roof, and beer [but] when I essayed to look at my watch, after having suffered excruciating torture for some five hours, and thought it 'time to get up' ... Having contrived to prop one eyelid open, and thereby managed to manoeuvre myself into my clothes, I went down in no very agreeable state of mind and body ... and on presenting myself before the landlord of the so-called hotel ... ere I could give vent to my feelings, as I intended, I was greeted with 'By the powers! – but they been and sarved you shameful! Come here man!' And before I knew what he was up to, I found my head grasped in one hand, while with the other, he knocked out the ashes of his pipe upon the table, and in an inconceivable short time manufactured a sort of mercurial-looking ointment, by means of – you may guess what; and in spite of my struggles, plentifully applied, and rubbed in, the pleasant compound into my eyebrows, cheeks, and forehead, then releasing one with a jerk, and surveying his manipulation with a grin of satisfaction, he said, 'There let it bide, if ye plaze, and ye'll be sound as an apple in five minutes.' This prophecy proved correct, and I thereby profited in the possession of a valuable recipe, which since (self-mixed, and self-applied), I have never known in similar, or cases of mosquito, gnat, or nettle sting, to fail.

Since Horton Rhys failed to mention the name of the innkeeper with the cure for fleas, it is impossible to know for certain just which of that town's several unpretentious hostelries was the scene of such miserable accommodation. Fleas, bedbugs, and other 'small game' were found in virtually every hotel, inn, or tavern in Upper Canada, so their presence offers few clues. Given the nationality and cheerful attitude of his host, however, the place could well have been Duffy's Tavern, a small stone hotel at the corner of King and East Streets in Prescott, near the first CPR station. Later known as the St Lawrence Hotel, the stone building is thought locally to have been Irishman Sylvester Duffy's hostelry, where he conducted business during the 1850s. He lived there with his wife, Mary, three sons, and a handful of paying guests.

If accommodation in Prescott was not to the liking of some travellers, those heading west by stage or bateau may well have preferred to press on to Maitland. That graceful village on the shore of the St Lawrence River boasted at least four hotels and a number of remarkably handsome houses, many of which add to its charm today.

Historian E.C. Guillet mentioned that the governor-general, Lord Elgin, once stayed at Dumbrille's Inn in Maitland. While the Elgin papers fail to mention such an event, it seems not unlikely that Elgin and his wife and baby might at least have stopped there during their eventful trip to Upper Canada in the autumn of 1849.

Lord Elgin's visit to the upper province was something of a calculated risk. Feeling was running high; in April of that year he had signed the controversial Rebellion Losses Bill, an act introduced to compensate Lower Canadians for losses sustained in the Rebellion of 1837–8. Opponents called it a payment for disloyalty, and Elgin was held personally responsible. Newspaper editors had a field-day in anticipation of the visit. Thundered the Toronto *Pilot* on 25 August 1849: 'let your eggs be stale and your powder dry! Down with Elgin! Down with the Rebels!'

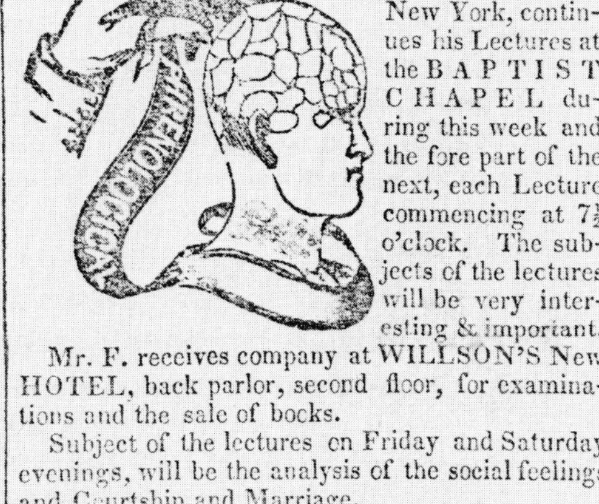
PHRENOLOGY.

MR. FOWLER from New York, continues his Lectures at the BAPTIST CHAPEL during this week and the fore part of the next, each Lecture commencing at 7½ o'clock. The subjects of the lectures will be very interesting & important.

Mr. F. receives company at WILLSON'S New HOTEL, back parlor, second floor, for examinations and the sale of books.

Subject of the lectures on Friday and Saturday evenings, will be the analysis of the social feelings and Courtship and Marriage.

Admittance to each lecture, 7½d.

Brockville, October 8th.

Orson Squire Fowler at work

The governor-general was well aware of the hazards but felt the trip to be imperative for symbolic reasons; in a letter of 6 August to Earl Grey, Secretary of State for the Colonies, he reported that: 'for the time, Her Majesty's dominions in North America are safe – whether they murder me at Brockville or not.'

Because of the volatile situation and the fact that Elgin was accompanied by Lady Elgin and the infant Lord Bruce, the party chose to avoid Brockville and any other community where riots were threatened. In fact, the boat on which Elgin sailed from Montreal to Niagara made only one stop, and that was at Prescott. Given the calibre of the inns at Prescott, Lord Elgin and his entourage were probably glad to travel six miles further to Maitland and the comforts offered at Dumbrille's Inn. A simple frame structure, the inn boasted eight rooms, eight beds, and stabling for a dozen horses.

Built about 1830 by Levi Davis, the inn was operated from 1836 to 1861 by Richard Dumbrille, an Englishman of Huguenot descent who, with his bride, Martha, settled first in Quebec in 1826 and then moved on to Maitland ten years later. From 1861 to 1881 the inn was known as Eldridge's Half-Way House. For many years an addition on the west end of the building housed the taproom, with its long mahogany bar. Early in this century that section was removed, as was the verandah that had once stretched across the front. These features had given the building a more 'inn-like' appearance and had disguised the curiously asymmetrical placement of door and windows.

To the east of Richard Dumbrille's inn is an impressive stone house that for several years was operated as an inn by Richard's cousin, William Dumbrille. One of the earliest buildings in the village, it was constructed in 1826 by Samuel Thomas, a local merchant whose shop still stands beside it. Thirteen years later, Thomas sold his property to Robert Howieson, a distiller who in short order set up a still on the river-bank behind the house. Howieson, a

The European Hotel, Maitland, run by innkeeper Dumbrille

Scot, was a Tory and an organizer of the demonstration in Brockville called to protest Lord Elgin's famous visit. There, on 15 September 1849, thousands of people from surrounding districts arrived 'to unite their voices with those of the assembled multitude, against ELGIN, LIES and POVERTY.' If indeed Lord Elgin stopped for a while in Maitland, it seems likely that his host was certainly not Mr Howieson.

The earliest of Maitland's many beautiful stone buildings is an inn that was built by David Dunham Jones in 1821. It looks today much as it did on the day that Jones completed its construction. For most of the last century, a verandah lent an air of graciousness to the façade and sheltered the two doors, one of which led to the taproom. That door, on the north-east corner, has now been replaced by a window. Of architectural interest are the stone parapets, which project above the roof, a feature more often seen in Scotland than in Upper Canada, although an almost identical inn was built in Brockville, suggesting that a Scottish stonemason was plying his trade in the area.

David Jones sold his tavern after a few years, and it became a residence for a succession of families until, in the late 1840s, it once more became an inn. In 1850, the new owners, Wardner, Nettleton, and Co, were advertising that 'the house has undergone a thorough repair and the furniture is new and of the best description; the rooms large and airy ... a porter will be in attendance.' For some reason the hotel changed hands the following year when a young Irishman, William Webster, took over, advertising that 'travellers will find a

Levi Davis's 1830 riverside inn, later Eldridge's Half-Way House

comfortable house, and conveyances are furnished when required.' Webster and his wife, Mary Ann, ran the inn for a time, but for the rest of the century it was a private home.

In the middle years of the nineteenth century Maitland was home to only two hundred or so people, and it may seem surprising that the village contained as many inns as it did. But until the coming of the railroad, the Queen's highway was a busy thoroughfare, and traffic along it created a demand for stopping places. Traffic on the road was heaviest in winter, for the roads were so bad that only when snow covered the ground was travel tolerable. Travellers had a variety of epithets for the roads, which were muddy and strewn with stumps and ruts. Captain Basil Hall was subjected to a coach ride in 1827 and

David Dunham Jones's inn, *circa* 1821

complained to his diary that the 'horrible corduroy roads' were pitted by 'deep inky holes which almost swallowed up the forewheels of the wagon.' Travellers preferred to go by bateaux or Durham boats, flat-bottomed barges propelled by sail and dragged across portages. This was singularly inconvenient, but better than travel on land.

In winter, the frozen St Lawrence became the major artery through that part of Upper Canada. Here too there were risks. Horton Rhys described the perils of travel at the spring break-up:

> After about ten minutes of the ordinary amount of bumping, an *extra*ordinary quantity of the same induced me to put my head out of the window, when I discovered that Scotchy, after all, was taking the short-cut across the river, and the unevenness of the ice corroborated what had been told me of the probability of a speedy 'break-up.' I did not tell Lucille or her mother of this immediately, but the jumping and jolting became every moment so much greater, and our progress, in proportion, so much slower, that the fact was soon patent to all, and the alarm consequently unmistakable. The track was marked by branches of trees, stuck up on either side at intervals of about one hundred yards, and the oozing of the water through the holes in which they were placed, was ominous. We were now about midway, and the fissures – yes, *fissures*, reader – becoming wider and more frequent, I began to think I ought to comply with Lucille's terrified entreaty to 'turn back,' and communicated our desire to Scotchy. What was our surprise on hearing him reply, 'Na, ye canna turn back – we maun mak' the beest of a bad beesness; hauld oop!' This last to the horse, who at the moment dropped his hind legs into a crack, and didn't seem able to get them out again.
>
> ... Of course, everyone knows we were *not* drowned ... we eventually got on to sound ice in shallow water, and thence on shore to receive quite an ovation from a large crowd who had assembled and watched our dangerous voyage, almost from its commencement. We were the last that crossed, and in an hour the *mail road* was a confused mass of rough waves and rugged blocks of floating ice.

The coming of the railroad after mid-century brought prospects of easier and safer, if less exciting, travel. At Gananoque, the potential of increased traffic when the railway was completed spurred the building of the Provincial Hotel at the corner of King and Stone streets in 1856. It was one of two hotels owned by a Mr Brophy, proprietor of Brophy's Hotel and the Provincial, the latter 'being reserved for commercial trade' while the former was frequented chiefly by tourists. Brophy was 'a veteran hotel keeper ... and deservedly popular with the travelling public.'

For some years the Provincial was known

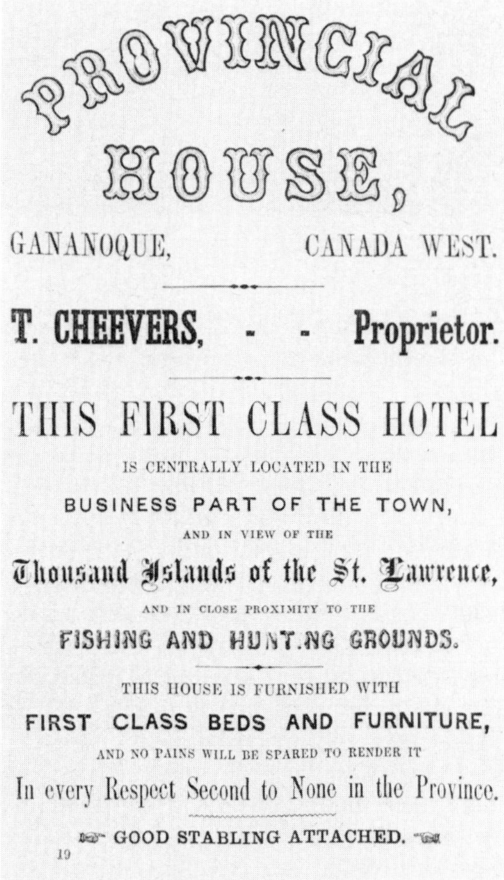

Grand Trunk Railway Gazetteer, 1862–3

Irishman Anthony English's popular inn, the first coach stop east of Kingston

as Cheevers House after Thomas Cheevers, its proprietor. It was sold in 1884 to A.M. Gamble but operated by the McCarney family, who still run the business today. It gained a measure of architectural distinction when additions were made early in this century. A third floor with a mansard roof provided more interior space, as did an addition to the west end of the building that housed the taproom. A large portico sheltered the front door and the local citizens who gathered there to watch the passing scene.

Fortunately for Gananoque, Anthony Trollope decided to take his critical pen and pass it by. His reason, incredible as it seems, was that he did not think the Thousand Islands were much to look at. He noted:

> I had on previous occasion gone down the St Lawrence, through the thousand isles, and over the rapids in one of those large summer steamboats which ply upon the lake and river. I cannot say that I was much struck by the scenery, and therefore did not encroach upon

my time by making the journey again. Such an opinion will be regarded as heresy by many who think much of the thousand islands. I do not believe that they would be expressly noted by any traveller who was not expressly bidden to admire them.

Anthony English was an Irishman who emigrated to Canada in 1816 and shortly thereafter built a modest stone house for himself and his bride, Martha. Situated beside the main road that led from Gananoque to Kingston (lot 3, concessions 2 and 3, Pittsburgh Township), it was the first stage-coach stop east of Kingston. English did not apply for a tavern licence until 1839, but it is likely that the house served as a wayside inn long before that time. According to English's descendants, the coaches that left Kingston heading east were equipped with the finest, sprightliest horses but, upon reaching the English Inn, these horses were exchanged for poorer beasts. The fine horses then made the return trip to Kingston, entering that place in high style.

In the 1860s the inn housed military personnel on occasion. A letter dated 29 January 1864 requested William English (presumably Anthony's son) to report to the commissariat at once 'any changes in the number of soldiers billeted.'

Today the house is owned by the fifth generation of the English family. They point with pride to a bottle, the bottom of which can be seen in one of the gable ends of the house. Coins and a Bible were placed in a cornerstone. This was, according to the family, to ensure that the house would always have within it money, God – and a drink. After all, English was an Irishman, one of a breed of men whom T.C. Haliburton's Sam Slick described in 1836 as 'always in love or in liquor, or else in a row. They are the merriest shavers I ever seed.'

Merry or morose, every innkeeper wanted his house to sound inviting. Some, like William Sumner of the Oakville House, enticed the customer with 'a larder as well stored as the market will admit – Good Liquors, purified by an addition of Ontario's beautiful waters – good fires to cheer the minds of his guests and warm their cold fingers.'

But clever as an innkeeper might be with words, the reputation of his inn took the flavour of his personality. In that department there were two types. The best were hosts such as Abner Cherry of the Fisherville Hotel on the Vaughan Road. Of his hostelry it was said that after receiving his fiftieth annual tavern licence, 'His little hotel has a place now in the history of Ontario ... Mr Cherry is pretty well but his aged wife is blind; but they are a happy couple ... They feed the man and the animal, and always have exceptional care for the latter.'

Then there was the other kind of reputation. Feltie Fisher had a log inn near Goderich. At Fisher's Inn tippling and brawling were pretty much a daily occurrence. One guest, while attempting a handstand on the staircase, killed himself when he fell. It was known that Feltie's wife had tried to improve the tone of the place by providing guests with wash-basins in their rooms. It was also known that as soon as Feltie saw the wash-basins he threw them out the window. He had an alternative to offer anyone who insisted on washing. Feltie led them to the public trough and gave them a towel.

The Ottawa Valley

has and intends keeping on hand a general as- of Hats and Bonnets, which he flatters himself as good quality and as cheap as can be had else-

All orders received with thankfulness and atten- punctuality.

th, 1829. 265z.

SALT RHEUM.—This inveterate dis- ease, which has long baffled the art of the most experienced physicians, has, at length, found a sovereign remedy in Dr. La Grange's genuine ointment. Few cutaneous diseases are met with more reluctance by the physician, in which he is so adversely unsuccessful. This has stood the test of experience, and justly ob- unparalleled celebrity. It immediately removes gives a healthy action to the vessels of the skin, ... It has in three or four weeks cured ... twenty years' standing, that had ... ry remedy that was tried. ... mediate relief in Salt R... commonly called Scald H... liar to unhealthy chil... here is nothing of a ... nay be used in i... es whatever.

PRICE

Sale, by

0th June,

t received

dicines.

known by Blacksmiths ... that it requires ... price of Common English ... an assortment of their CAST... consisting of Single and Double Sto... Franklin and Cooking Stoves, with ... ttles, Bake-pans, Tea-kettles, Sugar-ke... for Ploughs, &c. &c. &c. All of very fine metal executed, and will be sold lower than any ever sale in this Province.

PETER PATERSON, Agent.

Square, York. 272z.

SWEDES IRON.

Landing from the Ship General Wolfe, direct from ...TTENBURGH, ...ONS ASSORTED SWEDES IRON.

...y to WILLIAM BUDDEN, Point a' Calliere.

...al, August 18, 1829. 274-z

LOOKING GLASSES.

...received by the subscriber, a large and elegant ...ment of Looking Glasses; German Plate; a va- ...zes, and the prices remarkably low.

J. R. ARMSTRONG.

Sept. 10th, 1829.

YORK FURNACE.

F. R. DUTCHER continues his FURNACE in com- plete operation, where can be had, at short notice,

Castings of any description from one to thirty cwt:

Also on hand a general assort- ment of STOVES, HOLLOW WARE, PLOUGH CASTINGS and PLOUGHS.

F. R. D. having erected a first rate Lathe for ...on, is ready to complete any order at short notice. Sept. 22. 276z.

THEODORE BURLEY,

SMITH AND *Brass Founder:*

Yonge Street, next door to Judge Macaulay.

...CASTINGS for Millwork, &c. &c. done on ...shortest notice.

...White and Blacksmith's work done to order. ...highest prices, in CASH, will be paid for old ...per and tin.

...ept. 24th, 1829

JAMES FULTON.

Richmond Hill, Markham. Nov. 13th, 1829. 287z

Stray Ox and Steer.

Broke into the inclosure of the Subscriber, a LARGE OX, blind of the off eye, with seven wrinkles on his horn, a yellowish Red and White colour; also a RED STEER with him, nearly three years old; with a brindle face, and part white under his breast. The owner or owners are requested to prove proper- ty, pay charges, and take the animals away.

...RRELL.

...very low in- deed for cash, or if one half or one third of the purchase money is paid down. Immediate pos- session can be given, and, for further particulars apply to PHILIP CODY.

Toronto, Nov. 16th, 1829. 287z.

WHERE IS WILLIAM SUTHERLAND!

THE Subscriber is desirous of ascertaining the place of abode of Mr. William Suth- erland and family. They lived in or near Glen- garry, about the time of the last war, and were originally from the parish of Kindonan, Suther- landshire. Address a letter to the Subscriber, at Niagara, care of Messrs. Chrysler, Merchants.

N. B. Mrs. Sutherland's maiden name was Catharine Macpherson.

DANIEL MACPHERSON.

Niagara, 17th Nov. 1829. 2873.

Boarding.

THE Subscriber can furnish Boarding, Lod- ging, &c. for six steady mechanics, reason- able, on Dundas Street, between Mr. Willmot's Tavern and four doors from Mr. Bird's Tavern, in the house lately occupied by Mr. George Hutchison, Plaisterer.

JAMES PARKER.

Nov. 18. 87.

STRAYED, on the 10th October last, into the premises of ANDREW BIG- HAM, on lot No. 12, in the first concession of ETOBICOKE, A LIGHT IRON-GREY HORSE, rising five or six years of age.— The owner is requested to prove proper- ty, pay charges, and take him away.

Nov. 17. 873.

SAWYER & LABOURERS WANTED.

WANTED by the subscriber, a Sawyer who under- stands his business, and two men who understand Chopping; to whom liberal encouragement will be given. Apply to JAMES STEPHENS.

...also, TO LET, for one or more years, the SA... WORKS of the Subscriber.

For further particulars, apply to the subscriber, on premises.

Stoney Creek, Nov. 13, 1829. WILLIAM KENT 87z

THE SUBSCRIBERS have just received direct f... London, a general assortment of

Hosiery,

Black and Colored Gros-de-Naples,

Figured Norwich Crapes,

Black Silk and Cotton Velvets,

Sewing Silks,

Lace Thread Edgings,

Worked Insertions, and Scollop Muslins,

Reel and Ball Cotton,

Geo. the 4th Regulation Swords, Belts, &... Sashes,

...ware and Cutlery,

...eral Stock of Saddlery: also an extensive ...t of England Cloths, &c. &c.

J. C. GODWIN & Co

...29. 282z

...Subscribers, either wholesale

...rfine Mustard

...advantage to purchase it ...as it is commonly sold.

...rrels of

...D WHISKEY.

J. C. GODWIN & Co

282z.

...FERY.

...respectfully informs the ...ts vicinity, that she practic... ...wife in England, and will ...hat capacity, either in the To...

...et. 6th, 1829. 281z

NEWMARKET

MAIL STAGE.

WILLIAM GARBUTT, having taken the contract ... carrying His Majesty's Mails between York a... Newmarket, for the next four years, respectfully infor... the public that THE MAIL STAGE will start from J... seph Bloor's Hotel, York, on Mondays and Thursdays, 12 o'clock, noon, and arrive at nine o'clock, the same eve... ing in Newmarket;—and will leave Mr. Barber's Taver... Newmarket, for York, on Wednesdays and Saturdays, a... in the morning, and arrive in York at 2 P. M. on the sa... days.

Price for passengers conveyed between York and Ne... market, six shillings and three pence currency, and in pr... portion for shorter distances. Packages carried on th... route at moderate rates.

Mr. BARBER will accommodate passengers arrivi... with the Mail Stage at Newmarket; and they may be co... fortably conveyed to the Holland Landing, or in other ...rections if required.

York, March 30th, 1829. 254z.

NEW ARRANGEMENT OF STAGES

Between York and the Carrying Place at the head of the Bay of Quintie.

THE Public are respectfully informed that a Ma... Stage will run regularly twice a week between Yo... and the Carrying Place; leaving York every Monday an... Thursday at 12 o'clock, noon, and arriving at the Carryin... Place on Tuesdays and Fridays at 2 o'clock, P. M. W... leave the Carrying Place every Tuesday and Friday at ... o'clock A. M. and arrive at York on Wednesdays and S... turdays, at 12 o'clock noon. There will also a Stage leav... Cobourg every Monday at 10 o'clock, A. M. and arrive ... the Carrying Place the same day, and leave the Carryin... Place every Saturday at 9 o'clock, A. M. and arrive ... Cobourg the same day.

The above arrangements are in connexion with the Stea... Boats *Sir James Kempt* and *Toronto*, so that Traveller... going the route will find a pleasant and speedy conveyanc... between Kingston and York, as the line is now fitted up ... good order with good carriages, good horses and caref... drivers.

Every attention will be given to render passengers com... fortable while on the line, and the drivers instructed to st... at the best hotels on the route.

All Baggage at the risk of the owners.

Extras furnished to any part of the country.

The Stage Books will be kept at Mr. Bradley's Steam... boat Hotel.

*** The roads between Kingston and York are of lat... much improved.

CHAPTER TWO

The Ottawa Valley

STOPPING PLACES

'Take them all in all I love the shantymen. There is more of true manliness, of genuine unsophisticated right-heartedness among them than in any class of men I ever associated with.'

Joshua Fraser, *Forest and River Life in the Backwoods of Canada*, 1883

'An', Oh! 'twas the illegant whisky – its
like I never have seen
Since I went for my mornin's mornin
to Shanahan's ould shebeen.'

Gerald Brenan, 'Shanahan's Ould Shebeen,' n.d.

AT FREEZE-UP the lumbermen of the Ottawa Valley went into the bush. They travelled the frozen rivers in horse-drawn wagons, hauling men and supplies. Their pockets were empty, and life in the communal shanty would be temperate for the next five months. Tea was the staple drink – nothing stronger for men whose lives depended upon a steady hand on the razor-sharp broadaxe. They cut and squared the towering white pines until break-up in the spring and came out, down the rivers that fed into the Ottawa, riding the crest of a fortune in timber.

As the stands of magnificent white pine were depleted near the Ottawa River, it became necessary for the lumber barons to move their camps farther back in the bush, and so the shantymen of the valley went 'up the Clyde,' 'up the Madawaska,' 'up the Mississippi,' or to one of the other tributaries that flowed into the Ottawa River. For the men on the way in and for the teamsters who brought barrels of prime mess pork (hams and bacons only), mess pork (all the other parts), as well as flour, beans, potatoes, and other supplies, a stopover was necessary. And so the term 'stopping place' was coined. Although serving the same purpose as an inn in terms of providing sleeping accommodation, stopping places were unique unto themselves and to the Ottawa Valley, developing in a pragmatic way to suit the needs of their customers.

One such stopping place is located on the Pembroke-to-Mattawa Colonization Road (now Highway 17) on the southern outskirts of Deep River. The present city of Deep River is a mid-twentieth-century planned community, built to house the employees of Atomic Energy of Canada; but French explorers knew the area in the sixteen hundreds and called it La Rivière Creuse.

The Deep River stopping place, built in 1876, was operated by an Irishman, John Dowler, who ran it as a licensed establishment and sold whisky to the shantymen. Government regulations prevented him from selling liquor to local residents or anyone who lived less than five miles away. These same regulations prohibited all

Lumbermen's stopping place, Deep River, on the Pembroke-to-Mattawa road

gambling – in fact the only recreational activity allowed was billiards. But in spite of regulations, the evening's entertainment was likely to involve trials of brute strength.

Each area had its local strongman. These men of the valley were the raw material of legends, and the legends were as towering as the pines. Time may have added inches to their height, but the strongest of these Goliaths was reported to be well over six feet tall. Tales of the lumbermen's strength and dare-devilry grew, as did stories of their brawls. They told of the legendary Mountain Jack Thomson, Big Michael Jennings, and the giant Joseph Montferrand. When whisky combined with opportunity and the men were not in camp, the challenges went out – these huge men met head on, just to see what would happen. They met at stopping places such as Dowler's, and the fun began.

John Dowler had received his 122 acres from the Crown. Free land grants were offered to settlers on either side of the road for agricultural purposes, but the road, cut through in 1854, became instead an avenue of transport for lumbering interests that wanted year-round access to their camps. Dowler's was a typical stopping place – a cluster of log buildings that included the owner's house, a bunkhouse for travellers, a blacksmith's shop, and stables. The broadaxe used by Dowler to square the logs is still there.

In 1885 Dowler sold to John Ferguson from Nova Scotia, a Scottish Presbyterian and a man of principle. He refused to serve liquor. He was a venerable seventy-one at the time; his wife, Charlotte, was ten years younger. Their five daughters and three sons ranged in age from thirty-two to sixteen. Years later his sign with the words 'Temperance Hotel' was found in the loft. In spite of this rather abrupt (and to many, regressive) change in the character of the stopping place, business continued to thrive under John Ferguson and his son, George, who carried on until the 1920s.

Ferguson's was subsequently taken over by a nephew, John King, and run as a farm until it was purchased by Atomic Energy of Canada and restored. King, a riverman and bush worker, was interviewed by Joan Finnigan for her book *Some of the Stories I Told You Were True*. He remembered the heyday of lumbering when teams would pull into Ferguson's on their way to the camps owned by such lumber barons as J.R. Booth and James Gillies:

> ... if you wanted a meal they'd get it ready for you, but these portagers generally carried their own food in a box, cooked and all ... they'd have their blanket with them, rolled up, and they'd get them under their arm and their lunchbox and carry it in. Of course, it would be frozen, but they'd take it into the stove. They all had a teabag and they'd hand over their teabag and the woman cooks would put it in a great big vessel – ten cents to make the tea and twenty-five cents to keep the team overnight ... The portagers, lookit, they rolled their blankets out on the floor in rows and put a coat under their head. Some of them might have a pillow, but mostly it was coats and they'd be tired, all day out in the cold and up early. About eight o'clock was bedtime that time.

Stopping places were much more than shelters. They acted as supply depots for the lumber companies, whose responsibility it was to get food to the men in the bush. Usually a farm was part of the establishment, and livestock was raised to furnish food. As lumbering operations moved farther and farther back from the rivers, some companies set up small farms near the bush camp where they would leave 'an old Frenchman or a good chunk of a boy' to grow potatoes, feed the pigs, and generally meet the needs of the camp. John King, raised at Dowler's, remembered strings of loaded teams an eighth of a mile long followed by others of the same length at frequent intervals going 'back in.' This heavy traffic made it practical for a farmer to open a stopping place, and so these clusters of rugged log buildings became part of the valley landscape. (Today there are more log buildings in the Ottawa Valley than in any other part of North America, because their builders, unlike the lumber barons, never became rich enough to replace them with anything grander.)

The teamsters left Dowler's before daybreak and covered about twelve to fifteen miles before dark. As this was as far as a team was likely to make in a day, stopping places were located at intervals approximating a day's run along the trail into the bush. King recalled:

> Of course, they'd be up at four o'clock trying to get away early to get these drives in. And worse than that, a lot of these places, they'd be crowded out at night. There'd be no room and they'd have to go to the next stopover – and that wasn't easy. A tired team, tired right out after thirteen miles, and so slow, you know, slow going and out in the cold all day. Lots of times lots of them had to stay out and that was hardship, real hardship.

At spring break-up the felled white pine on the churning rivers became transportation for the lumbermen, replacing wagons on frozen pathways. Timber rafts became mobile stopping places. Twenty-four squared timbers of more than fifty feet in length were secured together to form a crib, which, mounted by the lumberjacks-cum-rivermen, catapulted through the slides built to traverse white water. Cribs were fixed together in a raft, which could be half a mile long.

As the logs were rafted down the Ottawa, over the slide at the Chaudière Falls, and on to Quebec, five months' thirst and full pockets frequently led to wild brawls. Joshua Fraser, who knew many of these strongmen, admitted that, in spite of his admiration for them, after a 'sojourn amid the pure bracing influences of the forest,' shantymen were likely to become 'groggily inclined.' In *Forest and River Life in the Backwoods of Canada*, Fraser recalled that there were frequent opportunities for the

After break-up: lumbermen on a timber raft in a moment of unaccustomed leisure

shantymen to gratify their appetites:

> Every few miles on the river side there are low taverns, or shabeen shops, licensed or unlicensed, where rank vitriolized poison under the name of good whiskey is sold by the glass or bottle to the thirsty drivers ... Now it is that ... the riverman can, if he pleases, give full fling to all that is sensuous, low and debasing within him. On Saturday night especially ... these riverside shabeens are often the scene of frightful orgies, and of most inhuman and brutal fights ... as he leaps with a light heart and a heavy pocket from the raft onto the shore he is at once beset with a host of hell-runners in the shape of calash drivers, boarding-house agents, brothel sirens and crimps and sharpies of the blackest stamp ... Between bad whiskey and worse men and women he is plucked as clean as a Christmas goose, and in an incredibly short time too.

On the other side of the ledger, shantymen were also known for their generosity. When, in 1847, news arrived of famine in Ireland, the Ottawa papers of the day carried long lists of names of shantymen and raftsmen who donated part of their winter's earnings to famine-relief committees.

Novelist Anthony Trollope adopted a romantic view of lumbering. During his tour of North America Trollope became smitten with the idea of going boldly into the bush with the shantymen, returning with them to leap nimbly from log to log along the turbulent river. In his journal (and from the safety of his armchair) he rhapsodized:

> I should love well to go up lumbering in the woods ... But if I were about to visit a party of lumberers in the forest, I should not be disposed to pass a whole winter with them. Even of a very good thing one may have too much. I would go up in the spring, when the rafts are being formed in the small tributary streams, and I would come down upon one of them, shooting the rapids of the rivers as soon as the first freshets had left the way open ... The excitement and motion of such transit must, I should say, be very joyous.

Up the Bonnechère River, Foy's stopping place had stabling for thirty-four teams.

Snedden's stopping place made the traveller 'oblivious to the comforts of his home.'

Standing by the water not far from Killaloe Station, it sheltered scores of shantymen on their way into Algonquin Park. Like Dowler and most settlers in the Ottawa Valley, Peter Foy was of Irish descent. (The Ottawa Valley accent still contains something of an Irish lilt.) Born in Quebec, Foy and his wife, Margaret McKibbon, a stern-faced, no-nonsense woman, raised their nine children at the stopping place they built in 1863. Eventually the business was taken over by their oldest son, Peter Henry, and later passed to Peter's younger brother, Norman.

Stopping places like Foy's and Dowler's were part of a pipeline that took men and supplies into the bush and brought timber out, supplying, from the earliest days of the nineteenth century, a desperate England with the raw material for its ships. The stopping place was fundamental to the economic development of the valley.

Lumber sold for twelve to fifteen cents a cubic foot at a time when thousands of acres and a seemingly limitless supply of blemish-free trees existed. Later the price rose to $1.00 per cubic foot as supplies of perfect specimens (no rot, no blemish, no crooks) diminished. It took a gang of six men a full day to cut and square one log of white pine.

Each 'stick' could be worth close to $100, and each carried a distinctive timber mark, to guard against theft and to allow for rapid identification when the logs were sorted and assembled into cribs and booms. In the peak years of the 1860s and 1870s more than 400,000 sticks were rafted down the Ottawa. Lumber barons such as John Rudolphus Booth made millions. When he died, Booth left an estate of thirty-three million dollars.

A traveller in 1846 described Snedden's stopping place as being kept 'in as good style as any inn in the province.' Fifteen years later a diarist of more poetic bent said of Snedden's:

> Who in this portion of Victoria's domain has not heard of Snedden's as a stopping place? Ask any teamster on the Upper Ottawa and he will satisfy you as to its capabilities of rendering the traveller oblivious to the comforts of his home.

These satisfied travellers spoke of a stopping place (on Highway 15, north of Almonte) in Lanark County owned by David Snedden, descendant of a Scottish family from Cambusland, near Glasgow. Here, on the Mississippi River, fast-moving rapids had prompted David's father, Alexander Snedden, to take an option on a mill site – a move that resulted in a prospering Snedden grist mill and sawmill and a business in squaring timber from local leases. The hamlet became known first as Norway Pine Falls, then Snedden's Mills, and later Blakenay. Alex Snedden garnered all he could from the timber trade. He owned, as well as his mills, a timber slide (a channel lined with parallel logs) where he charged for each log that went over the white-water bypass. He also became an agent for the railroad. He died in 1867.

Alex Snedden's son, David, David's wife, Mary, and their children, Minnie, David, and William, ran the stopping place, which, according to descendants still living in the house, was built in the 1840s. The heavy front door bears the original hardware and a deep axe scar – thanks to a drunken patron who, after being forcefully ejected from the premises, returned to avenge himself. The interior doors, pine with wide frames, have painted graining. The early diarists were right – Snedden's was more elaborate and provided travellers with better accommodation than did many stopping places. But the scarred door

The villain of the Valley – Laird MacNab

reveals that at Snedden's, too, many an argument was settled with fists, a well-placed kick, or, on occasion, an axe. Snedden's ceased operating as a hostelry in the mid-1860s; 1863 was the last year an innkeeper's licence was issued to the family.

One of the least-welcome lodgers ever accommodated at Snedden's had a characteristically devious manner of departing. He would produce a £20 note to pay for a minor bill and, since only rarely was there enough cash on hand to provide him with change, the scoundrel would march out, declaring his account was settled. This man was the villain of the valley – the notorious Laird Archibald MacNab.

A small log building, the blacksmith's shop of the White Lake stopping place, and MacNab's stone house at White Lake are reminders of the legendary man whose life was the stuff of Gothic novels. Archibald, Laird of the clan MacNab, inherited the title from the twelfth Laird, Francis the Great, a man said to be 'bacchanalian, the likes of which was never to be expected again.' Along with the title, Archibald inherited debts, a dwindling estate, and a mind-set not unlike that of his predecessor. His attempts to combine riotous living and the restoration of the clan's fortunes were unsuccessful and resulted in his hasty departure from Scotland for Canada in 1823. He left behind his wife, Margaret, four legitimate children, and at least two illegitimate children.

At some point during the long voyage across the Atlantic 'The MacNab,' as he called himself, realized that in the wilds of the new colony no one would know that he was only a few steps ahead of his creditors – his unsavoury past could be shrouded in the mist of his homeland. With this in mind, the Laird, a man of great charm and a master of the dramatic gesture, arrived on Canadian soil in memorable fashion. When his ship docked at Quebec City in 1823, Archibald MacNab strode down the ramp wearing the full regalia of a clan chieftain, while, bringing up the rear, two hastily recruited layabouts and a piper formed an appropriate retinue. The locals were duly impressed. This colourful event marked the beginning of a chaotic era of MacNab's autocratic rule in the Ottawa Valley. It would be seventeen years before the settlers there could rid themselves of this despotic Scot.

First impressions carried MacNab into the presence of the elite of Upper Canada and finally to Sir Peregrine Maitland, then lieutenant-governor. Maitland, an aristocrat who believed that men such as MacNab were born to lead, gave the chieftain an entire township to settle – 81,000 acres in the Ottawa Valley. He could choose the name himself. The Laird, with a glance in the direction of immortality, saw fit to call it MacNab Township, a name that remains to this day.

MacNab built a log mansion overlooking the Ottawa River and embarked on plans to re-establish his clan in his township. By 1825 he had twenty families booked for passage. When they arrived that summer the clansmen were greeted by their laird in his chieftain's bonnet and the welcoming wail of the pipes. Warm words and whisky were offered in an event that was to be the high point of their arduous journey. It was downhill from then on.

After a terrifying two-hundred-mile trek to MacNab Township from Montreal, the eighty-four men, women, and children settled into a new and toilsome life in the Canadian wilderness, unknowing victims of a feudal system virtually unheard of on this continent. Each head of household was required to sign a document that in essence made him a serf of the laird. Unaware that this was illegal in Canada, the settlers (most of them illiterate) pledged to mortgage their lands to MacNab in perpetuity and to pledge their timber and part of their crops as well. The commitment was made on behalf of their heirs, forever.

It was seventeen years before the settlers got title to their own land. During that period The MacNab, who felt that he owned both the land and the settlers, persecuted the few who had the temerity to

Burnstown's Leckie Hotel, where MacNab's settlers met secretly

defy him. He used his considerable power and his position as 'the law' to jail, ruin, and hound to their death men and women who had followed him as their chieftain. The beleaguered settlers held secret meetings at the Leckie Hotel in Burnstown in an attempt to get out from under MacNab's thumb. Finally, in 1842, he was brought to trial, and the settlers had their day in court, obtaining at last clear title to their lands.

The legal proceedings were complex, and when the trial came to an end MacNab thought he had won. He had been awarded damages, but the jurors made their feelings clear: the damages amounted to a mere five pounds for 'loss of character,' a stinging rebuke indeed for the arrogant Laird to deal with. He fled to the safety of Dundurn Castle, home of Sir Allan Napier MacNab. The men were cousins, a fact that Sir Allan had been understandably reluctant to acknowledge. But once under the shelter of his cousin's reputation, Archibald MacNab, as cocky as ever, was again seen on occasion parading along the streets of Hamilton in full regalia, preceded by a piper. The sight would not have surprised those who had known MacNab in the Ottawa Valley, as it was the way he always stepped out. Some said it was his 'presence' that allowed him to get away with his devious schemes.

In 1843 the unlamented MacNab left for Scotland where he had inherited a small estate, which he managed to deplete in the following fifteen years. He ended his days in France, living there on a small pension granted to him by his wife, the surprisingly loyal Margaret Robertson, from whom he had been separated since his hasty departure for Canada. The Laird MacNab was not an admirable individual by anyone's standards, yet his charm was undeniable. A settler who once shared a stage-coach with The MacNab remarked: 'He's a muckle fine man.' Many would have disagreed.

In the mid-1830s, when his growing unpopularity with the settlers of MacNab Township was making life uncomfortable, MacNab moved from his mansion on the Ottawa River to a spot near White Lake, where he built a stone house he called Waba Lodge. Here a stopping place was built, which, since he owned everything and everyone in the township, belonged to MacNab. The stopping place had the usual cluster of buildings, but today the blacksmith's shop is all that remains. It is a trim log building with large doors to admit horses and a small front door for the customers. Waba Lodge has been restored.

Not long after Archibald MacNab favoured the Ottawa Valley by leaving it, a young man from Merrickville arrived in the village of Pembroke and there entered the lumber business. He was Joseph Rowan, and for the following twenty years or so he and his partner, John Supple, were prominent in the Pembroke business community, with financial and family interests intertwined. Both were born in Ireland, both had wives named Esther, both had large families. By 1851 Supple had built a sawmill with 'one saw drove by water,' and owned a stone store as well as a log house.

For a brief three years, John Supple served as a Conservative MPP, but his bid for re-election in 1857 was unsuccessful. It was later discovered that some of the election procedures had been questionable – one township reported three hundred votes for Supple's opponent – a surprising number, since fewer than one hundred voters were living there. Supple did not run again.

Supple decided to stick to his growing lumber business. Both Supple and Rowan owned, at one time or another, a building generally known as Rowan's Hotel, a stone structure still standing today (somewhat the worse for wear) on McKay Street in Pembroke. Until Rowan's death, the property was in Supple's name, but it became part of the Rowan estate two years later, possibly to settle their joint business dealings. Known as 'the Stone House,' for many years it provided accommodation for workers at the sawmill, its fourteen bedrooms, two living-rooms, large dining-room, and kitchen offering ample space for the men's use.

When Joseph Rowan died intestate in 1867 his widow, the former Esther Livingstone, was left to administer the estate. Years later, she leased the building as a hotel. The *Pembroke Observer* of 17 March 1876 reported that the new proprietor was 'an American named Vickery' whose aim was to 'make Pembroke a summer resort for the indefatigable American tourist, an undertaking in which he will be well seconded by the magnificent scenery of the Upper Ottawa.'

During these years, lumbermen gathered at hotels such as Rowan's to be picked up en route to the bush. Hotels, part of the patchwork quilt of the lumbering business – as were most enterprises in the Ottawa Valley – served a totally different purpose from stopping places; the latter were keepovers and supply depots for the teamsters, whereas hotels were meeting places and served as employment offices. The hotel proprietor acted not only as a host but also as a link between lumber companies seeking men and local farmers seeking a winter's work. (Sometimes a lumberman would be 'bankrolled' by the proprietor, who knew his investment was safe.) Lumber baron J.R. Booth explained the system in a 1909 address to the Ottawa Board of Trade:

> The orders were given something like this. Joe you drive to Lavigne's Hotel and you get Alex Lafleur and Michael Rochon and you drive to Golden's Hotel and you get Pat Muldoon and Mickey Shea, then you drive to McCommet's Hotel and get Big Rory MacDonald and his crew ... and tell him not to forget his broad axe and his bagpipes ... and ... tell Rory to bring a black bottle with him, because it will be a long time between drinks.

The government brochure advertising the Ottawa-to-Opeongo Colonization Road lured potential immigrants with the tantalizing prospect of 'a vast extent of rich and valuable land,' an Eden available for the taking. 'One hundred acres [would] be given Free' if the settler agreed to build a house and cultivate twelve acres over four years while living on the property. The proposal sounded too good to be true. It

Charles and Eliza Raycraft's stopping place by the desolate Opeongo Road

was. One settler summed it up by noting that when his ancestors took down the trees and cleared away the rocks and bush they found that there was no soil. Another was more succinct: 'Around here, even the grasshoppers carry their lunch.'

Colonization roads were built as part of the government's scheme to promote immigration to the more remote parts of the province after earlier waves of settlement had skimmed off the best land in western and central Ontario. The province wanted to establish an agricultural base on, of all places, the pre-Cambrian Shield. Colonization roads were to be the means to that questionable end.

The Opeongo Road was one of them. Opened for part of its length in 1854, it was to lead from the Ottawa River at Farrell's Landing along the course of the Bonnechère and Madawaska rivers to Algonquin Park and then to Georgian Bay. But the dream was unrealized. Although some optimistic immigrants did settle by the Opeongo to eke out a living from the lumbering industry, life was not as advertised. Though the government report saw 'no obstacle to the raising of excellent crops,' the one necessary ingredient – good soil – was lacking. Many men and women, discouraged and disillusioned, left after their efforts resulted in little more than 'a harvest of stones.'

The unfortunate settlers could hardly be blamed for what happened. They had merely believed what the government, through its agent, T.P. French, wanted them to believe. Even today the land appears harsh and forbidding. It would have been even more rugged in 1857 when French reported in *Information for Intending Settlers on the Ottawa and Opeongo Road and Its Vicinity* that 'the country ... is composed of gently undulating and flat lands. Few of the very highest hills are incapable of cultivation, and it is strange that the best soil is not unfrequently found on their summits.' Even the stones, said French, while a source of annoyance, would not 'form any great obstacles to the raising of excellent crops.' For the new settler, 'the knowledge necessary for putting in his first crop will be acquired in a few weeks from his neighbours ... ' The entire approach verged on fraud.

And so the Opeongo, for many of the settlers, became a 'road of broken dreams.' A few determined souls, however, managed to persevere, among them Charles Raycraft who, like most of the settlers along the Opeongo, had come from Ireland. He settled near Clontarf (named after a famous battle in which the fighting Irish demolished the Danes), wisely establishing not only a farm but a stopping place as well. Raycraft is listed in the 1861 census, which fortunately records the date (1856) that his log house was built, suggesting that the Raycrafts were among the first immigrants to read and respond to the government's enticing prospects of good land and 'insatiable markets.'

Charles Raycraft and his wife, Eliza Beckett, were from County Mayo. With the help of their seven children, they managed to raise enough farm produce to support themselves and furnish food for their stopping place. The menu was limited: salt pork for dinner and a good supply of liquor made up the basic fare at meals, and space on the floor was allocated for sleeping. Still standing by the house are the original outbuildings that were once used to accommodate horses, teamsters, crops, and stored feed. The Raycrafts eventually built a second house, a squared-timber, one-and-a-half-storey gabled building set back from the road.

Not far from the Raycraft stopping place is St Clement's Anglican Church, built on land donated to the parish by the many Roman Catholics in the area. This gesture was surprising considering the animosity so prevalent at the time between Catholics and ever-aggressive Orangemen, but it exemplified the spirit of co-operation in which settlers rose above petty differences when faced with the harsh realities of pioneer life. They knew what was important.

The Opeongo Road was only one of more than twenty colonization roads that the government promoted in the area between Ottawa and Georgian Bay. Working enthusiastically on the assumption that soil in which trees grew would grow crops as well, the government forged ahead with its colonization roads; however, their plans were doomed from the start. The coming of the railroads in the late nineteenth century was the death knell for the many struggling communities along the roads that the railway bypassed. After frustrating initial efforts to carve out a farm many disheartened immigrants returned home, moved west, or left to start over again somewhere else. Today the numerous ghost towns on these colonization roads tell the sorry tale.

Ashdown is one such town. Once a small but busy village, it stood at the junction of the Parry Sound Colonization Road and the Nipissing Road. Some days thirty or more wagons loaded with provisions would pass through Ashdown, as hopeful settlers headed into the bush along the rutted, dusty road. Their next stop would be Seguin Falls where the King George Hotel offered food, drink, and the opportunity for a good night's rest. A frame, two-storey building, it stands alone beside a narrow overgrown trail, all that is left of the Nipissing Road. Built in 1897 when the railroad arrived and a measure of prosperity came to the hamlet, the King George replaced an earlier temperance hotel that had achieved a modest reputation for its 'most genial and hospitable host' and 'the excellent cuisine of his good lady.'

North of Seguin Falls, in Spence, another temperance house served those who were abstemious by choice or by circumstances. Called the Spence Inn, it was built in 1878 and run by Levitt Simpson. The 1881 census showed that Simpson, an Englishman, was then fifty-seven and running this remote hotel with the help of his wife, Ann, and their four children. Spence's functioned as a public house until 1911. It was privately owned until 1977, when the

On the dusty Nipissing Road, the King George Hotel, Seguin Falls, offered a respite.

Verandah, King George Hotel

Rotary Club of Huntsville purchased it and moved it to the Muskoka Pioneer Village, where it stands today, well restored and offering, by its presence, a reminder of Ontario's colonization roads and of the well-intentioned but misguided scheme that brought discouragement and despair to so many.

While travellers may have had difficulty in finding strong drink in Seguin Falls and Spence, the residents of Parry Sound lived under regulations that were ludicrous – and therefore challenging. The original terminus of the Parry Sound Colonization Road, Parry Sound was a viable mill town on the shores of Georgian Bay. Its founder, William James Beatty, was a militant teetotaller, who did his best to ensure that not a drop of liquor would be sold in the town during his lifetime and well after. Beatty, who owned most of the land on which Parry Sound was developed, was able to place a

Levitt Simpson's 1878 temperance establishment, the Spence Inn

restrictive covenant on the sale of his holdings, thereby preventing the sale of 'any spiritous or intoxicating liquors' in any building built on any property. He also managed to enforce this edict from beyond the grave. The covenant, dated 1872, covered the period 'during the lives of the grandchildren of Her Majesty Queen Victoria ... and during the period of twenty-one years after the death of the survivors of such parties and such grandchildren.' It was not until 1950 that legislation was passed to release the descendants of the early purchasers from this agreement.

The thirsty citizens of the town, then called Beatty's Rapids, were nothing if not enterprising and, as usually happens with any kind of prohibition, they soon found a variety of creative approaches to the problem. Some would simply go across the harbour to Codrington, a collection of miserable shacks known locally as 'Parry Hoot,' thanks to the proliferation of brothels and bars that sprang up in the 1860s to cater to the lumbermen, fishermen, longshoremen, and railway men in the area. The Kipling Hotel is the only building still standing as a reminder of those rip-roaring days.

In Parry Sound itself, most hotels managed to disguise liquor with 'soft stuff.' According to one old-timer, 'the boys [would] ask for pop and give the password.' In time strangers learned to use the 'Parry Sound wink' when ordering soda water; or they would patronize the Palace Hotel,

The Stage will

LEAVE Parry Sound

AT SIX O'CLOCK, A.M.

Monday and Thursday

MORNINGS,

Returning will

LEAVE Bracebridge

ON

Tuesdays and Fridays

AT NOON.

—:o:—:o:—

Northern Advocate, 19 April 1876

where the proprietor, Billy Johnson, had his own creative way of dealing with the situation. According to the Huntsville *Forester* of 25 June 1897:

> Johnson ... got the adjoining township to grant a shop license. It was a mile from the Palace. He put up a telephone between the two places. The liquor store was known as 'The Lean-To' because it touched the corporation [Parry Sound] but wasn't in it. Any guest asking Brér Johnson for a bottle of ale would find that he nearly fainted. 'Sir, are you not aware this is a temperance town? But you can call up the telephone, ask for what you want and they will send it over.' And they did. It was served up in about 10 seconds. The guests would sometimes remark that it didn't take long to get it, if the shop was a mile away. 'No sir,' said Bill, 'our horses do move in this country.'

Drugstores also did a thriving business dispensing everyone's favourite cure-all. As the same old-timer recalled:

> ... while a friend of mine was getting 'something' for a lame back, another fellow called for 'lung balsam,' and a third had a bad headache. Strange but true, the bottle that fixed my neighbor was also the correct thing for the other fellows' lungs and headache. In most towns this remedy is known as 'Seagram's' or 'Club,' but in Beatty's Rapids it is known as The Universal Temperance Beverage.

The Rideau Waterway

Subscriber.

JAMES FULTON.

Richmond Hill, Markham, Nov. 13th, 1829.

Stray Ox and Steer.

Broke into the inclosure of the Subscriber, a LARGE OX, blind of the off eye, with seven wrinkles on his horn, a yellowish Red and White colour; also a RED STEER with him, nearly three years old; with a brindle face, and part white under his breast. The owner or owners are requested to prove property, pay charges, and take the animals away.

deed for cash, or if one half or one third of the purchase money is paid down. Immediate possession can be given, and, for further particulars apply to PHILIP CODY.

Toronto, Nov. 16th, 1829. 287z.

WHERE IS WILLIAM SUTHERLAND!

THE Subscriber is desirous of ascertaining the place of abode of Mr. William Sutherland and family. They lived in or near Glengarry, about the time of the last war, and were originally from the parish of Kindonan, Sutherlandshire. Address a letter to the Subscriber, at Niagara, care of Messrs. Chrysler, Merchants.

N. B. Mrs. Sutherland's maiden name was Catharine Macpherson.

DANIEL MACPHERSON.

Niagara, 17th Nov. 1829. 2873.

Boarding.

THE Subscriber can furnish Boarding, Lodging, &c. for six steady mechanics, reasonable, on Dundas Street, between Mr. Willmot's Tavern and four doors from Mr. Bird's Tavern, in the house lately occupied by Mr. George Hutchison, Plaisterer.

JAMES PARKER.

Nov. 18. 87.

STRAYED, on the 10th October last, into the premises of ANDREW BIGHAM, on lot No. 12, in the first concession of ETOBICOKE, A LIGHT IRON-GREY HORSE, rising five or six years of age.— The owner is requested to prove property, pay charges, and take him away.

Nov. 17. 873.

SAWYER & LABOURERS WANTED.

WANTED by the subscriber, a Sawyer who understands his business, and two men who understand Chopping; to whom liberal encouragement will be given.

Also; TO LET, for one or more years, the SALT WORKS of the Subscriber.

For further particulars, apply to the subscriber, on the premises.

WILLIAM KENT.

Stoney Creek, Nov. 13, 1829. 87z

THE SUBSCRIBERS have just received direct from London, a general assortment of Hosiery, Black and Colored Gros-de-Naples, Figured Norwich Crapes, Black Silk and Cotton Velvets, Sewing Silks, Lace Thread Edgings, Worked Insertions, and Scollop Muslins, Reel and Ball Cotton, Geo. the 4th Regulation Swords, Belts, and Sashes,

J. C. GODWIN & Co.

NEWMARKET MAIL STAGE.

WILLIAM GARBUTT, having taken the contract for carrying His Majesty's Mails between York and Newmarket, for the next four years, respectfully informs the public that THE MAIL STAGE will start from Joseph Bloor's Hotel, York, on Mondays and Thursdays, at 12 o'clock, noon, and arrive at nine o'clock, the same evening in Newmarket;—and will leave Mr. Barber's Tavern, Newmarket, for York, on Wednesdays and Saturdays, at ... in the morning, and arrive in York at 2 P. M. on the same days.

Price for passengers conveyed between York and Newmarket, six shillings and three pence currency, and in proportion for shorter distances. Packages carried on this route at moderate rates.

Mr. BARBER will accommodate passengers arriving with the Mail Stage at Newmarket; and they may be comfortably conveyed to the Holland Landing, or in other directions if required.

York, March 30th, 1829. 254z.

NEW ARRANGEMENT OF STAGES

Between York and the Carrying Place at the head of the Bay of Quintie.

THE Public are respectfully informed that a Mail Stage will run regularly twice a week between York and the Carrying Place; leaving York every Monday and Thursday at 12 o'clock, noon, and arriving at the Carrying Place on Tuesdays and Fridays at 2 o'clock, P. M. Will leave the Carrying Place every Tuesday and Friday at ... o'clock A. M. and arrive at York on Wednesdays and Saturdays, at 12 o'clock noon. There will also a Stage leave Cobourg every Monday at 10 o'clock, A. M. and arrive at the Carrying Place the same day, and leave the Carrying Place every Saturday at 9 o'clock, A. M. and arrive at Cobourg the same day.

The above arrangements are in connexion with the Steam Boats *Sir James Kempt* and *Toronto*, so that Travellers going the route will find a pleasant and speedy conveyance between Kingston and York, as the line is now fitted up in good order with good carriages, good horses and careful drivers.

Every attention will be given to render passengers comfortable while on the line, and the drivers instructed to stop at the best hotels on the route.

All baggage at the risk of the owners.

Extras furnished to any part of the country.

The Stage Books will be kept at Mr. Bradley's Steamboat Hotel.

SWEDES IRON.

WILLIAM BUDDEN, *Point a' Callure.*

LOOKING GLASSES.

J. R. ARMSTRONG.

YORK FURNACE.

F. R. DUTCHER continues his FURNACE in complete operation, where can be had, at short notice,

Castings of any description from one to thirty cwt:

Also on hand a general assortment of STOVES, HOLLOW WARE, PLOUGH CASTINGS and PLOUGHS.

THEODORE BURLEY, SMITH AND *Brass Founder:*

Yonge Street, next door to Judge Macaulay.

CHAPTER THREE

The Rideau Waterway

ENTERTAINMENTS IN INNS

'If a journey to Ottawa is bad, the journey from it is worse, and could only be supported by the strong sense of relief experienced at getting away from such a place.'

George Rose, MA, *The Great Country; or Impressions of America*, 1868

NO ONE who set foot in Ottawa could understand why it had been chosen to be Canada's capital. According to George Borrett, an Englishman who visited the place in the 1860s, there was much speculation as to why this remote, scruffy, rowdy, undistinguished lumber town had beaten out Montreal, Quebec, Toronto, and Kingston for the honour. 'Some say it was selected by mistake,' he reported, while others 'think it was done by the Queen to spite the Canadians.' The American press, however, saw some wisdom in the choice and remarked that Ottawa would be easy to defend since 'the invaders would inevitably be lost trying to find it.'

Like it or not, Ottawa was chosen by Queen Victoria in 1857 as Canada's capital. For many years afterwards travellers took pains to report on the deficiencies of the town, with particular emphasis on the dreadful roads, the overpowering smells, and the poor hotels. Say what you will about Canada's Founding Fathers, they had to be a hardy lot to withstand the raw frontier flavour of early Ottawa.

Brawling lumbermen, muddy roads, flimsy wooden sidewalks, the clutter of shops, and the smells of markets made up the Sussex Street of the mid-nineteenth century. Here stood most of Bytown's early inns, establishments that catered to the hordes of migrant workers who twice yearly invaded the town. They came in the fall in search of work at lumber camps. Team bosses canvassed the hotels to recruit their shantymen. Innkeepers played their part in the proceedings by staking men to food and accommodation of sorts, knowing that in the spring the lumber companies would pay once the lumber was sold. The arrival of spring saw the return of the shantymen who, after a long and lonely winter in the bush, lustily celebrated the end of the logging season. And local innkeepers, merchants, and prostitutes obligingly assisted them in getting rid of their winter's earnings.

In 1961, the National Capital Commission was empowered to buy properties and restore them in conjunction with local entrepreneurs, and since then Sussex Street has become Sussex Drive. It has acquired a new face – a cleaner and more refined one than the original. As a result many fine limestone buildings, some of which were early hostelries, have been restored. In their new-found dignity, they have come a long way from the era of their construction when itinerant raftsmen and a population of bois-

Ottawa's bustling Byward Market

terous Irish labourers presented a scene that filled newly arriving civil servants with serious doubts about the judgment of their sovereign and their own wisdom in agreeing to come to such a place.

The British Hotel still stands at the corner of Sussex Drive and George Street. Here Donald McArthur built a two-and-a-half-storey stone inn in 1828, operating it with his wife, Jane. They called it the Ottawa Hotel. This was the first time in the area that the name 'Ottawa' had been applied to anything but the river itself. McArthur was a successful innkeeper, and business was brisk. His inn provided the town with its first library and also operated as a civic centre. Outside the Ottawa was a communal well lighted by a whale-oil lamp, so that residents could draw their water at any hour of the day or night.

By 1844 McArthur had renamed his inn the British Hotel and was considering an addition. The terminus of the Bytown-to-Prescott railway was to be built at the end of the street, so prospects for increased business looked good. McArthur replaced his first hostelry with the four-storey limestone building still occupying the corner of George and Sussex. When completed it faced Sussex Street with a splendid façade consisting of a massive, ornately carved verandah that provided a gallery for each floor. By 1853 the enlarged premises were open for business, a fact McArthur announced on 10 January of that year in a local paper whose name advertised its bias, the *Orange Lily and Protestant Vindicator*.

> In returning thanks to the public for the liberal support hitherto extended to his Establishment ... the subscriber would respectfully announce to his old friends throughout the country and the travelling community generally, that he has re-opened the British Hotel and is now prepared to receive and entertain all those who may favour him with their patronage.

Ten years later the building was purchased from McArthur by the Honourable

James Skead, a wealthy lumber baron, businessman, and politician. Skead built a wing along George Street that greatly enlarged the building, but he had no opportunity to reap the benefit of additional business, for the government immediately took over the hotel to use as a barracks for the British troops who arrived in 1866, a time when fears of Fenian attacks were widespread. When the British military presence in Ottawa ended, the building stood empty for a time, as Skead was unable to find a tenant. Then, in 1875, it was taken over and refurbished by the enthusiastic but ill-fated William Mills.

Mills decided to call his hotel the Clarendon, promising that, 'The table will be furnished with the choicest delicacies of the season and that ... the patrons of the Clarendon may rely upon the reputation of the Proprietor to please them in every particular.' Opening festivities consisted of a gala banquet. One well-fed reporter announced that 'the viands disappeared like frost in the sunshine.' So, unfortunately, did the reputation of William Mills. One year later Ottawa was horrified to read about a 'Manitoba MPP Charged with Committing Rape upon a Young Girl.' The girl was Minnie Mills, daughter of the proprietor. The incident was alleged to have taken place in Mills's hotel, the Clarendon. When the case came to court, the defendant received a verdict of not guilty. The jury accepted the defence's claim that the girl had been prompted by her mother to make a case against the defendant. The ensuing notoriety forced Mills, who was near bankruptcy, to give up the business. For some time after this the building was vacant.

In 1880 the Marquess of Lorne, then governor-general, and his wife, Princess Louise, encouraged an exhibition of art, which would be shown in the old building, once again called the British Hotel. Held under the auspices of the Canadian Academy of Arts, the exhibition was a huge success, although sceptics had claimed that there was not enough good Canadian art to bother with. Sales amounted to seven thousand dollars. This first collection at the British Hotel became the nucleus of the National Gallery of Canada. The building now serves as government offices.

The Revere House, Clarence and Sussex

After a winter in the bush, itinerant shantymen arrived in Bytown. Their pockets were full, and they were looking for a good time. They took over the inns in Lower Town. One of their many haunts was the Revere House, built in the 1870s, at Clarence and Sussex streets. It stood amid a jumble of shops where merchants sold lumbermen's supplies, tobacco, watches, and other merchandise. Directly adjacent to it was the Byward Market, named after Colonel By, the town's founder. Here the noise of the hawkers in their stalls added to the general tumult. After its wilder years were over, the Revere was purchased by the Institut Jeanne d'Arc, an institution devoted to assisting girls in need of help. Gradually the institute absorbed the neighbouring merchants' buildings, and a mansard roof united them structurally, covering the survivors of a raucous past with a measure of architectural dignity.

The antics of the shantymen were to become the stuff of legend, but they were based on fact. The Ottawa *Daily Citizen*, for instance, reported on 30 July 1873 an

Innkeeper Bernard Larivière's Champagne Hotel once catered to boisterous lumbermen.

Mayor Martineau's four-inns-under-one-roof, on Murray Street, near the market

incident suggesting that Ottawa, even after Confederation, was still a rollicking frontier town. A handful of exuberant celebrants were tossed out of one hotel but decided, a few hours later, to pay a return visit:

> They secured two bears which were chained to a tree in close proximity to the house, and after waiting for a few hours to allow the proprietor of the bar to fall asleep, they stole noiselessly to the bar-room window and succeeded in raising it up. They then put the bears in and, after giving them a few lashes, closed the window. No sooner had they done this than the bears began to howl fiercely and the men scampered off. The landlord was awakened by the noise and springing to his feet he seized a double-barreled shotgun and rushed down stairs to annihilate the disturbers of his peace. On the way down he stumbled and fell, striking the dilapidated weapon on the bannister and causing discharge of both barrels at once. The force of the explosion sent him flying four steps up the stairs, and there he remained standing on the back of his head, with his feet against the bannisters. As soon as he had recovered from the shock he rose from his uncomfortable position and bolted for the bar-room where he was met by what he pictured (as) a double-headed bear. He fell with fright and the two bears walked over him and, making a bolt through an open door that led to the kitchen, jumped through a window much to the relief of the frightened proprietor. He is in bed today.

The four-storey stone building at 343 Sussex Drive has served a variety of purposes since it opened its doors in 1852 as the College of Bytown, a bilingual institution that was the forerunner of the University of Ottawa. Today it is the LaSalle Academy, a parish school run by the Roman Catholic Separate School Board. But for a period of ten years (1856–66), it led a more informal life as the Champagne Hotel, part of the busy Sussex Street scene. It did not voluntarily close its doors to the lumbermen who frequented it. Instead, hotel keeper Bernard Larivière was notified on 23 October 1866 that he had twenty-four hours to vacate. The inn was being taken over, as were several of its neighbours on Sussex Street, to serve as barracks for Viscount Monck's British troops brought out to protect the governor-general and Parliament from Fenian attack. Larivière got $500 compensation for the loss.

On his arrival in Ottawa in 1872, Lord Dufferin, Monck's successor as governor-general, found that there was little to offer anyone of gentle breeding. The place was very desolate, he wrote, 'with a wilderness of wooden shanties spread along long strips of mud.' His wife described the place as 'a small town with incongruously beautiful buildings crowning its insignificance.' But the situation improved somewhat that year with the construction of the Martineau Hotel, an impressive limestone structure built in the Byward Market area near Sussex Street (47–61 Murray Street) by Ottawa's mayor, Eugene Martineau. A successful merchant from St Nicholas near Quebec City, Martineau became mayor at the age of thirty-four. Having constructed a seventy-room building, he leased it out as four separate inns. Recently restored and renamed the Carriageway, the building now contains retail and office space. The exterior remains virtually unchanged, and its presence adds immeasurably to the atmosphere of the revitalized Byward Market area.

In fact the building, like its neighbours, undoubtedly looks better today than it ever did, thanks to wide paved streets, attractive lighting, and the overall charm of the market area. In earlier days, the streets of Ottawa were rutted and either muddy or dusty, depending on the weather. Garbage was strewn about, pigs and cows wandered at will, and the resulting mess caused a pervasive foul smell that became even worse when it rained. Polluted wells and disease followed. These streets were, according to Julius George Medley in *An Autumn Tour in the United States and Canada*, 'the vilest roads I ever saw.' Ottawa itself was 'a second-rate town, which appears to live on the lumber trade.' Toronto journalist and academic Goldwin Smith summed up the prevailing feeling with the scathing 'Ottawa is a sub-arctic lumber village converted by royal mandate into a political cock-pit.'

The hostelry boasting the longest unbroken innkeeping record in Ottawa, the Albion, is in the Sandy Hill district, at 1 Daly Avenue. A large stone structure, it was built by Allan Cameron some time prior to 1844, when it was advertised as having 'comfortable Bed Rooms, private parlours ... [and] a spacious Ball Room – 45 feet by 16.' Today it looks somewhat forlorn, but structurally it has changed little since its heyday more than a century ago.

Walter Shanley, the chief Engineer of the Bytown and Prescott Railroad, endured living conditions in both towns during the time he was responsible for the railway's construction. In letters to his brother, Francis, in July 1851, he implied that one place was about as bad as the other. 'A greater set of ruffians than the whole population of Bytown it would be hard to find outside Tipperary,' he remarked. There, 'between treacherous Papists and truculent Orangemen, it is hardly safe to walk the streets in daylight.'

Shanley found his business dealings continually hampered by the casual attitude he encountered in his Bytown employers:

> ... the people of Canada are the D——d's fools in a business point of view that are anywhere to be found. I was very busy in my office last week in Bytown and was disturbed half a dozen times one day by the President [of the railway] rushing in to try and force me out to play cricket ... I have fallen immeasurably in his opinion as a fit and proper person to carry successfully to completion the Bytown and Prescott Railway, and yet he is altogether the best of the lot of Directors, indeed, the only one to do business with.

The situation was anathema to Walter Shanley's precise engineering mind and professional approach, but it was typical of the time and the place. Business was conducted and decisions were made not only in offices and on playing fields but in the lobbies of the town's crowded and noisy hotels. By far the most important was the Russell House at the corner of Sparks and Elgin. It opened its doors in 1845 as Campbell House, a modest three-storey inn, and then in the 1860s was taken over by the Russell family and, as it became increasingly popular, was enlarged three times. Located near Parliament Hill, the Russell House (and its popular bar) was generally acknowledged to be the place where most of the action in town took place. Affairs of state were conducted there, as were affairs of the heart. As one wag wryly put it:

> Ottawa is composed of the Parliament Buildings and the Russell House. In the daytime the government employees spend their time in the former place, and the greater part of the night in the latter.

Until the Château Laurier opened in 1912, the Russell was unquestionably the best hotel in town. That is not to say, of course, that it met with universal approval. The ubiquitous British traveller, ever anxious to impress the world with his taste and discernment, could be depended upon to voice scathing criticism. Few managed to be more disparaging than George Rose, an Englishman who visited Ottawa in the mid-1860s. In *The Great Country; or Impressions of America* (1868), Rose spoke disdainfully of Canada's capital city and described his arrival there one crisp winter day as follows:

> ... there was an open sleigh waiting to convey one to the hotel, the Russell, which is said to be one of the best in Canada; if it be so, I'm sorry for Canada.
>
> As I have spoken elsewhere of American hotels as not being ... first rate, I may as well state on this occasion that I do not consider allegiance to Queen Victoria has had the

effect of improving them, for in Canada they are so like similar establishments in the United States, that there is no perceptible difference.

Dinner was served at 6:15, and had it never been served at all, no one would have regretted it, for never did mortal man have worse.

Rose went on to describe with an almost audible sniff the interior of the Russell House:

The office of the hotel at Ottawa is the chief place of resort for the guests, where they lounge and spit about as they discuss their baccy and politics, both being highly popular, especially during the session of parliament.

... the hotel was crowded with members who forsake home, business, pleasure, comfort and all, to serve their country at the low charge of six dollars ... per diem and their travelling expenses.

Why Ottawa should have been selected as the seat of the great Canadian legislature one can't imagine, except under the hypothesis that every other place wished to get rid of the nuisance. It is simple banishment, for Canada at best is the Siberia of Great Britain. One doesn't know what can induce a man to accept the post of Governor-General, unless he should be a misanthrope, or have hosts of relations at home whom he is anxious to make distant.

Of course, then as now, people who approached new experiences with a positive attitude usually saw things in a different light. Not long after George Rose made his withering comments, Peter O'Leary wrote in *Travels in Canada, the Red River Territory, and the United States* (1877) that the Russell House was

one of the largest and best hotels in North America ... in a larger room in the front [were] comfortable arm chairs ranged round for visitors to sit in, reading, smoking, chatting, or perhaps manipulating some scheme or organizing some enterprise; the room in the evening is the resort of most of the leading men in the city, and a stranger wanting to see any prominent man has only to ask for him at the office as he is sure to be heard of there.

In the early 1880s the Russell House was entirely rebuilt and refurbished, its 250 well-appointed rooms supplying the best accommodation that Ottawa had to offer. Until the Château Laurier usurped its position, the Russell House was the place to go for those who wished to see and to be seen. This famous landmark was destroyed by fire in 1928.

The hotels in Ottawa, as elsewhere, offered a variety of entertainment, both legal and illegal. Donald McArthur's Ottawa Hotel, built in 1828, housed a library, a not-uncommon amenity. Innkeeper McArthur provided the lamps, while his readers had to furnish their own coal-oil – or purchase it from him. Along with a collection of newspapers, McArthur carried a number of esoteric publications, among which was the *Dublin Philosophical and Scientific Review*. Thomas Need, travelling in the 1830s, published his recollections in *Six Years in the Bush*. Having asked the host of his country inn for a book, he noted the result:

... after a while he produced a volume of *Johnson's Dictionary*, and a *History of the United States, by an American* – he had somewhere besides a volume of Extracts from various English authors, published at Boston, under the imposing title of *British Classics* ... these books are the staple, I afterwards found, of most North American Inns.

But not all the evening's entertainments were as edifying as a perusal of *Johnson's Dictionary* by the light of a coal-oil lamp. Many of the activities that took place were illegal. Any form of gambling with dice – commonly for money, knives, or other valuables – or through games such as skittles or ninepins, was forbidden by law, and the innkeeper could lose his licence or be heavily fined for permitting it. Nevertheless gambling went on. In some inns there were boxing or 'purring' matches. (Purring was a form of boxing with the feet. With trousers rolled up over the knees the contestants faced each other, hands on their opponent's shoulders, and kicked each other's shins with their feet.)

But the most despicable diversions were those involving purposeful cruelty to animals. The Ottawa landlord who had a visit from the two bears he had kept chained to a nearby tree probably got no more than he deserved. John A. Williams of Oakville lived next door to an inn where a chained bear was fed the occasional live pig in order to amuse the local drunks.

Nor was this the only form of sadistic entertainment. Cock-fights too were staged to entice the bloodthirsty customer. As late as 1860 the *Mail* in Niagara reported a cock-fight at an inn in Queenston where the customers got more than they bargained for:

> ... between three and four hundred people assembled at Queenston on Tuesday week to witness a grand cock-fight which took place in the large room of an Inn in that village – paying half-a-dollar-a-head for admission to see the cruel spectacle of poor birds tearing one another to pieces. During the performance the weight of people in the room caused the floor to yield and sag with a loud crack; it did not fall, however, but the company was dreadfully alarmed, many of them jumped out of the windows and others were bruised and cut by their tumultuous exit ...

The cock-fight no doubt took place in that all-purpose room no self-respecting inn could be without – a ballroom. In many cases the term ballroom conjures up the picture of a far more elegant chamber than actually existed. The room was usually a large loft running the length of the building – in fact for some innkeepers this one room was the sum total of their sleeping accommodation, and mattresses were spread across the floor each night. John Mactaggart, chief engineer for the Rideau Canal, arrived one winter night at a crowded inn near Bytown and found that not only was the ballroom occupied by numerous sleeping guests but also, under a blanket on a table, lay the body of a young man: 'One side of his head seemed to be mangled in a shocking manner and covered with clotted blood.' Mactaggart and friends decided to look elsewhere for sleeping space. They found upon inquiry that 'the body ... was that of a young Irishman who had been killed two days before by a shot from a gun carelessly let off by one of the sons of the landlord.'

When John Howison, stopping at a Brockville hostelry, was led to the ballroom to sleep, he too was greeted with snores coming from all parts of the room. He asked the innkeeper how often balls were held there and was told: 'I calculate upon there being one next winter; in these times people ain't as spry as they used to be.'

But Susanna Moodie, author of *Roughing It in the Bush*, noted that dancing was the only thing that made the long Canadian winter bearable. 'I never met a Canadian girl,' she recalled, 'who could not dance and dance well.' Dancing was the chief entertainment in inns, and when a ball was held, drudgery was temporarily set aside. Settlers were known to travel two hundred miles by sleigh to dance to the fiddler's polkas, mazurkas, jigs, and hornpipes, and the dance lasted all night. A fee ranging from two to five dollars was charged by the innkeeper. That allowed a man to bring one or two partners and enjoy wines, liquors, and supper. The tone of the ball depended upon the calibre of the establishment, the host himself, and the 'class' of the guests. If the ball was a public affair there was that mixing of the classes that never failed to startle the British. Susanna Moodie commented on the phenomenon in her inimitable manner, explaining just how the system worked: 'As long as they are treated with civility, the lower classes shew no lack of courtesy to the higher.'

Bell's Corners, a hamlet nine miles west of Ottawa, had several busy inns. They catered to the throngs of farmers heading to the Ottawa market and to teamsters hauling freight from Ottawa to the lumbering shanties along the Madawaska, Bonnechère, and Mississippi rivers. Supplies moved in caravans of teams during the autumn months, and it was not unusual to see as many as fifty wagons or sleighs filling the yard at each hotel.

Adding to the commotion at times were cattle drovers on their way to the semi-annual cattle fairs. Drovers, lumbermen, and farmers all welcomed the conviviality and the brouhahas that not infrequently enlivened the stop at Bell's Corners.

The Hartin Hotel is now the only remaining hostelry at the Corners. Built of limestone and sandstone, it was originally a simple, pleasant structure with a five-bay front. A verandah sheltered the main door and stretched across the front of the building, offering protection from the elements and an inviting spot from which the patrons could watch the passing parade. Livery stables and a blacksmith's shop were at the rear.

Hartin's was built shortly after a fire in 1870 destroyed an earlier hotel on the property. David Hartin had purchased the building only a month before the fire, but, seemingly undaunted, he started business again when his new stone building was completed.

Bell's Corners was named after pioneers William and Hugh Bell, Irishmen who settled in the area before 1820. Hugh Bell made his living as a farmer and innkeeper. When the Bells arrived, the community was known as Steele's Tavern and later as Boyd's Tavern.

Not far south of Bell's Corners, a man named Chapman settled by the Jock River and kept a stopping place there as early as 1815. Four years later in this remote, unlikely, and decidedly undistinguished location, Charles Lennox, fourth Duke of Richmond and governor-in-chief of North America, died. In his honour the community was named Richmond.

It was 1819, a year after his arrival in Canada, and the Duke had embarked on a tour of the upper province to study its internal communications and defences. He arrived at Perth on 23 August, and it was there that he first experienced symptoms that soon proved fatal. He died of rabies, having been bitten a few weeks previously by a rabid animal – either a pet fox or a dog, depending on which report one reads. In a letter to the British government, Charles Cambridge provided details of the Duke's untimely demise:

> ... the Duke dined with a detachment of officers stationed at Perth, and it was only on the 25th that the first symptoms of that cruel disorder presented themselves ... Early on that morning his valet found His Grace alarmed at the appearance of some trees which were near a window where he slept, and which he insisted were people looking in, and shortly afterwards when a basin of water was presented to him, he elicited evident abhorrence at the sight it, and on several other occasions on that day, and on the 26th, the same symptoms were but too obvious whenever any liquid was presented to him, and which it now appeared His Grace partook with extreme reluctance.
>
> The same evening an assistant surgeon, the only one in the vicinity, was sent for, who bled him, and His Excellency apparently found so much relief from the operation, that he arose early next morning, and proposed walking through Richmond Wood to the new settlement of that name, which had recently received its appellation from its illustrious founder, who was now about to immortalize it, by the catastrophe of his death.
>
> He had in his progress thro' the wood started at hearing a dog bark, and was with difficulty overtaken and, at the sight of some stagnant water, His Grace hastily leaped over a fence and rushed into an adjoining barn, whither his dismayed companions eagerly followed him. The paroxysm of his disorder was now at its height. It was almost a miracle that His Grace did not die in the barn. He was removed to a miserable hovel in the neighbourhood and early in the morning of the fatal 28th, the

Duke of Richmond expired in the arms of a faithful Swiss who had never quitted his beloved master for a moment.

John M'Donald, member of a conducted emigration from Scotland, arrived at Perth in 1822. He described it as 'a thriving place' that boasted two churches, 'two bakers, several store-keepers, two or three smiths and a post office.' It also had a least one inn, the place where the ill-fated Duke of Richmond had stayed before leaving for Richmond and his death in that 'miserable hovel.'

That small inn still stands at 53–5 Craig Street, with little in its quite ordinary appearance to suggest its colourful past. The inn was owned by Lieutenant John Adamson from Guernsey in the Channel Islands, and what little we know of the man suggests that he was a something-less-than-admirable character. According to the Reverend William Bell, a Presbyterian missionary who had settled in Perth two years earlier, 'I was informed that a Mr. A—— who kept the head inn, had behaved very ill while the Duke was in his house, beating his wife and servants and turning them out of doors.'

But in spite of himself, the stern Reverend Mr Bell was impressed with the significance of the Duke's visit. Bell presented a welcoming speech and described the dinner as 'rather too expensive ... but a splendid one ... the idea of dining with a Duke so far flattered my vanity as to induce me to join in it.' The Duke, however, didn't quite measure up to the reverend gentleman's high, rigid standards – few people did – and Bell felt compelled to add:

> His Grace certainly discovered much civility and good nature but I must confess I saw nothing in his conduct to call forth all that wholesome panegyric, that was bestowed on him on that occasion. Though he remained one Sunday in Perth, he did not attend public worship, which gave me an unfavourable idea of his piety.

At the time of the Duke's visit, Adamson's Inn was a log structure. It was not until 1910 that the clapboard siding seen today was placed over the logs. In the intervening years the inn served as a centre of community activities and political rallies with, traditionally, the winning candidate and his hangers-on repairing to the inn to celebrate the victory. As well, the building was used as a Masonic hall, one of the first in this part of the province.

The village of Perth was only about three years old when the Duke of Richmond arrived on his tour of inspection. It was part of a military settlement – an expensive scheme devised by the British government after the Battle of Waterloo. There were several objectives: to help solve a serious unemployment problem in Britain; to relocate the thousands of military personnel who had become superfluous after the Napoleonic Wars; and to reinforce the dangerously underpopulated corridors of settlement along the United States northern border. Within six years of Perth's founding there were eleven thousand settlers in the Rideau corridor, about 30 per cent of whom were disbanded soldiers.

Transportation was one of the most difficult and hazardous aspects of pioneer life. Even at their best, roads, so called, were the stuff of which nightmares are made. The estimable Reverend Mr Bell, remarking on the Duke of Richmond's arrival in Perth, said that 'His landlady at the inn stated that, on the evening of his arrival in Perth, he drank seven glasses of brandy and water which clearly proved that he had been very thirsty.' This thirst, of course, may have been caused by the Duke's incipient attack of rabies, but it was just as likely that it was the result of many hours' travel through the bush. (Five years later, when the first road from Kingston to Perth was declared 'open,' it was at the same time described as 'impassable.')

With the completion of the Rideau Canal in 1832, travel in the area became easier and Ottawa more accessible. The canal,

For the exchange of news and views, plus a pint and a pipe: the Russell Hotel lobby.

which had been conceived as an alternate military route between Montreal and Kingston, linked the Ottawa River with Lake Ontario at Kingston. Designed and constructed under the supervision of Lieutenant-Colonel John By, the canal, about 125 miles long, was a remarkable engineering feat. Fifty dams were needed to control water levels along its length, and the entire project required the efforts of two thousand men, most of them Irish labourers, who built it by hand under conditions of great hardship. Because of malaria, accidents, and alcohol excess, many of them lost their lives. Yet for the people in that part of Upper Canada, the canal was a godsend. For more than a century small steamboats carried freight and passengers along its length. For settlers desperate for a link with 'civilization' it provided a good system of still-water navigation that bypassed the St Lawrence River and placed the entire Rideau corridor on a direct line with Montreal via the Ottawa River.

At Merrickville, however, the canal proved something of a mixed blessing to the family that virtually owned the town. The construction of the Rideau Canal damaged much of the land and mills belonging to the town's founder, William Merrick, but the government was disinclined to compensate him for his losses. The quarrel went on for years; even after Merrick's death in 1844, his sons were still attempting to obtain redress.

Merrick had arrived in the area almost forty years earlier to take up land grants received as a Loyalist. He built the first sawmill in 1802 and, shortly thereafter, a grist mill. Within two years he had secured title to the townsite. Described as a 'patient, plain-dealing, hard-working man ... imbued with a sense of adventure and a willingness to take risks,' William Merrick prospered, and his town prospered with him. The settlement became known as Merrick's Mills but, when the coming of the canal promised a glowing future, the town fathers decided it was time for a new name. They asked Merrick to choose one. Having been put on the spot, the modest founder declined to do so, for 'reasons of delicacy,' and thus the name Colborne was decided upon. In time it was discovered that two other communities in Upper Canada had chosen the same name and so, with a certain belated sensitivity, Merrick's Ville was named.

By 1829, when the building of the canal brought increased business and an attendant construction boom, there were several stores, fifty houses, and 'three or four respectable taverns.' Not surprisingly, the Merricks, who owned various commercial enterprises, also owned one of those 'respectable' hostelries.

Merrick's tavern – a small stone building still standing on the north side of the river – is within sight of the blockhouse built by Colonel By for the defence of the Rideau Canal. The tavern was an early business venture for Aaron Merrick, one of nine children born to William Merrick and his wife, Sylvia Comstock. Aaron, following in his father's footsteps, became the town's leading citizen, serving as JP, reeve of Wolford township, and the first reeve of Merrickville. Today the small tavern is a private home.

Thanks to the building of both the Rideau Canal and also, earlier, fortifications and a dockyard at Kingston, that town became home to a fair number of trained masons. Their presence, along with the wealth generated by Kingston's position as a commercial and shipping centre, changed the town from a community of wood buildings to one of stone. From the time of the War of 1812, when Kingston served as navy and sometimes army headquarters, the town grew dramatically, and hopes were high that it would in time be named as Canada's capital. When Ottawa won that honour in 1857, the choice proved a blow, both psychologically and economically, to the citizens of what was then one of the largest cities in the province.

Kingston had been built to fulfil a promise that never materialized. When actor Horton Rhys arrived, not long after the bubble had burst, he found

> public buildings ... ridiculously large for the requirements of the place; they are, moreover, handsome; – but there is nothing in them, and they stand alone in melancholy magnificence. The shops go in couples – two music stores, two drapers, two printers; – two everything side by side in inert rivalry. They are all fast closed at seven o'clock, as are the eyes of their proprietors by eight; and the lamps when they *are* lighted, go out simultaneously with the cats – who, by-the-way, are the most rampaginous I have ever had the misfortune to listen to.

But for the first half of the century, Kingston was a town surging with vitality and the certainty of its own importance. Sir George Head, who was there in 1815, secured lodging for the night and then went off for a walk. When he returned to his room he found that it was full of people – guests at a ball – who were using it as a card room.

> What with the good spirits of the young ladies and the good humour of the old ones, it was past three o'clock in the morning before the house was clear of its guests, when, the beds having been all taken down for the occasion, I betook myself to a mattress spread for me on the floor.

One of the more noteworthy tourists to

A 'respectable tavern' by the Rideau at Merrickville

visit Kingston and write of the experience was Charles Dickens. His impressions in 1842 were not favourable; the pen that brought to life the impressions of that celebrated traveller Mr Pickwick wrote:

> The seat of government in Canada [Kingston was then the capital of the United Canadas] is a very poor town, rendered still poorer in the appearance of its marketplace by the ravages of a recent fire. Indeed, it may be said of Kingston that one half of it appears to be burnt down, and the other half not to be built up.

Dickens was perceptive. Kingston, like so many other communities, experienced frequent spates of unplanned urban renewal brought about not by civic pride but by recurring, disastrous fires that periodically ravaged entire blocks. Given these hazards and the innate instability of the hostelry business, it is surprising that today there are several early inns still standing in Kingston. One of the earliest is John Moore's Coffee House (75–7 Princess Street), which was built in 1820, shortly after stage-coach service began along the York–Kingston road. Moore not only catered to the travelling public, but attracted local customers as well by accommodating the occasional circus in his yard. In June 1820, an elephant could be viewed there for 1s. 6d., children half price.

In the 1830s, one S. Carmino took over the Mansion House, and provided amenities such as a library and a ballroom. By mid-century the building had become a military hospital and, in 1856, a temperance group was holding meetings in the ballroom.

Not long before John Moore built his Coffee House, one of Kingston's leading citizens had built a home for his family a short distance away at 200 Ontario Street. He was Lawrence Herkimer, and his imposing limestone house stood across from the waterfront, giving the Herkimers a front-row seat from which to observe the never-ending activity there. Kingston was a thriving town in those early years, and many of the ships entering the harbour tied up at the wharf across from Lawrence Herkimer's house where, on the ground floor, he operated a wholesale liquor business.

When Herkimer built his splendid home, some time prior to 1816, Ontario Street was lower than it is today, so customers from the commercial ships and Durham boats that landed at the wharf across the way found that getting Herkimer's liquors to and from the house was an easy matter. Lawrence Herkimer's liquor business, however, was only one of his many concerns. He was also involved in shipping – he was among those responsible for building the SS *Frontenac*, the first steamship to sail Lake Ontario – and he had large land holdings, both in Kingston and in York. When he died unexpectedly in 1819 at the age of fifty-two he was already a wealthy man.

The son of Loyalist Captain Johan Jost Herkimer, Lawrence Herkimer was highly respected in Kingston. In its obituary of Herkimer, the *Kingston Chronicle* of 22 October 1819 described him as a gentleman whose character

> was marked by rectitude of principal and propriety of conduct. He was scrupulously exact and honorable in his private business, unassuming in his manners, and distinguished by a pious discharge of the duties enjoined by our Holy Religion. His unexpected death, while in the apparent possession of a robust frame and unbroken constitution, is a heavy loss to the domestic circle wherein his earthly happiness was centred and leaves a melancholy blank in the community.

That domestic circle consisted of Herkimer's wife, Elizabeth Kirby, three sons, and two daughters. Elizabeth inherited the property, but eventually it came into the hands of the younger daughter, Jane Catherine, who, about ten years after her 1838 marriage to John McPherson, turned the house into a hotel. No sooner had this been done than a mysterious fire almost destroyed the building. For nearly half a century it endured a series of owners and various attempts to enlarge and renovate the once-handsome structure. The name changed as frequently as the proprietors, and at one time or another the building was called the Albion House, the Oregon Saloon, the Hotel Iroquois, the Stanley House, and then, in 1918, the Prince George Hotel.

One of the oldest buildings in Kingston, the Prince George has been a hotel for nearly 140 years. Its appearance changed dramatically in 1895 when architect W. Newlands was retained. His addition of a mansard roof and a central tower not only provided the hotel with a third floor and more rooms, but gave it a more imposing appearance, in keeping with the flamboyant tastes of the day. The stately verandah at the front provided the finishing touch.

At about the time Herkimer's daughter and her husband were changing the family home into a commercial establishment, a man named Cicolari was achieving success in the saloon business by providing meals and liquid refreshment to customers at Kingston's bustling market. Cicolari's tavern was one of a pair of buildings at 324 King Street, all that remains of a range of stone shops built in 1837. By the 1880s, the shops, in uneasy proximity to one another, housed (at number 324) the Marble Hall Saloon, and (at number 326) the Temperance Dining Room.

Three years before Dickens's inauspicious visit to Kingston, another British traveller recounted his experiences at a time when feelings were still running high following the rebellions in Upper and Lower Canada. Kingston still was very much a frontier community. One day in 1839, two hangings took place.

The Herkimer home, now the Prince George Hotel, Ontario Street, Kingston

One was a rebel; the other was one of Bill Johnston's men ... In the evening the officers of the 83rd gave a grand ball and supper in the British-American Hotel. Over three hundred guests were present and they danced and made merry until five o'clock in the morning. In front of the jail two corpses swirled and swung in the bitter wind. The happy young women hardly glanced at them as they were tucked warmly beneath their fur rugs by their escorts. The bells jingled merrily on the horses' harness as the sleighs drove off.

In 1840 a major fire destroyed most of Brock Street, the Market Square, and Ontario Street – an event that probably accounted for Dickens's unflattering description of Kingston two years later. That fire damaged Thomas Bamford's Steamboat Hotel at 33 Brock Street, but in 1842 he rebuilt it. At about the same time, a more substantial building was going up at 16–20 Market Street and it, like Herkimer's building, was able to take advantage of its proximity to both the market and the harbour. Number 16 was called the Duke of York by its owner, John Medcalf, and then the British Empire Hotel by a later proprietor, Mr Loomis.

Charles Dickens didn't linger long enough in Kingston to witness the next great fire, a calamitous event that wiped out much of Princess Street, destroying thirty buildings, including the well-known City Hotel. Cornelius Stenson, the owner, rebuilt immediately. The new and larger building provided room for 52 guests; its dining-room could seat 150. Business prospered and, for as long as stage-coaches operated between Toronto and Montreal, they stopped to pick up passengers at the new City Hotel as well as at Irons' Hotel (178–86 Ontario Street), at Stenson's British Empire Hotel, and at Kingston's finest, the British American Hotel.

Considering the fulsome praise that their proud owners lavished upon these establishments, it seems somewhat strange to read of the difficulties encountered by one traveller at a time when the City Hotel's Archie McFaul was claiming that his place was 'the best $1.50 per day house in the Dominion.' Timothy Bigelow, during his 1875 visit to Kingston, inquired about the inns from his friend Judge Cartwright, who 'lamented that their village could not afford better accommodations.' After investigating three or four establishments that were 'small, filthy and ill-supplied,' Bigelow and his companion appealed to

> Walker, who keeps the hotel here, notwithstanding he said his beds were all occupied. While we were dining, two young British officers, who were at table, and who were lodgers in the house, politely offered us their beds, with the aid of which, by dividing them and spreading them upon the hall floor, we made out to sleep very comfortably.

Walker, the innkeeper referred to by Bigelow, was probably one of three Walker brothers who were the proprietors of the most famous hostelry in Kingston. It stood at the corner of Clarence and King and was known first as Walker's Hotel and later as the British American.

Timothy Bigelow's friend Judge Cartwright seemed surprisingly uninformed about Kingston's hostelries. He must have known, for instance, of Grimason House, a meeting place for the local Tory establishment and the unofficial political headquarters of Kingston's favourite son, Sir John A. Macdonald. At Grimason House, 344 Princess Street, Bigelow would have been assured of comfortable surroundings and a warm welcome – assuming of course that he was a Tory. The proprietor, Eliza Grimason, had stated publicly that she hated 'them damn Grits!'

The friendship between John A. Macdonald and Eliza Grimason began when he was a young lawyer and she a girl of sixteen. In 1856, according to Grimason family tradition, Eliza's husband, Henry, purchased

Grimason House

a Kingston building from John A. When Henry died eleven years later, the building was not entirely paid for. Macdonald, as Eliza's adviser, did not press her for the balance of the payments. The widow, by then forty-six years old, was left to raise two daughters and a son. She took on the running of Grimason House, and in this she succeeded admirably. The building (now called the Royal Tavern) was near John A.'s office and a handy spot for political gatherings. On election nights the hotel, crowded at the best of times, became a rallying place for the Tory faithful, with the landlady dispensing free drinks when a celebration was called for. After one successful election, Eliza and John A. were seen careering along a Kingston street in a carriage – she wearing his top hat and he wearing her bonnet!

No one ever had a more devoted follower than Sir John A. had in Eliza Grimason. When he and Lady Macdonald invited Eliza to Ottawa, she was thrilled almost beyond words. 'There's not a man like him in the livin' earth,' she claimed. And when she was shown through Earnscliffe, her joy was complete for 'in the fine big library there was my picture up beside o' His, just where He sits.'

What Eliza Grimason lacked in education, she more than made up for in intelligence and enthusiasm. Her fortune was eventually estimated at $50,000, a remarkable sum for someone who had been left a near-destitute widow. She was ninety-five years old when she died. She is buried in Cataraqui cemetery in the plot next to her adored Sir John A. – a plot she had shrewdly purchased well before her death.

One letter to her beloved friend proved that Eliza, although unlettered, was nobody's fool – she knew when and how to use her political connections:

My dear Sir John as you have not rote to me since you come hoam, I thought I would rite you. I went to Mr Kilpatrick to find out how you ware an I trust you may be spared for many a long day and especially while I live. It was my intention to see you at Ottawa but the weather is so cold that I was afraid to leave hoam and this will do as well as for one thing I want you to be so good as to apoint Tomas deputy inspector. Now Sir John it is in your power and I think if any living soul deserves it from a son I deserve it of you for you know thair is not a friend on earth I would do as much for as you all you would have to do is to tell me. Mr Kilpatrick told me to rite to you now. Sir John this once I will never ask any more from you and I was requested to ask you not to appoint that Faghey girl matron for they are the biggest grits in Kingston if you give it to a Papist be good enough to apoint Mrs Sulivan as she is the Conservative candidat and he always suported you that you know what do you care for this rotton hole of Kingston now. I wont trouble you no more but I hope you will grant my request from you ever loving friend.

Eliza Grimason

rite soon.

Grand Caravan

OF

LIVING ANIMALS,

WILL BE EXHIBITED

AT Mr. JNO. MOORE'S MANSION HOUSE,

STORE STREET, KINGSTON,

From Monday Noon, the 15th Aug. 1825

UNTIL

THURSDAY EVENING, the 18th Inst.

THE ANIMALS

CONTAINED IN THE GRAND CARAVAN,

ARE AS FOLLOWS:

NO. I.

TIPPOO SULTAN—THE

Great Hunting Elephant

OF INDIA.

The Performances of Tippoo Sultan, together with the dexterity and intrepidity of Mr. MARTIN, his keeper, produce a spectacle not only curious and diverting, but, in some instances, both horrible to the Spectator and dangerous to the keeper. Among a variety of singular marks of sagacity in this Elephant, he takes a stand in the middle of the yard, and moves briskly round, his hind feet remaining in the centre, forming a circle with his head—places his keeper on his tusks, and in continued repetition, round the circle, tosses him up to the height of fifteen or eighteen feet, and with the most singular, and seemingly studied accuracy, catches him upon his tusks and trunk, and in conclusion give him a toss into the air—the keeper turns a Somerset in his flight, and safely lands upon the back of the Elephant.—The nature of the circumstance, and want of security of the keeper, renders this exploit more dangerous and intrepid than the hanging feats of the celebrated Mr. Stoker. This very superior Elephant is superior in size to any in the country, being nine feet high, and weighing between six and seven thousand pounds.

NO. II.

Upper Canada Herald, 9 August 1825

The Danforth Road

JAMES FULTON.
Richmond Hill, Markham. Nov. 13th, 1829.

Stray Ox and Steer.

Broke into the inclosure of the Subscriber, a LARGE OX, blind of the off eye, with seven wrinkles on his horn, a yellowish Red and White colour; also a RED STEER with him, nearly three years old; with a brindle face, and part white under his breast. The owner or owners are requested to prove property, pay charges, and take the animals away.

...deed for cash, or if one half or one third of the purchase money is paid down. Immediate possession can be given, and, for further particulars apply to PHILIP CODY.
Toronto, Nov. 16th, 1829. 287z.

WHERE IS WILLIAM SUTHERLAND!

THE Subscriber is desirous of ascertaining the place of abode of Mr. William Sutherland and family. They lived in or near Glengarry, about the time of the last war, and were originally from the parish of Kindonan, Sutherlandshire. Address a letter to the Subscriber, at Niagara, care of Messrs. Chrysler, Merchants.

N. B. Mrs. Sutherland's maiden name was Catharine Macpherson.

DANIEL MACPHERSON.
Niagara, 17th Nov. 1829. 2873.

Boarding.

THE Subscriber can furnish Boarding, Lodging, &c. for six steady mechanics, reasonable, on Dundas Street, between Mr. Willmot's Tavern and four doors from Mr. Bird's Tavern, in the house lately occupied by Mr. George Hutchison, Plaisterer.

JAMES PARKER.
Nov. 18. 87.

STRAYED, on the 10th October last, into the premises of ANDREW BIGHAM, on lot No. 12, in the first concession of ETOBICOKE, A LIGHT IRON-GREY HORSE, rising five or six years of age.—The owner is requested to prove property, pay charges, and take him away.
Nov. 17. 873.

SAWYER & LABOURERS WANTED.

WANTED by the subscriber, a Sawyer who understands his business, and two men who understand Chopping; to whom liberal encouragement will be given. Apply to JAMES STEPHENS.

SALT RHEUM.—This inveterate disease, which has long baffled the art of the most experienced physicians, has, at length, found a sovereign remedy in Dr. La Grange's genuine ointment. ...

PETER PATERSON, Agent.

SWEDES IRON.

WILLIAM BUDDEN, Point a' Calliere.
August 18, 1829. 274-z

LOOKING GLASSES.

...ceived by the subscriber, a large and elegant ...of Looking Glasses; German Plate; a variety, and the prices remarkably low.
J. R. ARMSTRONG.

YORK FURNACE.

F. R. DUTCHER continues his FURNACE in complete operation, where can be had, at short notice,

Castings of any description from one to thirty cwt:

Also on hand a general assortment of STOVES, HOLLOW WARE, PLOUGH CASTINGS and PLOUGHS.

THEODORE BURLEY,

SMITH AND *Brass Founder:*

Yonge Street, next door to Judge Macaulay.

THE SUBSCRIBERS have just received direct from London, a general assortment of
Hosiery,
Black and Colored Gros-de-Naples,
Figured Norwich Crapes,
Black Silk and Cotton Velvets,
Sewing Silks,
Lace Thread Edgings,
Worked Insertions, and Scollop Muslins,
Red and Bell Cotton,
Geo. the 4th Regulation Swords, Belts, & Sashes,
...ware and Cutlery,
J. C. GODWIN & Co.

WILLIAM KENT.
Stoney Creek, Nov. 13, 1829.

NEWMARKET MAIL STAGE.

WILLIAM GARBUTT, having taken the contract for carrying His Majesty's Mails between York and Newmarket, for the next four years, respectfully informs the public that THE MAIL STAGE will start from Joseph Bloor's Hotel, York, on Mondays and Thursdays, 12 o'clock, noon, and arrive at nine o'clock, the same evening in Newmarket;—and will leave Mr. Barber's Tavern Newmarket, for York, on Wednesdays and Saturdays, at ... in the morning, and arrive in York at 2 P. M. on the same days.

Mr. BARBER will accommodate passengers arriving with the Mail Stage at Newmarket; and they may be comfortably conveyed to the Holland Landing, or in other directions if required.
York, March 30th, 1829. 254z.

NEW ARRANGEMENT OF STAGES

Between York and the Carrying Place at the head of the Bay of Quintie.

THE Public are respectfully informed that a Mail Stage will run regularly twice a week between York and the Carrying Place; leaving York every Monday and Thursday at 12 o'clock, noon, and arriving at the Carrying Place on Tuesdays and Fridays at 2 o'clock, P. M. ...

Every attention will be given to render passengers comfortable while on the line, and the drivers instructed to stop at the best hotels on the route.

All baggage at the risk of the owners.
Extras furnished to any part of the country.
The Stage Books will be kept at Mr. Bradley's Steamboat Hotel.

CHAPTER FOUR

The Danforth Road

STAGE-COACH TRAVEL

'Half a log, half a log
Half a log onward,
Shaken and out of breath,
Rode we and wondered.
Ours not to reason why
Ours but to clutch and cry
While onward we thundered.'

Carrie M. Hoople, 'The Corduroy Road,' 1909

WHEN THE first stage line opened on the York–Kingston road in 1817, passengers had to stretch their imaginations to find words to describe the experience. 'Bone-jarring,' 'head-cracking,' 'violent,' 'primitive,' 'fatiguing to the last gasp': these, of course, were descriptions penned by the lucky ones who were not pitched out of the coach as it was 'forging, like a ship in a head-sea' into one hole after another. The alternative to being pitched out was to be thrown against the roof, and so it was considered wise to travel with a hat on in order to prevent direct contact between the head and the ceiling. And then there were those other unwelcome exits from the coach, when all hands had to help push the vehicle out of the mud or up a hill. It seemed that the trip was a combined effort, with the coach sometimes transporting the passengers and the passengers sometimes propelling the coach. Some travellers found it safer and faster to walk to York from Kingston. By so doing they could get there a day ahead of the stage-coach.

Stage-coach travel, however, in spite of the difficulties, was a boon to settlers in the early nineteenth century. It brought with it a mail system with some degree of regularity and enabled travellers to cover distances that would otherwise have been virtually impossible, particularly when any amount of baggage was involved. By mid-century, when William Weller was the stage-coach king of the area around Lake Ontario, travel was almost pleasant. Roads had improved, and coaches had such amenities as springs. This was the heyday of the stage-coach era. It lasted until the railways began to arrive in the mid-1850s.

The stage-coach business was part of an extensive travel network. It involved the coaches and drivers of the stage line, toll-gate keepers, ferry operators, blacksmiths, and innkeepers, who provided drink, food, and overnight lodging for the battered passengers. (The word 'stage-coach' was originally applied to a coach that ran from station to station over a number of stages in the road, with fresh horses supplied at each stage.)

No one appreciated a stop more than the stage-coach drivers, a hardy breed for whom jolting and jostling was a way of life. Frequently they and the innkeepers had some mutually satisfactory financial arrangement, so that a prolonged stop meant fuller pockets for both. The result was predictable. One traveller on the Brantford road, realizing that the driver was drunk, got off the coach when it slowed momentarily. Proceeding on foot he soon caught up with the coach and found that the unlucky passengers had 'been tossed about by fast driving over the stump of a tree, all having been thrown from the wagon, one breaking his shoulder blade and another being unconscious.' The horses had bolted and the wagon lay in pieces.

For the coach driver, however, it was an exciting life, one that attracted many adventurous immigrants, particularly the Irish. They wanted the work, not so much for the pay of ten to twelve dollars a month, but for the challenge and variety it offered. Drivers were often injured, sometimes fatally, when thrown from their coaches. They were also the first to suffer when the occasional robbery occurred. (Local legends tell of adept drivers hiding a payload in gold from pursuing highwaymen. Stories like these have led to fortune-hunting forays along the old York-to-Kingston Road.)

Samuel Purdy started stage-coach operations in 1816, between Kingston and Bath (in the next year the road was extended to York). His was the first stage run on the Danforth. For the Kingston–York run he charged eighteen dollars and allowed twenty-eight pounds of baggage per person. Initially his service lasted only until the ice broke up each year, for passengers preferred travel by water when it was feasible. It lacked the 'bone-jarring' and 'head-crunching' aspects of travel by land.

With the opening of Purdy's line in 1816, inns sprang up along the route. At Amherstview, the Fairfield family allocated a few rooms of their large home to travellers. The licence required that they have at least three rooms over and above family requirements and that they provide their guests with adequate stabling.

The Fairfields' imposing two-storey house faced south overlooking Lake Ontario and the steamships that plied its waters. The narrow road that led from Kingston to Bath passed conveniently a few yards from their back door. What better location could there be for an inn? The Fairfields could, and did, entertain travellers all year long.

William Fairfield, his wife, Abigail, and their six children were among the first United Empire Loyalists to settle along the north shore of the lake. By 1793, Fairfield, with the help of his four slaves, had built his spacious house, which, in the ensuing years, gradually filled with more Fairfield offspring. Six children were born to the Fairfields after their arrival in Canada, and so it was not until the 1820s that the family found itself with the space necessary to become innkeepers. Tavern licence records show licences issued in the Fairfield name from 1826 to 1850.

The Fairfields were far from being the first innkeepers along the Bath Road. To the west, in the village of Bath, Henry Finkle had been dispensing food, drink, and a rudimentary style of justice since shortly after the Loyalists arrived in 1784. His tavern (no longer standing) catered to travellers and, when necessary, served as a courthouse as well. One of the first courts held in Upper Canada took place at Finkle's Tavern when a black man was tried for stealing a loaf of bread, found guilty, and sentenced to thirty-nine lashes. Sentence was meted out on the spot, with the recipient tied to a nearby tree.

Henry and his wife, Lucretia Bleecker Finkle, were Loyalists, among the first to be aware of the commercial potential in serving the travelling public. The Finkles operated their tavern and also started a steamship business. Their grandson later opened a stage-coach line and a factory to build coaches. Henry's brother, John, with similar entrepreneurial spirit, operated the first brewing and distilling business in Upper Canada.

Among the first to patronize Finkle's Tavern was surveyor Asa Danforth, who used the place as his headquarters while he and his men were building the first road

Beside the Bath Road, the splendid Fairfield White House

from Kingston to York in 1799.

The old Bath Road ended just west of Adolphustown. From the beginning of the nineteenth century, a ferry routinely carried travellers, their vehicles, and livestock from Adolphustown across the Adolphus Reach to Glenora in Prince Edward County and the continuation of the Danforth Road. The early ferries used horse power, with two horses working a treadmill, which moved the barge. Once across the water, travellers had to venture only a short distance before reaching the next inn, although most of that distance was in an upward direction.

The Stone Mills Stage and Ferry Inn stands atop a steep hill overlooking the mills at Glenora and the beauties of Adolphus Reach. Built not long after 1807, when recent immigrant Elephalet Adams purchased the property, it was a spacious but spare utilitarian structure, lacking even a verandah to soften its exterior plainness. The Stone Mills Inn was already a well-known landmark when in 1831 its owner, Jacob Adams, decided to sell:

LOOK AT THIS

To be sold and possession given on the first of May next, the well known tavern situated near the Stone Mills in Marysburgh with the ferry across the bay of Quinty and 200 acres of excellent land. Its proximity to the Stone Mills and in the direct road from the thriving village of Hallowell to Kingston makes it a desirable stand for business.

Thomas Eyre's Inn, Bridge Street, Picton

The inn was later purchased by John Green, foreman in the iron foundry and owner and operator of the ferry. Like many others who served the travelling public, Green recognized the possibilities inherent in linking related business enterprises – it was not unusual to find stage-line operators who owned steamships, others who developed reciprocal arrangements with innkeepers, ferry owners who owned inns, innkeepers who owned blacksmith's shops, and farmers who ran inns. One thing led to another in a pragmatic chain of related enterprises.

Glenora was the site of mills built in 1796 by Loyalist Peter Van Alstine. Here Hugh Macdonald, father of Canada's first prime minister, ran the flour and carding mill. Here also the young John A. lived and, in later years, campaigned. He was said, of course, to have spent many a happy hour in the taproom of the Stone Mills Stage and Ferry Inn – and few would argue the likelihood that that occurred.

Down the road at Hallowell Bridge (Picton's original name) was Thomas Eyre's inn. It too opened to the public in 1807, and so for many years was the next stop for travellers after they had refreshed themselves at the Stone Mills Inn. The building standing at 64 Bridge Street is not the original structure but was built in the 1830s or 1840s to replace its more primitive predecessor.

Township records dating from 1798 show that Eyre's first home was a centre for the town's activities. In 1806 the annual meeting was held 'at the dwelling house of Thomas Eyre' and, the following year, at 'the Inn of Thomas Eyre,' so undoubtedly this was the year that Eyre started providing food and drink for profit.

Meetings at Eyre's were presided over by two of 'His Majesty's Justices of the Peace,' and all official appointments for the coming year were made there – town clerks, wardens, highway overseers, poundkeepers, and fence-viewers. Here too the

Hayes' Tavern: restored elegance near Waupoos

locals fought to decide the town's name – an issue that polarized the community. One faction wanted Hallowell, after the colourful Benjamin Hallowell, a former British customs officer from Boston who terminated his responsibilities there pursued by 160 members of the Continental Cavalry at full gallop. The other side opted for Sir Thomas Picton, a British general and a relative of the pious William Macaulay, an influential local clergyman. Arguments at Eyre's were heated, with the Hallowell proponents charging that Macaulay had weighted the scales in favour of his relative by heavy contributions towards the construction of a new court-house and jail.

On 16 June 1837, a skilled hand carved the date into the first planks to be used in the construction of Hayes' Tavern, a few miles west of Picton in the village of Consecon. When construction was finished more than a year later, the date 'October 1838' was added. These marks were made either by Martin Miller, the carpenter and joiner responsible for the superior workmanship, or by the proud new owner, Richard Hayes. It is anyone's guess as to who later carved the pithy 'R.H. Esq. Rogue and Liar' into the woodwork.

Martin Miller was only twenty-three when he built this refined and beautifully detailed inn in a remote Prince Edward County village. He was an American, and he and his Irish-born wife, Elizabeth, had four children.

Just three years after it was completed, the inn became the property of George Hayes, probably Richard's brother. The deed of sale, dated 9 October 1841, gave a good description of the property: ½ acre

The Farmers and Drovers Inn at Westbrook

with buildings thereon erected known by the name of Hayes' Tavern which said building is at present occupied as an inn by the said Richard Hayes with all the out-buildings consisting of barn, stables, sheds, yards and all the other apurtenances thereon.' George Hayes paid one thousand pounds for all this.

George's wife, Susan Marsh, was a great-granddaughter of Colonel William Marsh, whose services to the Crown during the American Revolution had reaped a reward of thousands of wilderness acres in Upper Canada. He never settled in Canada but left the land to his sons, one of whom, Matthias, eventually became the owner of two thousand acres and the father of two dozen children. One of those twenty-four, Archibald, was the father of Susan Hayes. George's father-in-law owned all of Consecon and much more of the surrounding land as well. George ran the inn for six years, and then it passed to the Pennock family, first Samuel and then John, both merchants.

By 1869, Consecon was a busy village, and the inn had become the Porter Hotel. It was run by Robert Porter and his wife, Hannah, until 1895. Over the years, as Consecon's fortunes diminished, the hotel fell into disrepair, and its days seemed numbered. But by great good fortune it was rescued in 1966 by a discerning and far-sighted purchaser and moved, board by board, to the village of Waupoos – on the opposite shore a few miles to the east, but still in 'The County.' Now years of laborious, painstaking restoration have made the building a thing of rare beauty. It stands in incongruous splendour beside a curve in the road, its fine proportions and classical detailing causing passers-by to catch their breath in delighted astonishment.

From Kingston to York the most direct route led through Cataraqui and along what is now Highway 2. One of the first stage stops was at Westbrook, where James Sproul, who had emigrated from Ireland in the mid-1850s, operated a modest hostelry he called the Farmers and Drovers Inn.

Sproul was living in his two-storey stone dwelling in 1851 and was still in business fourteen years later when the *Kingston Directory* of 1865 listed him as sawmill owner, hotel proprietor, and farmer. Clearly his operations had prospered as travel along the Kingston Road increased.

The hazards of travel between coaching stops involved discomfort not only from swaying carriages and unspeakably bad roads but often from the disparate nature of the passengers themselves. Stages were confining, journeys were long, and tempers were short, particularly after several forays out of the coach to extricate it from yet another cavernous, mire-filled hole. Some passengers who would sooner have stayed at arm's length – or farther – from their fellow travellers found themselves squeezed uncomfortably close to one another. Given the lack of facilities for bathing in those days, this meant that the trip could often be a highly sensory experience.

Few passengers disliked each other's company more than the proud, uppity British and the upstart Yankees. Frances Trollope, mother of writer Anthony Trollope, summed up her disgust in *Domestic Manners of the Americans*. She concluded that they had none. On an 1832 trip, the unfortunate woman found herself in a coach already crowded with seven hefty passengers when a Yankee arrived carrying his lady friend's hat-box. He suggested that a British passenger get out to make way for the hat-box. The Britishers indignantly refused, causing the Yankee to rail against 'British tyranny,' claiming that 'we makes our own laws, and governs our own selves ... we don't want no foreign power to tyrannize over us.' Mrs Trollope summed up the incident by noting tersely that it 'revived our doubts whether the invading white men, in chasing the poor Indians from their forests, have done much towards civilizing the land.'

Anna Jameson, another of those intrepid British women who travelled extensively and penned acerbic descriptions of their adventures, wrote of a journey during which she found herself close to a man who was not only a Yankee but a drunk one at that. She knew that he was an American because 'his nasal accent, and his drunken objurations against the old country and all who came from it, betrayed his own birth and breeding to have been on the other side of the Niagara.' He was 'degraded, haggard and inflamed with filth and inebriety.' For the Yankee, the feeling was mutual, and he finally 'exclaimed, with a scowl and a hiccup of abomination at every word, "I should like – to know – madam – how – I came under your diabolical influence?"'

Inns were frequently used as polling places during elections. Fralick's Inn (lot 28, concession 5, North Fredericksburgh), east of Napanee near Morven, served this purpose and was the scene of many lively and often physical 'discussions' of matters political. Because there was a rival inn across the road, competition for business was as brisk as the competition for votes. Polling at the time went on for several days because some settlers had to travel very long distances to exercise their franchise. These weary voters were unlikely to turn around and head for home immediately after casting their ballots. Few of them did. For years there were no regulations requiring the closing of taverns during an election – with the inevitable result. John Fralick, like most innkeepers, welcomed elections, which were good for business.

A visit to Fralick's in 1817 was a memorable event for the elegant young Charles Fothergill, a writer and artist who found conditions at the inn shocking to say the least:

> Frelick's inn by no means so good as represented, full of people, obliged to take tea with divers Yankees of no agreeable cast ... The kind of freedom of manner, amounting to downright impertinence, & a great mixture of rank & persons in Yankee inns or where Yankee customs are prevalent, is extremely disagreeable to an Englishman. Indelicacy too prevails, decent & even pretty girls hawking & spitting ab^{t} the room, occasionally scratching &

Fralick's Inn, east of Napanee, once a polling station

rubbing themselves & lounging in attitudes in their chairs in a way that in Britain w[d] be unpardonable & throwing out more than broad hints, occasionally as to the sexual intercourse.

Because stumps, rocks, and potholes frequently made coach travel a nightmarish experience, winter travel was preferred when at all possible; the smoother ride on snow more than made up for the biting cold weather. Snuggled down under fur robes, passengers found travel by sleigh to be exhilarating – if, of course, the next tavern was not too far distant. John Mactaggart whose *Three Years in Canada* was published in 1829, described sleighs as

neither all of one name nor construction. The Traineaux are the simplest ... built on low runners or slides, drawn from a bar below, which shoves the snows before it, and forms the cahots or waves on the road, which are so troublesome ... The Burline is the travelling sleigh of the Canadians; it is just large enough to hold two comfortably ... It is on low runners, and not easily upset; it has horns by which the driver balances it; it will glide over very rough roads and untrod snows. The Cutter is on high runners. The Americans are very fond of this sort: they are easily upset; but on smooth roads, or where the snows are not deep, they are more commodious than the Burline. The Carriole is the noblest vehicle of the whole, and will carry a whole family. Some of these are constructed in a very genteel manner, silver-mounted, and in every respect as elegant, if not more so than an English coach ... The Grandees make a wonderful display in them.

Mactaggart was aware, however, that

Proctor's Halfway House, on the Kingston Road, west of Brighton

travel by sleigh on the frozen lake, although inviting, was hazardous at best. He cautioned that, although Lake Ontario froze about two feet thick, the safest route for the traveller was near the shore, because

> the ice is more safe there and ... should it break in, he has a better chance to get out. Often horses and sleighs will break smack through, sink beneath the ice, and be seen no more ... If the horses are allowed to plunge much, there is no chance of saving them: they have therefore to hang them, to keep them quiet, until they are pulled out, when the noose on the neck is slackened, and life permitted to return.

When a traveller approached Brighton, whether by sleigh or stage-coach, he had a choice of inns. There were two at the corner of Main and Ontario streets, or he could go west of town to Proctor's Inn. If he was a temperance advocate then the choice was simple – he headed for Bettes' Temperance Hotel, still standing on the south-west corner of the intersection of Main and Ontario streets.

While Bettes's hostelry met the needs of temperate travellers or those who simply wanted a good night's sleep, it also served the community at large by housing the local doctor, who set up his offices in the building – a not-uncommon occurrence in those days.

If the occurrence was common, not so the doctor. He was A.E. Fife and, as he announced to the world in the *Brighton Sentinel*, 12 August 1853, he had found the following diseases prevalent in Brighton:

> Affection of the Lungs, Liver, Kidneys, Spleen and their attendant symptoms as Rheumatism, Dropsy, Shortness of breath, Asthma, Palpatation, Faintness or weakness at the pit of the Stomach, Dyspepsia, Melancholy, Acidity, Flatulency, Costiveness, Piles, Diarrhaea, Catarrh, Nervousness, Dizziness, Pain in the Head, Nausea, Numbness, Cold Hands and Feet, Weakness and pain across the small of the back, Pain in the Sides and Shoulders etc. etc.

The good doctor went on to claim that 'my practice is eclectic; based upon true

Bettes' Hotel, where Doctor Fife cured his patients' every ill

philosophical principles; employing such remedies to remove disease as act in perfect harmony with the laws of nature and animal life.'

Those seeking a cure for any of the above ailments could reach Dr Fife at Bettes' Temperance Hotel. Best of all, the doctor added the magic words 'free of charge.'

If Bettes' Temperance Hotel held no appeal for a traveller, whisky was always available across the road at Hodges' Tavern, a two-storey frame building at 156 Main Street. It had been in operation since 1835, when Ira Hodges first received his tavern licence. Later the inn became known as Turkington's Hotel.

On the west side of Brighton (lot 6, concession 2, Brighton Township) stands Proctor's halfway house. In 1856 the crown patent went to Isaac C. Proctor, who built the sizeable frame building to serve as a stage-coach stop. Isaac was the brother of John Proctor, Brighton's leading entrepreneur, owner of ships and mills and a good deal of Brighton itself.

The arrival of the stage-coach was an event made more or less theatrical at the whim of the driver. One coachman well remembered in Brighton and beyond was George Mink, who enjoyed making an entrance by careering down Brighton's lengthy main street with horn blowing and horses at full gallop. Mink, the son of a slave, was popular with his customers and had a successful career operating inns both in Toronto and Kingston. He also liked to drive his own coaches.

Though he was financially successful, George Mink's life was beset by tragedy. According to John Ross Robertson, in *Landmarks of Toronto*, George Mink retired with quite a fortune for the time and spent approximately ten thousand dollars of it to attract an eligible white husband for his beloved daughter. In time a candidate appeared and the couple were married; they then left for the United States, where the scoundrel sold his bride into slavery. Mink, distraught, spent the remainder of his wealth to free her, which he eventually did.

Old Joe Keeler's frame tavern, Colborne

Winter Arrangements.

THE ROYAL MAIL STAGE

WILL leave the North American Hotel, Division Street, for Kingston, every morning at 8 o'clock, or after the arrival of the Mail Stage from Toronto, calling at all intermediate places between Cobourg and Kingston.

This mail having changed hands, the subscriber wishes to inform the public that he will use his utmost exertions for the comfort and safety of those who may favor him with their patronage.

GEO. MINK, Proprietor.
N. C. ENGLISH,
General Agent.

Cobourg, Jan. 10th, 1852. 21

Parcels sent by this line will meet with all possible care and attention.

Cobourg Star, 19 January 1853

His last years were spent with his daughter in Toronto, where they lived simply, as dictated by their now impoverished circumstances.

Keeler's Tavern, at King and Parliament streets in the village of Colborne, was restored in 1970. Removal of the ugly insulbrick revealed what had been a simple but pleasantly proportioned frame structure beneath. It had operated as an inn from the early nineteenth century, bearing the name of a family that had settled there in 1789. Joseph Keeler came from Vermont and, before the turn of the century, had encouraged forty families to settle with him on the shores of Lake Ontario at what became Colborne's harbour, a settlement now called Lakeport.

Joseph Keeler's son and grandson were both named after him but, to avoid confusion, the three were known locally as Old Joe, Young Joe, and Little Joe. It was Young Joe who founded Colborne by establishing a store and post office in 1815. Before the village adopted a new name honouring Sir John Colborne, it was simply known as Keeler's Tavern, after its first and most important citizen, Old Joe Keeler.

Old Joe owned an illegal still in Colborne's harbour. But in 1808 the law caught up with this sideline, and he was fined two pounds for operating without a licence. By January 1817, Keeler was legally operating a 56-gallon still. This amount seemingly failed to meet demand, and the following year he increased his output and was licensed for 'a wooden still of 124 gallon capacity.'

Old Joe was well known for his kindness to travellers. Phoebe Roberts, a member of the Society of Friends (Quakers) travelling on a missionary tour in 1821, had a meeting scheduled to take place at Keeler's Tavern. As she noted on 31 October 1821:

> got to our Inn agreeable to the time appointed but there was no meeting on account of the great rain. Joseph Keler treated us kindly, free gratis.

West of Colborne, at Grafton, Charles Fothergill, the intrepid traveller who was so displeased by the behaviour of the women at Fralick's Inn, found when he arrived at Grover's Inn that his concerns now centred on the character of the landlord:

> Found Grover a one-eyed, dark complexioned & very shabby & suspicious looking fellow & drunk withal & very loquacious & very consequential in his own eyes. Settled here 15 years ago (1802) when there was not a soul within many miles of him ... I did not like his manners nor the continual surprize he expressed at my travelling alone in such a country & his frequent interogatory whether I was not afraid of being robbed & murdered ... As he lifted my portmanteau into my bedroom remarked on its weight saying it must be full of money. I did not like his manner of handling & pointing my double-barrelled gun ...

The next morning brought a more assuring impression. 'My landlord sober was a very superior man, as may be readily supposed, to my landlord drunk.'

Grover's was sold to Edward Pepper; whereupon, to no one's surprise, it assumed the name of Pepper's Tavern. Pepper in time developed loftier ambitions for his establishment and so placed a notice in the *Cobourg Star* on 11 July 1832:

> For Sale – All that excellent and well known Tavern stand in the village of Grafton with Outhouses, Sheds etc. ... known for many years by the name of Grover's Tavern and now in the occupation of Mr Pepper.

After that portion of the property on which the old tavern stood was sold, Pepper built the impressive Mansion House, a building that still dominates the centre of the village today under the name of the Grafton Village Inn. So imposing was the Mansion House that it prompted one traveller to extol its virtues, in particular that of its new sign, in the *Cobourg Star* of 27 November 1833:

> A beautiful sign ... had just been elevated, displaying the British Arms in bold relief, under which are emblazoned the national emblems of the constituent parts of the United Empire. May the Rose, the Thistle and the Shamrock ever be in unity, and then we can bid defiance ... to a world in arms against us.

Back in the days when Grover still owned the inn, a meeting was called in order to choose a name for the village. Grafton had been the home of the Grover family in Massachusetts – a fact that explains why the hospitable Mr Grover provided amply for the many toasts to the choice, toasts that continued well into the night. Grover's was also the spot where a meeting of a different cut took place: the 'Grafton and Haldimand Moral Society for the Suppression of Vice Etc.' was formed in the tavern. Political candidates were nominated there and, until the town hall was built in 1859, the inn, by then the new Mansion House, was the scene of most public meetings.

It was, however, not the only choice. There were, unbelievably, six inns in the village of Grafton, one of them the well-known inn built by Thomas Spalding when the York Road opened in 1817. That structure was either replaced by or formed part of the handsome two-storey brick building Spalding built in 1835, a building that stands today as a landmark at the west end of town.

Upper Canada's best-known coach-line entrepreneur was Cobourg's William Weller. His fame derived from his fine coaches, his reliable service, and some valuable publicity he garnered in 1840. That year Weller bet one thousand pounds that he could convey the governor-general, Lord Sydenham, from Toronto to Montreal in time to catch a ship. Weller insisted upon driving the entire 375 miles himself, with the governor, snug under fur rugs, stretched out in the sleigh. He made the trip in thirty-five hours and forty minutes, stopping only to change horses. Weller won his thousand-pound bet, earned one hundred pounds for the passage, and received as well a gold pocket watch and a good deal of prestige.

Built in Cobourg, William Weller's coaches were handsome vehicles, the acknowledged ultimate in style. In an 1832 letter, one early traveller, Mrs William Radcliff, noted:

> There are three rows of seats ... the centre seat moves on a pivot so as to clear the doorway and allow free ingress and egress, for those who occupy the other two.

The most elaborate of the Weller coaches boasted rosewood or mahogany writing desks, only of use, of course, when the coach was stationary. In 1837 the *Cobourg Star* proudly announced that the latest Weller coach was

> a very handsome coach and six, driven in hand, intended for the line of six-horse stages newly established by him between Toronto and Hamilton. The carriage is of improved construction and being painted a light yellow, with the harness entirely new and drawn by six spirited bay horses, it made an imposing appearance.

Not all coaches were as splendid as Weller's. The average stage-coach in Upper Canada consisted of a wooden carriage, which could be colourful, streamlined, or simply a nondescript wooden box, depending on the whim of the builder. It was suspended by leather straps attached to the framework of the vehicle. The open sides

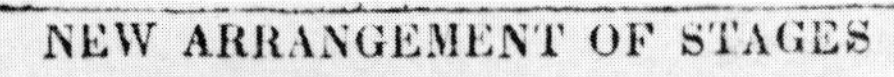

NEW ARRANGEMENT OF STAGES

Between York and the Carrying Place, at the head of the Bay of Quintie.

THE Public are respectfully informed that a Mail Stage will run regularly twice a week between York and the Carrying Place; leaving York every Monday and Thursday at 12 o'clock, noon, and arriving at the Carrying Place on Tuesdays and Fridays at 2 o'clock, P. M. Will leave the Carrying Place every Tuesday and Friday at 9 o'clock A. M. and arrive at York on Wednesdays and Saturdays, at 12 o'clock noon. There will also a Stage leave Cobourg every Monday at 10 o'clock, A. M. and arrive at the Carrying Place the same day, and leave the Carrying Place every Saturday at 9 o'clock, A. M. and arrive at Cobourg the same day.

The above arrangements are in connexion with the Steam Boats *Sir James Kempt* and *Toronto*, so that Travellers going the route will find a pleasant and speedy conveyance between Kingston and York, as the line is now fitted up in good order with good carriages, good horses and careful drivers.

Every attention will be given to render passengers comfortable while on the line, and the drivers instructed to stop at the best hotels on the route.

All Baggage at the risk of the owners.

Extras furnished to any part of the country.

The Stage Books will be kept at Mr. Bradley's Steamboat Hotel.

*** The roads between Kingston and York are of late much improved.

WILLIAM WELLER.

York 30th June, 1829. 267-z.

Colonial Advocate, 16 July 1829

Such beauty promised a warm welcome: Thomas Spalding's 1835 inn, Grafton

had leather curtains for protection from the elements, and luggage was stored at the back or on the roof. The driver perched on a ledge at the front and was sometimes accompanied by the occasional passenger, who probably preferred to see the potholes before sinking into them, or perhaps simply wished to escape from the other inmates.

Weller, the highly respected king of the Toronto-to-Montreal line, had various secondary lines, a carriage works and stable in Cobourg, and an inn at Gores Landing on Rice Lake. The inn, much altered, is still there.

William Weller's many enterprises prospered through the 1850s, and so did he. A successful politician, he was elected mayor of Cobourg three times. Local papers reported the 'almost proverbial security and regularity' of his line. This security was tested in an 1839 incident that received much press in Cobourg. On one run the driver and passengers had been forced to get out and walk up a steep hill near Port Hope. On this occasion, when the coach finally heaved up to the hill top, the driver stopped to inspect the trunks that had been strapped to the 'hind boot.' Mysteriously, the straps had been cut, and the trunks were gone. The driver, on horseback and with the coach lamp in one hand, made a heroic pass through the woods, raised the local inhabitants, and eventually recovered the loot.

The press reported Weller's tragedies, too. On a winter day in December 1855, his two young sons

> were playing on the ice near their father's residence when the eldest, an interesting lad of about nine years of age fell through. The younger brother, prompted by the case of duty

The Kennaleys' fourteen-room hostelry built in Keene and now at Century Village, Lang

and affection, attempted to extend relief; but alas, he with his brother were drowned before assistance arrived.

Eventually, the arrival of the railway brought an end to stage-coach travel between the major centres. This, and the failure of the Cobourg-to-Peterborough Railway, in which Weller had invested heavily, spelled disaster for the flamboyant entrepreneur, and he was forced to liquidate his holdings. He died a poor man, in 1863.

A sturdy two-storey stone building in Hamilton Township (lot 26, concession 2) served as an inn on the Burnham Road north of Cobourg. This was part of a route that wound through the villages of Camborne, Cold Springs, and Bewdley, joining the road to Peterborough.

The Burnham Road inn, a typical rural hostelry, was built in 1857 by John Ford. At one time a verandah offered a sheltered place for guests to sit or escape from inclement weather. (Verandahs were commonly seen on inns, their presence adding a decorative touch but serving a practical purpose as well. Sad to say, harsh climatic conditions gradually caused most of them to deteriorate.)

Ford's Inn was sold to Thomas Dayman in 1873. But there were many other inns in the area to serve travelling farmers. The road continued to be used for local traffic and the occasional passer-by of more exotic mien. Thomas Dayman's descendants, present owners of the building, tell tales that have been handed down in the family about a travelling circus (including elephants) that once lumbered by on its way to Cobourg.

A small frame building, stuccoed with

lime, was built in the village of Keene (just north of Rice Lake, south-east of Peterborough) some time before 1836. Initially it housed Thomas Carr, son of Andrew, an early settler in Peterborough County. But like many other houses located on a sparsely settled stretch of road, the old Carr house expanded its walls and its purpose and became an inn. Travellers heading west to Millbank or north to the main Peterborough-to-Ottawa road (now Highway 7) were welcomed by Martin and Mary Jane Kennaley, listed as innkeepers in 1878.

Shortly after it was built, the Carr house was sold to Thomas Short, a merchant who held positions as councillor, justice of the peace, and warden of Peterborough County. Short doubled the size of the building by adding a two-storey addition at the rear, but lost the house when he became bankrupt in 1862. When the Kennaleys purchased the house sixteen years later there were fourteen rooms to fill. This, however, was no problem. They had eight children of their own, raised Mrs Kennaley's sister's orphaned children, and took in guests as well.

But the building was accommodating for the purpose. The restoration, planned by architect B. Napier Simpson, Jr, reveals the layout of the inn. The front section, the original Carr house, had a main hallway with waiting room and ladies' retiring room on the left. The barroom was on the right with the usual separate exterior entrance. Behind the barroom were the innkeeper's office and storeroom. The second floor had four rooms, one of which could be used as a sample room for salesmen. Short's addition at the rear contained the dining-room and kitchens on the main floor and three rooms above that housed guests and the Kennaley's large brood. Also on the second floor, a 'flop room' would have been supplied with thin, straw-filled mattresses on the floor to serve those unlucky travellers who arrived when the inn's regular beds were occupied. Given the size of the Kennaley family, no doubt this room often had a full complement of weary bodies on the floor. The Keene inn is now open to the public. It has been moved to become part of the Century Village at Lang.

Within a day's journey of the Kennaley hostelry lay the comforts of Peterborough and Richard Welch's hotel. The stone building, built in 1849, still stands, in good condition, at 179–81 Simcoe Street.

North and west of Cobourg (lot 4, concession 1, Hamilton Township) is a building that, according to legend, sheltered Major-General Sir Isaac Brock en route to Niagara during the War of 1812. But this building was likely built immediately after that war, replacing an earlier, more primitive inn on the property. Although it is now covered in insulbrick, a discerning eye can tell that the Half Way House was once a very imposing structure. A door with beautifully detailed framing once led to the three-storey verandah, now a sorry victim of wind and weather. On the third floor a spacious ballroom provided accommodation for travellers or a space for meetings or community revelries.

Travellers who reached the Half Way House in its early days before there was a passable stage route came on foot or by horseback, or, during the winter, by sleigh. The inn stood beside the Danforth Road, which, when completed in 1803, was little more than a blazed trail. At the conclusion of the War of 1812–14, the government began to open what became known as the Kingston Road. This road was located several concessions back from the lake because the powers that be believed that the Danforth, which ran for much of its length beside the shore, was too accessible to attack by the Americans. So the Kingston Road (1817) became the stage-coach run. Some sections of the original Danforth Road were incorporated into the Kingston Road, and parts of it, like this section between Grafton and Cobourg, are still in use.

Not far north is Baltimore. It is difficult today to imagine that this tiny, gentle hamlet once hummed with commercial activity. Only five miles from Cobourg,

By Baltimore's once-busy Main Street: Barnabus Jaynes's Arlington Hotel

Detail, Arlington Hotel

little Baltimore managed to support three grist mills, a carding and fulling mill, two sawmills, an axe factory, a pump factory, a cheese factory, and several carriage and wagon shops. As well, there were stores, two churches, a school, a number of private homes, and, of course, hotels – two of them: Cockburn's and the Arlington.

Still standing by the road, its exterior unchanged in well over a century, is the handsome, recently restored Arlington Hotel, built in the mid-1840s by Barnabus Jaynes. It catered to the constant flow of traffic along the gravel road that led from Cobourg through well-populated farmland to Hastings at the top of Rice Lake. In 1847 Edmund Pickering and his wife, Mary, purchased the building. A native of Lincoln, England, Pickering operated the hotel until his death in 1876, at the age of sixty-one. Pickering bequeathed the building to his second son, Christopher, requesting that he 'carry on my hotel business.' This the young man did (although he was only about nineteen when his father died), and in time the establishment became known as Pickering's Hotel.

The taproom, entered from a door on the south side, had a fireplace to add to its charm. A long parlour occupied the north half of the building. There were eleven bedrooms above. For many years, a frame wing at the rear of the building provided

Built in the 1840s and recently restored: the Midland Hotel, Port Hope

added kitchen space below and several bedrooms above. A rear exit led across a walkway to the privy. That wing is no longer there, nor is the privy, but the original Baltimore fire department's fire-hall (wide enough for a wagon) can still be seen, tucked into the hill behind the hotel.

West of Baltimore, a back road led through the villages of Precious Corners and Bethesda to Welcome, where it met the Kingston Road, now Highway 2. To the west of Welcome, on the north side of the road, was Marsh's Inn, which at one time housed a fair number of guests in an east wing that also contained a taproom and the essential ballroom. Built by William Marsh in 1825, the inn had eight fireplaces and, as an added attraction, a deer park at the east end of the property.

Stage-coach passengers on the Kingston Road, as elsewhere, were endlessly innovative in the epithets they chose to describe their sufferings. William Kingston, travelling in 1853 when coach travel was supposedly more tolerable, coined the phrase 'limb-dislocating.' The driver was

> a good-natured, jolly fellow, in a straw hat, white shirt, with red under-sleeves showing, and an unbuttoned waistcoat ... In a few minutes we began a series of bumpings, thumpings, joltings, and other dislocating movements, which ended not till the termination of our journey.

The second lap of Kingston's trip took place at night. They set out

> across the rugged road, over which our primitively constructed vehicle went jolting and

The Liverpool Hotel, Pickering: home to the bigamous Robert Secker and his 'wives'

Window detail, Liverpool Hotel

> bumping, and creaking along, though almost at a snail's pace, yet with no less violence than before. There we all sat, our legs firmly wedged in among sundry boxes and carpet-bags, securely jammed down with a big, dusty buffalo-robe; we often giving way to uncontrollable fits of laughter, in spite of our misery, our unlucky persons bounded and rebounded on the benches; our vehicle sometimes leaning over at an angle of 45 degrees, as the wheels of one side sunk into a deeper rut than usual.

The amiable Adam Fergusson, a Scots writer and agricultural expert who settled near Hamilton, described the endless bounding and rebounding as a 'harlequinade.' Every so often, said Fergusson, the driver cried out:

> 'Gentlemen, please a little to the right or to the left' as the case might require when ... there was an instantaneous and amusing scramble to restore the equilibrium. Broken heads on such occasions are by no means rare.

The arrival of the railway was a threat to

innkeepers along country roads. It promised the eventual end of stage-coaching and heralded the day of large urban hotels. Towns served by the railways were sure to grow, while those that were bypassed withered and, in time, settled into quiet lassitude. In Port Hope, the arrival of the Midland Railway ensured the town's survival and created a demand for additional hotel rooms. The Midland Hotel on John Street was one result.

The Midland has been recently restored under the watchful eye of restoration architect Peter John Stokes. Construction details suggest that the Midland was built in two stages, the southern, three-bay section during the 1840s, and the northern section about ten years later.

The basement of the Midland housed a kitchen, a storeroom, and a scullery at the south end. At the north end, separated by a crawl space, were the still room / beer cellar, with a barrel slide to admit beer barrels from the street, and a separate wine cellar. At street level there were public and private dining-rooms and bars. The door to the public bar can be seen on the left side of the façade. Over the years the fine old building deteriorated, and its days seemed numbered until it was rescued by a far-sighted buyer and restored. It now houses apartments.

After mid-century, travellers reaching Pickering found a pleasant hostelry awaiting them at Liverpool Corners near the Pickering harbour (Highway 2 and Liverpool Road). Known as Secker's Hotel or the Liverpool Hotel, it was built in 1878 by Robert Secker, an enterprising Englishman who settled there in the mid-1850s and achieved notable success with his hotel and also, the records show, with the ladies.

Although illiterate, Robert Secker succeeded in the hotel business even at a time when traffic along the Kingston Road was diminishing. Part of his success may have resulted from an unusual domestic situation that provided him with added (and free) female help. Secker had a legal wife, Harriet, in England, as well as two more 'wives' in Canada. The census of 1861 recorded that Robert Secker had a 'wife' named Eleanor (sometimes Helen or Ellen). Ten years later, the census showed that two children, William and Susan, had been born to them. When the census-taker returned in 1881 he found Secker involved in a *ménage à trois* that was, to say the least, unusual. Eleanor / Ellen (now aged fifty-three) was still in residence, but a younger woman was also on the scene, listed as the mother of his 'natural' daughter, Minnie. The new 'wife' was Sarah Newman, and she became Secker's sole legatee. His will clarified matters a bit, as he left everything to 'Sarah Newman, generally known as Mrs Sarah Secker, who has lived with me for a number of years' and to 'our natural daughter, Minnie Secker.'

Shortly before Christmas 1878, the *Whitby Chronicle* reported in detail one of the many festive dinners held at Secker's. Thirty guests were in attendance. After a sumptuous meal 'served early and in splendid style by Mrs Secker' and 'a very temperate use of the ample liquids,' the guests settled back to enjoy singing and toasts. The final toast was made to 'our Host and Hostess, and success to their new hotel which they propose building.' That new hotel, now the Liverpool House, contained, when completed, thirty-two rooms, including a parlour for the ladies. The second floor was a rabbit-warren of small rooms, most of them no larger than nine feet by seven.

When Robert Secker died, the *Pickering News* of 27 November 1896 wrote of him:

> Deceased was 75 years of age, and has been a resident of Liverpool for many years where he conducted an hotel business until some 3 or 4 years ago, when he retired, being a man of considerable means.

East on the Kingston Road at Midland Avenue in Scarborough stood another Half Way House, a stopping place for coaches

Alexander Thompson's hotel on the Kingston Road, now in Black Creek Pioneer Village

running between Dunbarton, near Pickering, and Toronto. Today it stands, restored and shiningly beautiful, in Black Creek Pioneer Village, as the village's example of a typical, mid-century country inn. And that it was.

Thought to have been built in the late 1840s, it was owned by Alexander Thompson and his wife, Mary Ann McClure, great-granddaughter of Sarah Ashbridge, a Scarborough pioneer and first owner of the property. The inn soon became a centre for community activities. In every way it met the strict criteria outlined in the Regulations of Inns and Houses of Public Entertainment that became law in Scarborough in 1851. The Thompsons provided exactly 'five, clean, comfortable beds and bedding, exclusive of the bedding used by the family,' adequate stabling for horses, and so on. As well, they lived with stringent regulations aimed at the prevention of alcohol abuse and other social problems. They could not serve alcohol to children under fifteen, nor allow 'any evil disposed person' in the house, nor allow 'tipling ... for more than one hour except on business.' That exception undoubtedly proved the rule on many occasions, for, at least in the 1890s, it was customary for the innkeeper at the Half Way House to leave a jug of whisky on the bar after he had retired for the night. Farmers arriving late helped themselves and left money for their host to find in the morning. It was, of course, thought unnecessary ever to lock the door.

Rather than stopping at the Half Way House, William Weller's coaches stopped at the Nelson Gates Inn, a few miles to the east. But there were other coach lines operating along the Kingston Road, and the traffic was heavy enough to warrant charging (in Scarborough) an additional two pounds and two shillings to license the inns that sprang up along its length.

As the stage-coaches approached Toronto they were usually drawn by the finest horses, saved by the sagacious operator of the line so that the approach of the coach and four would be as impressive as possible. The stage thundered into town, with a blast from the coachman's horn announcing its arrival, so that when it finally pulled up in front of the Toronto General Stage Office at the intersection of Front, Church, and Wellington streets, the world was there to meet it.

The spirited horses that made the dramatic entrance into Toronto were the lucky ones. Others endured the trip along the Kingston Road, across the frozen lake, or through the pot-holed roads under conditions like those described by the long-suffering John McDonald in 1822. He noted in his journal the day's trials for an exhausted horse. The unfortunate animal

> laired in a miry part of the road, where he stuck fast, and even after he was loosed from the yoke the poor animal strove so much to no purpose, that he fell down in a state of complete exhaustion three times in the mire. The mire was so tenacious, being a tough clay, that we were compelled to disengage his feet from the clay with hand spokes, before we got him freed, and yet he still struggled long to get our waggon out of the mire.

Nor did McDonald himself escape unscathed for 'as I was standing in the waggon, the horses advanced a step, and I fell out of the vehicle on my back, and broke one of my ribs.' At the end of such a journey no inn, even with its unwashed Yankees and disrespectful colonials, could be anything but a haven for man and beast.

Toronto

JAMES FULTON.

Richmond Hill, Markham, Nov. 13th, 1829. 2873

Stray Ox and Steer.

Broke into the inclosure of the Subscriber, a LARGE OX, blind of the off eye, with seven wrinkles on his horn, a yellowish Red and White colour; also a RED STEER with him, nearly three years old; with a brindle face, and part white under his breast. The owner or owners are requested to prove property, pay charges, and take the animals away.

deed for cash, or if one half or one third of the purchase money is paid down. Immediate possession can be given, and, for further particulars apply to PHILIP CODY.

Toronto, Nov. 16th, 1829. 287z.

WHERE IS WILLIAM SUTHERLAND?

THE Subscriber is desirous of ascertaining the place of abode of Mr. William Sutherland and family. They lived in or near Glengarry, about the time of the last war, and were originally from the parish of Kindonan, Sutherlandshire. Address a letter to the Subscriber, at Niagara, care of Messrs. Chrysler, Merchants.

N. B. Mrs. Sutherland's maiden name was Catharine Macpherson.

DANIEL MACPHERSON.

Niagara, 17th Nov. 1829. 2873.

Boarding.

THE Subscriber can furnish Boarding, Lodging, &c. for six steady mechanics, reasonable, on Dundas Street, between Mr. Willmot's Tavern and four doors from Mr. Bird's Tavern, in the house lately occupied by Mr. George Hutchison, Plaisterer.

JAMES PARKER.

Nov. 18. 87.

STRAYED, on the 10th October last, into the premises of ANDREW BIGHAM, on lot No. 12, in the first concession of ETOBICOKE, A LIGHT IRON-GREY HORSE, rising five or six years of age.—The owner is requested to prove property, pay charges, and take him away.

Nov. 17. 873.

SAWYER & LABOURERS WANTED.

WANTED by the subscriber, a Sawyer who understands his business, and two men who understand Chopping; to whom liberal encouragement will be given.

Also; TO LET, for one or more years, the SAW WORKS of the Subscriber. For further particulars, apply to the subscriber, on premises.

WILLIAM KENT.

Stoney Creek, Nov. 13, 1829. 87z

THE SUBSCRIBERS have just received direct from London, a general assortment of Hosiery, Black and Colored Gros-de-Naples, Figured Norwich Crapes, Black Silk and Cotton Velvets, Sewing Silks, Lace Thread Edgings, Worked Insertions, and Scollop Muslins, Reel and Ball Cotton, Geo. the 4th Regulation Swords, Belts, and Sashes, Hardware and Cutlery.

J. C. GODWIN & Co.

D WHISKEY.

J. C. GODWIN & Co. 282z

NEWMARKET MAIL STAGE.

WILLIAM GARBUTT, having taken the contract for carrying His Majesty's Mails between York and Newmarket, for the next four years, respectfully informs the public that THE MAIL STAGE will start from Joseph Bloor's Hotel, York, on Mondays and Thursdays, at 12 o'clock, noon, and arrive at nine o'clock, the same evening in Newmarket;—and will leave Mr. Barber's Tavern, Newmarket, for York, on Wednesdays and Saturdays, at in the morning, and arrive in York at 2 P. M. on the same days.

Price for passengers conveyed between York and Newmarket, six shillings and three pence currency, and in proportion for shorter distances. Packages carried on the route at moderate rates.

Mr. BARBER will accommodate passengers arriving with the Mail Stage at Newmarket; and they may be comfortably conveyed to the Holland Landing, or in other directions if required.

York, March 30th, 1829. 254z.

NEW ARRANGEMENT OF STAGES

Between York and the Carrying Place at the head of the Bay of Quintie.

THE Public are respectfully informed that a Mail Stage will run regularly twice a week between York and the Carrying Place; leaving York every Monday and Thursday at 12 o'clock, noon, and arriving at the Carrying Place on Tuesdays and Fridays at 2 o'clock, P. M. Will leave the Carrying Place every Tuesday and Friday at o'clock A. M. and arrive at York on Wednesdays and Saturdays, at 12 o'clock noon. There will also a Stage leave Cobourg every Monday at 10 o'clock A. M. and arrive at the Carrying Place the same day, and leave the Carrying Place every Saturday at 9 o'clock, A. M. and arrive at Cobourg the same day.

The above arrangements are in connexion with the Steam Boats *Sir James Kempt* and *Toronto*, so that Travellers going the route will find a pleasant and speedy conveyance between Kingston and York, as the line is now fitted up in good order with good carriages, good horses and careful drivers.

Every attention will be given to render passengers comfortable while on the line, and the drivers instructed to stop at the best hotels on the route.

All Baggage at the risk of the owners.

Extras furnished to any part of the country.

The Stage Books will be kept at Mr. Bradley's Steam boat Hotel.

PETER PATERSON, *Agent.*

SWEDES IRON.

Landing from the Ship *General Wolfe*, direct from GOTTENBURGH.

ASSORTED SWEDES IRON.

WILLIAM BUDDEN, *Point a' Callieres.*

August 18, 1829. 274-z

LOOKING GLASSES.

Received by the subscriber, a large and elegant assortment of Looking Glasses; German Plate, &c. &c. and the prices remarkably low.

J. R. ARMSTRONG.

YORK FURNACE.

F. R. DUTCHER continues his FURNACE in complete operation, where can be had, at short notice,

Castings of any description from one to thirty cwt:

Also on hand a general assortment of STOVES, HOLLOW WARE, PLOUGH CASTINGS and PLOUGHS.

THEODORE TURLEY,

SMITH AND *Brass Founder:*

Yonge Street, next door to Judge Macaulay.

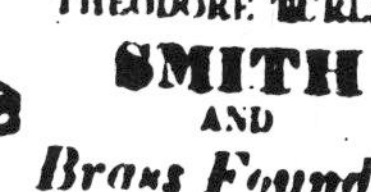

CHAPTER FIVE

Toronto

THE JUDICIAL, POLITICAL, AND LEGISLATIVE FUNCTIONS OF INNS

'Toronto as a city is not generally attractive to a traveller.'

Anthony Trollope, *North America*, 1862

UPPER CANADA'S first courts were held in its taverns. When English civil law was introduced to Upper Canada, a meeting was held in Wilson's Hotel in Niagara at which the prestigious Law Society of Upper Canada was founded. Inns also played a role in the political process, as a venue both for the hustings in front of the inn and for the polling station inside. And in Toronto an inn served temporarily as the Legislature of Upper Canada.

Before the province's stately courthouses and town halls were built, the ubiquitous inns and taverns successfully filled the void. Everything from criminal trials to coroners' courts were held at the local inn. The first issue of the *Colonial Advocate* described a court of inquiry held in an inn to investigate the mysterious death of a Colonel Nichol who fell (or was pushed) one dark night from a high cliff at Queenston. The foreman of the jury was none other than Toronto's first mayor, William Lyon Mackenzie. The paper reported that the jury saw the body of the deceased, viewed other evidence, and then 'adjourned to Mr Wynn's Inn,' where the inquiry was concluded. (Nichol's fall from the cliff, they decided, was likely due to the consumption of too much port.)

At Montgomery's Inn in Etobicoke prisoners were held in a basement lock-up and brought to trial in the courtroom above. The stairs leading from the jail to the court were a local version of the Bridge of Sighs.

Jordan's Hotel in York had the singular distinction of holding within its walls the 1814 session of the Legislature of Upper Canada. Jordan's had opened in 1801 on what is now the south side of King Street between Berkeley and Ontario Streets. When it was built it was the last word in inns for, although small – one and a half stories – it had a ballroom. It was here that the government of Upper Canada held its session of the Legislature after the parliament buildings were burned by the invading Americans.

While the new legislative buildings were being built and the House was sitting at Jordan's, members felt very much at home, for Jordan's was where many out-of-town members stayed during sessions. The inn was considered to be luxurious and John Jordan a fine host who could produce meals of unrivalled quality. But when its days of glory came to an end, the hostelry quickly deteriorated. Sir George Head, who stayed there the following year, described his room as cold and dirty and his steak as 'dry, black and tasteless.'

Jordan's York Hotel, home of Upper Canada's legislators and York's first Sunday School.

The Mansion House across the road then became the more popular of the two, even though the landlord there was a rather strange character who had both ears missing, a lack he concealed by the clever arrangement of his hair. The Mansion House had the added attraction (to some) of housing a resident circus in a barn at the rear.

While Jordan's was in its prime its host welcomed an unlikely group of guests – the children attending York's first Sunday school. According to historian E.C. Guillet, the youngsters came to the inn to be taught by a Methodist minister, the Reverend John Lever. (It may seem strange that a Methodist minister taught Sunday school in a tavern, but so was the fact that Toronto's three major breweries were run by staunch Methodists: John Doell, Joseph Bloor, and George Rowell.)

The 1801 Court of Quarter Sessions, sitting to issue tavern licences, met in a York tavern to decide on the number of taverns to be licensed in that town. This seemingly incongruous situation was repeated throughout the province. Inns were the only buildings with both the necessary space for meetings and the ability to provide food and drink for the judges and magistrates who presided over the courts.

That 1801 court decided that 'six persons

The Red Lion, Yorkville, site of political rallies and one crucial election

are a sufficient number for Keeping Tavern in the Town of York.' In order to preserve the peace most efficiently, five of those six innkeepers were made constables, so that offenders could be apprehended on the spot. (The sixth innkeeper was a woman.) By 1837 six innkeepers had long since become insufficient. The town then had fifty taverns in the tiny area bounded by King and Front streets and Yonge and Church streets. Signs swung enticingly advertising such establishments as the Dog and Duck Tavern, the Neptune Inn, the Black Bull Tavern, the Stag Tavern, the Edinburgh Castle, the White Swan, and the Blue Bonnet.

By this time the fiery William Lyon Mackenzie was talking rebellion and many were listening. York's inns became the site of political rallies, heated speeches, and quiet plans. Each establishment had its own political bent. The host would often declare for one of the candidates. Several inns had a particularly close affiliation with the rebel leader and the major political events of 1837. One of these was an inn on Yonge Street just north of Bloor, where the sign of a lion rampant had been welcoming guests since 1808. The Red Lion, built by Daniel Tiers on his two-hundred-acre grant when it was virtually all forest, became the rallying point for the village of Yorkville. In 1832 an election was held at the Red Lion, and history was made.

In December 1831, William Lyon Mackenzie had been expelled from the Legislature for publishing seditious articles in his paper, the *Colonial Advocate.* An election was called for 2 January 1832, to be held at the Red Lion. Mackenzie ran for re-election. His popularity with the farmers north of York was such that more than two thousand of his supporters came down to vote for him and assembled in front of the Red Lion. The practice was for the town clerk to call for nominations from the assembled crowd, following which the candidates would climb up and speak from the hustings, a temporary platform erected for this purpose. Voting would then begin and

The Sun Tavern, Queen and Yonge, where crowds heard W. L. Mackenzie urge rebellion

could carry on for a week or so, with, of course, frequent visits to the taproom and equally frequent rows. But in Mackenzie's case, it was over in no time. Voting began at 1:30, and within an hour the count was 119 for Mackenzie and 1 lone vote for his opponent, Mr Street, who felt it wise at that point to withdraw.

The Reverend Henry Scadding described the triumphal procession, which, he noted,

> was formed at the Red Lion Inn on Yonge Street ... where the hustings were. In front of it was an immense sleigh belonging to Mr Montgomery, which was drawn by four horses, and carried between twenty and thirty men and two or three Highland Pipers. From fifty to one hundred sleighs followed, and between one and two thousand of the inhabitants ... One of the most singular curiosities of the day was a little printing-press, placed on one of the sleighs, warmed by a furnace, on which a couple of boys contrived, while moving through the streets, to strike off their New Year's address, and then throw it to the people ... It should be stated that on the apex of Mr Montgomery's pyramidal sleigh stood the hero of the day himself, wearing the golden chain and medals presented to him a few hours previously, at the Red Lion, by his constituents.

Two other inns were focal points in pre-Rebellion days. At the corner of Queen and Yonge stood the Sun Tavern, a frame hostelry owned by a family connection of Mackenzie's. Like the Red Lion, it became a favourite spot for farmers on their way to market who wanted to air their grievances against the government. Here Mackenzie made rousing speeches from the balcony, and here he and his committee prepared their 'Declaration of the Independence of Upper Canada.' John Montgomery's inn on Yonge Street north of Eglinton became the rebels' headquarters.

For many people, the prospect of running a tavern was inviting. By 1836 there was one such establishment for every 127 persons, including every man, woman, and child in town. (On Dundas Street there were three popular inns in a row: Collard's, the Brown Bear, and the Queen Street Tavern.) The obligatory words 'licensed to sell wine and spiritous liquors' seemed to be posted everywhere. Some of the better inns became institutions, and each developed its own character and its own clientele. At the corner of King and Ontario streets was the house run by Mrs Hayes, a 'stout, good-natured woman, a good cook and manager and the embodiment of a hospitable landlady.' Hayes' Boarding House was the haunt of the legislators who did not choose Jordan's. For three or four dollars a week members could stay with the jovial Mrs Hayes and, if they chose to entertain, she could put on an impressive spread. The renowned Colonel Thomas Talbot, who walked about town wearing his sheepskin coat with the wool side out, preferred to stay with Mrs Hayes.

At King and York streets, the British Coffee House opened its doors in 1834. Designed by architect J.G. Howard, it was the scene of public balls and also housed a private club and reading room, later the nucleus of the Toronto Club. In 1845 there was a sensational suicide there – a visiting major from Woodstock took prussic acid – but this did nothing to deter its customers or gentlemanly club members from frequenting their favourite haunt.

Colonel Thomas Talbot, in his sheepskin coat

The Ontario House at Church and Wellington streets was a three-storey building with pine columns soaring from its base to the eaves, behind which a double gallery offered guests a sheltered spot from which to view the scene below. In 1837 it was run by David Botsford, an innkeeper from Niagara-on-the-Lake. Advertising in the *Patriot* that year, Botsford proclaimed that his hotel was 'beautifully fitted up for the reception of ladies and gentlemen' and that 'its accommodations are second to none in Canada in point of comfort.' After noting the extreme comfort of his beds he added the ultimate factor in their favour: 'they are warranted free from vermin or insects of any kind.' (This pledge meant a lot to travellers. Guests arriving at night found it difficult to check the state of the insect community in their beds. As a guest at the Steam-boat Hotel on Front Street noted after a bad night, 'I could not have remained a second night, or gone to bed the first one, had light enabled me to see the actual state of things.')

In the 1840s the Ontario House became Wellington's and attained fame for its large dining-hall that featured one long table where guests were seated, each, according to John Ross Robertson, with a bottle of sherry or port at his place. Food was placed on the table all at once, and diners fell to in what often became a mêlée. Wellington's had a private sitting-room, the first room William Lyon Mackenzie entered when he returned from exile.

Before the mid-nineteenth century, a number of blacks were successfully keeping tavern in Toronto. One such was George Mink, whose innkeeping and stage-coaching ventures made him a fortune, all of which he lost when he bought his daughter's freedom from slavery. Mink's tavern was at the top of Toronto Street. At

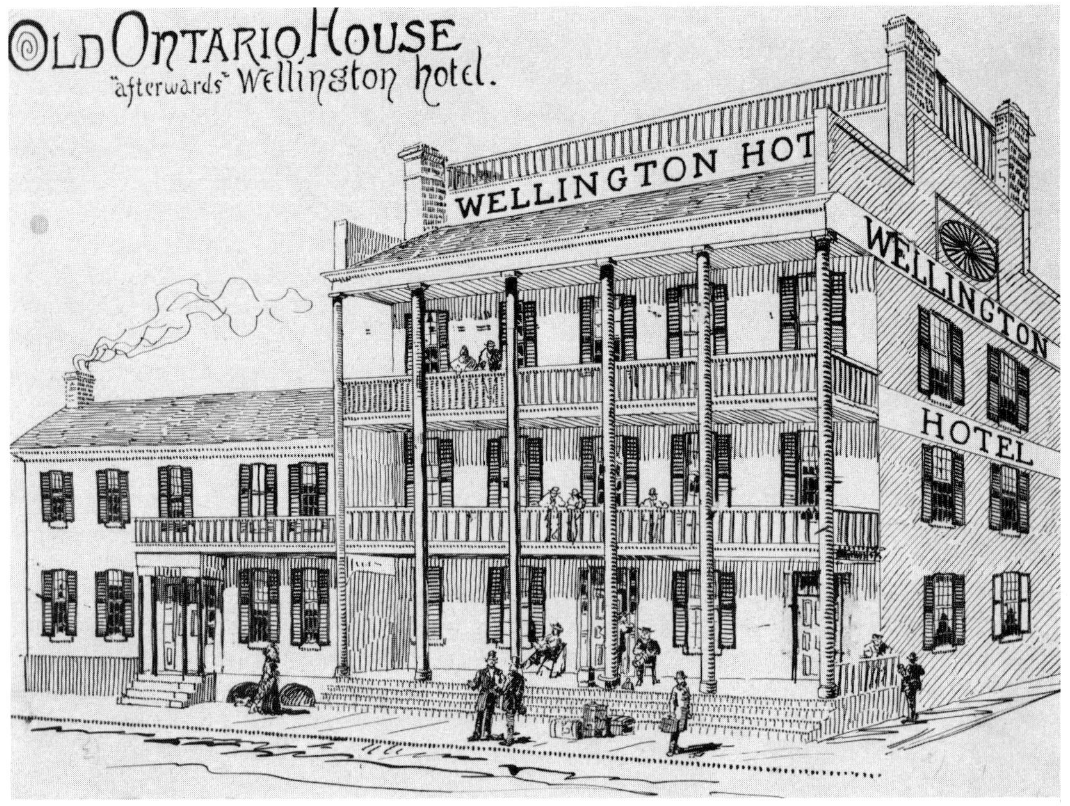

The Wellington Hotel, where beds were 'free from vermin or insects of any kind'

Church and Colborne a black man named Snow opened what became one of the most popular inns in town, latterly known as Russell's. The original frame structure, Snow's Inn, was replaced with a brick building, and the inn changed hands several times before Azro Russell took it over. His tenure began with promise but ended in disgrace.

Russell's was the scene of continual hustle and bustle. Enthusiastic members of the Orange Lodge and the Masonic Lodge met there, as did virtually everyone of importance in town. John Ross Robertson called it the 'popular hotel of Toronto.' But not everyone agreed. Isabella Lucy Bird kept journals during her tour of America, published as *The Englishwoman in America* (1856). She peremptorily dismissed Russell's (and all the other hotels in town) as follows:

> From my praise of Toronto I must except the hotels, which are of a very inferior class ... The bedrooms at Russell's swarmed with mosquitoes; and the waiters, who were runaway slaves, were inattentive and uncivil.

Isabella Bird would not have been surprised, given her opinion of the place, to hear two years later that the proprietor of Russell's had absconded with valuables belonging to many of the hotel's guests. As the *Conservative Standard* of 20 August 1858 noted:

> considerable consternation was created in Toronto on Sunday morning by the discovery of the departure [of] Mr Russell the well-known proprietor of Russell's Hotel, corner of Church and Colborne Street. Mr Russell it seems absconded from his establishment about 5 o'clock on Sunday morning, taking with

Russell's Hotel. Its popular host absconded with his guests' belongings.

him fifteen trunks containing household personal property ... the notification of Mr Russell's departure created an extraordinary scene of astonishment and dismay, as he was indebted largely to a number of his boarders, to the inhabitants of the city and to his domestics to some of whom he owed as much as $120.

Farmers on their way to market often chose Joseph Bloor's Farmers' Arms by the market (on the site of the present St Lawrence Hall) at King Street. This area was known as the 'devil's half acre' because of the preponderance of inns and taverns there. Bloor later moved to Yorkville, where he established a brewery and was instrumental in the development of the village of Yorkville.

Colourful signs proclaiming the innkeeper's hospitality swung in front of every tavern – a centuries-old tradition. Toronto had its share of imaginative ones. The Green Bush was famous for its pine tree; the Gardener's Arms for its gardening tools displayed in a heraldic crest; the Bond Head Inn, named after the reformers' nemesis, boasted his portrait and the words, 'Let them come if they dare.' At Front and John streets the sign in front of the Greenland Fishery depicted an Arctic scene on one side and a whaling expedition on the other. The most inventive sign was at the Rescue, an inn popular with sailors. It depicted a desperate mother atop a cliff, reaching for her baby, who was perched precariously in an eagle's nest to which the bird had carried the screaming infant.

Around 1840, a pleasant brick hostelry

The busy Toronto market scene near the Butcher's Arms

was built at the north-east corner of Palace and New streets. (Today those streets are known as Front and Jarvis.) The building has recently been restored and, now a restaurant rather than a taproom, is patronized by customers from the St Lawrence Market across the street. The first market and the weigh-scales have disappeared from the streetscape, but happily this building remains, one of the last links to the days when floggings, duels, and hangings were all part of the frenzied activity in this part of York.

A building dispensing spirits has occupied this corner since 1800. In a scenic view of York, painted by a Scottish artist in 1820, Thomas Robson's frame store was shown in this location. Like most grocers, Robson undoubtedly sold spirits. Once the hotel was built (at some point prior to 1850) to cater to the market crowd, it changed its owners and proprietors with a frequency that was a hallmark of the hotel business.

By 1856 the business was being operated by John Cornell as Cornell's Hotel, and it remained under his management for a relatively long six-year period, until Mary Ann Trotter took over in 1863, followed in quick succession by proprietor Charles Luke in 1864 (he called it Waverley House) and, in 1866, by James Turner.

In 1867 the hotel got a new proprietor and a more appropriate name – John Bolam ran it as the Butcher's Arms, in recognition of its proximity to the market, which, by this time, was a covered market, part of the beautiful St Lawrence Hall (1850) that fronted on King Street. Diagonally across the Front and Jarvis intersection was the Town Hall, built in 1844. For a hotel, the location could not have been better.

John Bolam ran the Butcher's Arms until 1875. Towards the end of his tenure he changed the name to Bolam's Hotel, possibly because there was another Butcher's Arms in the city's east end. (That notorious establishment was known for its cock-fighting.)

From 1875 until 1888 the hotel was run

The recently restored Butcher's Arms, Front and Jarvis streets

by Messrs Hook and McCulley, who called it the International Hotel, perhaps a reflection of the crowd-drawing performances at the nearby St Lawrence Hall. Such singers as Jenny Lind, 'the Swedish Nightingale,' a host of politicians, among them Sir John A. Macdonald and the Hon. George Brown, and an eclectic array of lecturers, choral concerts, and social events attracted the public. Proprietor McCulley was from Brockville and had earned his living as a shoemaker before entering the hotel business. He came to Toronto in 1871, married Amelia Marsh the following year, and three years later began to operate the hotel. According to one account, he tried 'in every way to make his guests comfortable.'

A change of proprietors brought another change of name in 1888 when the International became Reid's Hotel at the Haymarket and again, in 1890, Fielder's Hotel at the Haymarket. Both proprietors advertised as follows:

> Importer of
> Irish and Scotch Whiskies, English Ale
> and Dublin Stout on Draught
> FINEST 5 CENT CIGAR IN THE CITY

For a century or more the hostelry at Front and Jarvis was part of the noisy, bustling scene around the Town Hall, the market, and the St Lawrence Hall. Even as early as 1790 something of interest was sure to be going on at the market square. Here the sentences handed down by the courts were enacted – everything from the stocks to the gallows was nearby. Convicted felons were publicly punished there, and justice was quick and severe, sometimes lethal. A visitor might witness an assortment of events.

As the York *Oracle* reported, on 1 December 1798:

Last Monday William Hawkins was publicly whipped and Joseph McCarthy burned in the hand at the market place.

The Reverend Henry Scadding described a flogging he had seen at the market place:

A discharged regimental drummer, a native African, administered the lash. The sheriff stood by, keeping count of the stripes. The senior of the two unfortunates bore his punishment with stoicism, encouraging the negro to strike with more force. The other, a young man, endeavoured to imitate his companion in this respect but soon was obliged to evince by fearful cries the torture endured.

And, the *Oracle*, York, 4 January 1800, reported:

Yesterday morning a duel was fought back of the Government buildings by John White, Esq., his Majesty's Attorney-General and John Small, Esq., clerk of the Executive Council, wherein the former received a wound above the right hip which it is feared will prove mortal ... [White died from the wound and Small was acquitted.]

SLAVE FOR SALE. To be sold – A healthy, strong Negro woman, about 30 years of age, understands cookery, laundry and the taking care of poultry. N.B. She can dress ladies' hair.

Penalties were imposed on any innkeeper who allowed tippling in his tavern. Such penalties ranged from fines to loss of licence; or, 'the court may order the offender to be set in the stocks for the space of four hours.' The practice of putting offending innkeepers in the stocks, which was still allowed for in the by-laws in 1835, had been used as a deterrent from the days when the first innkeeper hung up his sign in York. In 1804 Elizabeth Ellis was convicted of keeping a disorderly house and sentenced to six months in prison and 'two sessions of two hours each on the pillory on market days, opposite the Market House.'

The establishment at Palace and New was not only handy to the activities at Market Square, but was also just down the road from the jail, scene of many public hangings. Men, women, and children came in their holiday best when there was a hanging. Those who attended the execution of Elijah Dexter in 1818 saw some high drama. When the jailer invited Dexter to ascend the scaffold the prisoner adamantly refused to do so. The august Reverend John Strachan encouraged him pleasantly: 'Oh, Mr Dexter, do please come up,' he urged, 'do come up, please.' But, in spite of this gracious invitation, the stubborn Dexter still refused to budge. Finally a horse-drawn cart was found, and Dexter was put into it with his back to the scaffold. The noose was placed around his neck and, when the horse was whipped, Mr Dexter was launched into eternity.

The hostelry at Front and Jarvis changed its name with such monotonous regularity that patrons could hardly be expected to know, from one visit to the next, just where they were. This was also the case with the hundreds of other taverns that dotted the neighbourhood and the city at large. But the regulars at the Wheat Sheaf Tavern, at King and Bathurst streets, had no such problem. That popular tavern has kept its name since shortly after Bernard Short received the Crown grant in 1841. In fact, for the first fifty years of its life, it had only two families as owners.

In 1843, a Toronto directory listed Bernard Short as an innkeeper and baker on the Garrison Common. Short, with the help of his first wife, Rose, and his second wife, Mary Anne, owned and leased a

The unique Wheat Sheaf Tavern served men from Toronto's garrison in the 1840s.

Window, Wheat Sheaf Tavern

Tower, Wheat Sheaf Tavern

complex of buildings on the south-west corner of King and Bathurst for thirty years. Tenants included a cooper, a blacksmith, members of the military, and various tenants of the six 'cottages' the Shorts built and owned. A number of proprietors leased and operated the tavern from time to time, but it was always in Bernard's hands. He died in 1865, and his widow, Mary Anne, took over the business, a common occurrence in the innkeeping trade. She ran the inn and was landlord to her group of tenants for the next seven years until, at the age of sixty-six, she died.

In 1874 ownership passed to Moses Furlong and then to his widow, Mary, who, in her will, mentioned that her son should have first option on buying what was and is a prime tavern location. Mary Furlong, although illiterate, had enough income from the Wheat Sheaf to leave two hundred dollars, for a 'substantial and permanent' monument for herself and Moses. The Wheat Sheaf, in business continuously since the 1840s, remains a well-known 'watering hole' in Toronto today.

Not far away, at 298 Queen Street West, the Black Bull Tavern (said to have been built in the 1830s) vies with the Wheat Sheaf for the honour of being Toronto's oldest tavern. It was originally a simple two-storey structure. A series of additions and alterations (none of which improved its appearance) resulted in what is today a rather nondescript building.

Toronto taverns reverberated with the sounds of political wrangles, court sessions, town meetings, fancy dress balls, and every possible community activity; but there could be risks when the strength of the building proved unequal to the size of the crowd, as the residents of Mount Forest north of Toronto found out. The *Examiner* reported on 12 February 1863 that:

> At the County meeting held in Matthew's Hall of Friday last, an accident occurred which for a time created considerable excitement among the attendant crowd ... The Hall, it may be stated, is immediately over the Hotel Stables, the carriage way being under the middle of the Hall floor. Now it so happened that as Mr Ryan was addressing the meeting ... a dull cracking sound, as of timber breaking, was heard, and, in an instant, down went the floor over the carriage way, the whole width of the hall and about twelve feet in length, carrying with it the crowd who were upon it, numbering somewhere about sixty persons, into the carriage way below. So sudden was the crash that not one upon the breaking timbers had time to escape, and the momentary panic created among those at the further end, who were cut off from retreat was such that several foolishly jumped out of the windows ... so sudden and unexpected was the catastrophe that not a word escaped from the victims, if we except one individual who evidently did not comprehend the crisis and shouted 'Fire' as he went down.

Yonge Street

JAMES FULTON.
Richmond Hill, Markham. Nov. 13th, 1829. 2873

Stray Ox and Steer.

Broke into the inclosure of the Subscriber, a LARGE OX, blind of the off eye, with seven wrinkles on his horn, a yellowish Red and White colour; also a RED STEER with him, nearly three years old; with a brindle face, and part white under his breast. The owner or owners are requested to prove property, pay charges, and take the animals away.

... deed for cash, or if one half or one third of the purchase money is paid down. Immediate possession can be given, and, for further particulars apply to PHILIP CODY.
Toronto, Nov. 16th, 1829. 287z.

WHERE IS WILLIAM SUTHERLAND!

THE Subscriber is desirous of ascertaining the place of abode of Mr. William Sutherland and family. They lived in or near Glengarry, about the time of the last war, and were originally from the parish of Kindonan, Sutherlandshire. Address a letter to the Subscriber, at Niagara, care of Messrs. Chrysler, Merchants.

N. B. Mrs. Sutherland's maiden name was Catharine Macpherson.

DANIEL MACPHERSON.
Niagara, 17th Nov. 1829. 2873.

Boarding.

THE Subscriber can furnish Boarding, Lodging, &c. for six steady mechanics, reasonable, on Dundas Street, between Mr. Willmot's Tavern and four doors from Mr. Bird's Tavern, in the house lately occupied by Mr. George Hutchison, Plaisterer.

JAMES PARKER.
Nov. 18. 87.

STRAYED, on the 10th October last, into the premises of ANDREW BIGHAM, on lot No. 12, in the first concession of ETOBICOKE, A LIGHT IRON-GREY HORSE, rising five or six years of age.— The owner is requested to prove property, pay charges, and take him away.
Nov. 17. 873.

SAWYER & LABOURERS WANTED.

WANTED by the subscriber, a Sawyer who understands his business, and two men who understand Chopping; to whom liberal encouragement will be given. Apply to

Also; TO LET, for one or more years, the SALT WORKS of the Subscriber.
For further particulars, apply to the subscriber, on the premises.
WILLIAM KENT.
Stoney Creek, Nov. 13, 1829. 87z

THE SUBSCRIBERS have just received direct from London, a general assortment of
Hosiery,
Black and Colored Gros-de-Naples,
Figured Norwich Crapes,
Black Silk and Cotton Velvets,
Sewing Silks,
Lace Thread Edgings,
Worked Insertions, and Scollop Muslins,
Reel and Ball Cotton,
Geo. the 4th Regulation Swords, Belts, and Sashes,
...ware and Cutlery,
...eral Stock of Saddlery: also an extensive ... of England Cloths, &c. &c.
J. C. GODWIN & Co.

NEWMARKET MAIL STAGE.

WILLIAM GARBUTT, having taken the contract for carrying His Majesty's Mails between York and Newmarket, for the next four years, respectfully informs the public that THE MAIL STAGE will start from Joseph Bloor's Hotel, York, on Mondays and Thursdays, at 12 o'clock, noon, and arrive at nine o'clock, the same evening in Newmarket;—and will leave Mr. Barber's Tavern, Newmarket, for York, on Wednesdays and Saturdays, at ... in the morning, and arrive in York at 2 P. M. on the same days.

Price for passengers conveyed between York and Newmarket, six shillings and three pence currency, and in proportion for shorter distances. Packages carried on the route at moderate rates.

Mr. BARBER will accommodate passengers arriving with the Mail Stage at Newmarket; and they may be comfortably conveyed to the Holland Landing, or in other directions if required.
York, March 30th, 1829. 254z.

NEW ARRANGEMENT OF STAGES

Between York and the Carrying Place at the head of the Bay of Quintie.

THE Public are respectfully informed that a Mail Stage will run regularly twice a week between York and the Carrying Place; leaving York every Monday and Thursday at 12 o'clock, noon, and arriving at the Carrying Place on Tuesdays and Fridays at 2 o'clock, P. M. Will leave the Carrying Place every Tuesday and Friday at ... o'clock A. M. and arrive at York on Wednesdays and Saturdays, at 12 o'clock noon. There will also a Stage leave Cobourg every Monday at 10 o'clock, A. M. and arrive at the Carrying Place the same day, and leave the Carrying Place every Saturday at 9 o'clock, A. M. and arrive at Cobourg the same day.

The above arrangements are in connexion with the Steam Boats *Sir James Kempt* and *Toronto*, so that Travellers going the route will find a pleasant and speedy conveyance between Kingston and York, as the line is now fitted up in good order with good carriages, good horses and careful drivers.

Every attention will be given to render passengers comfortable while on the line, and the drivers instructed to stop at the best hotels on the route.

All baggage at the risk of the owners.
Extras furnished to any part of the country.
The Stage Books will be kept at Mr. Bradley's Steamboat Hotel.

SALT RHEUM.—This inveterate disease, which has long baffled the art of the most experienced physicians, has, at length, found a sovereign remedy in Dr. La Grange's genuine ointment. ...

PETER PATERSON, Agent.

SWEDES IRON.

...ing from the Ship *General Wolfe*, direct from ...NBURGH.
ASSORTED SWEDES IRON.
WILLIAM BUDDEN, *Point a' Calliere.*
August 18, 1829. 274-z

LOOKING GLASSES.

...ived by the subscriber, a large and elegant ... of Looking Glasses; German Plate; a va... and the prices remarkably low.
J. S. ARMSTRONG.

YORK FURNACE.

F. R. DUTCHER continues his FURNACE in complete operation, where can be had, at short notice,
Castings of any description from one to thirty cwt:
Also on hand a general assortment of STOVES, HOLLOW WARE, PLOUGH CASTINGS and PLOUGHS.

F. R. D. having erected a first rate Lathe for ... is ready to complete any order at short notice.

THEODORE TURLEY,
SMITH AND *Brass Founder:*
Yonge Street, next door to Judge Macaulay.
...ASTINGS for Mill work, &c. &c. done on ... notice.
...White and Blacksmith's work done to order. ...hest prices, in CASH, will be paid for old ... tin.

CHAPTER SIX

Yonge Street

ALCOHOL ABUSE

'Die I must, but let me die
  drinking in an inn!
Hold the wine cup to my lips
  sparkling from the bin!
So, when the angels flutter down
  to take me from my sin,
"Ah, God have mercy on this sot,"
  the cherubs will begin.'

Walter Map, 1140–1210

In nineteenth-century Upper Canada, any cherubs looking for sinners to usher to the heavens (or elsewhere) had to look no further than the inns that stood every half mile or so along Yonge Street. From its foot at Lake Ontario to its terminus at Holland Landing, Yonge Street boasted inns and taverns in abundance – a welcome sight to bone-weary travellers who needed little urging to rest a while and sample whatever the proprietor had to offer.

By the time he reached Holland Landing after a long day's journey and numerous stops for refreshment, a traveller might well have had trouble putting a steady foot on the ground. The mood in the coach became more boisterous after each stop; at the best of times a formidable experience, the journey often became a rollicking, noisy, and occasionally dangerous adventure. Nor was it unknown for the driver to be somewhat unsteady as well, since it was customary for tavern-keepers to treat him to free drinks in exchange for his continued patronage. One traveller recalled that the driver of his coach (obviously new to the route) knew only three English words: 'How far tavern?'

Whisky, welcome as it was to exhausted travellers, created immeasurable problems for the pioneer society of Upper Canada. Cheap, readily available, and sometimes of lethal quality, its use and abuse became a topic of concern to settlers and visitors alike. Indeed one traveller suggested that anyone who couldn't handle liquor should forget coming to Canada: 'men of irregular habits are the most unfit persons for emigration, spiritous liquors being exceedingly cheap, and as such easily attainable by such troublesome members of society. Therefore I would honestly advise such men ... to remain at home.'

His concern was understandable. Life was hard and whisky was cheap – by mid-century, it sold for twenty-five cents a gallon at general stores and taverns. In the numerous grog shops there was no lack of drink at a penny a glass or five cents a grunt, a grunt being as much as the customer could swallow in one breath. There are frequent references in travellers' journals to the numbers of inns and taverns. Goderich, for example, in 1833, had forty houses and three taverns.

Whisky was a way of life. It was served to the family at breakfast. Children grew up on it. Men took it with them to the fields as they worked. Whisky was the fuel that powered the pioneer, weary of hard physical labour and always at risk of death by accident and disease. Whisky was the motivator. Every major work project was, of necessity, a community effort, and these 'bees' became central to pioneer life. For many lonely men and women they were the only social outlet available. Liquor was an expected and integral part of the proceedings – without a pail of whisky going around, few men would stay to work.

And of course there were funerals. In 1817 a woman named Mrs Hewitt died in Queenston. It seems unlikely that anything in her life surpassed the manner of her leaving it. The list of her funeral expenses remains to intrigue anyone studying drinking customs in Upper Canada:

1817 October 26th	1 qt Madeira wine	12.0
	1 qt spirits*	8.0
	1 qt brandy	12.0
	1 qt shrub*	8.0
October 27th	1 qt Teneriffe wine	12.0
	1 qt port, 26th	12.0
	1 qt spirits	8.0
October 28th	1 qt Madeira wine	12.0
	1 qt shrub	
	1 qt Teneriffe wine	12.0
	1 qt port wine	12.0
	1 qt brandy	12.0
	1 qt spirits	8.0
	1 pint gin	6.0
	1 qt Madeira wine	16.0
	1 pint gin	6.0
	1 quart gin	12.0
	1 pint Madeira wine	8.0
October 29th	Cash for liquors at Queenston and digging the grave	3.0.0

The whole amounting to £12.0.0

*Spirits were distilled liquor; shrub was a prepared drink of lemon or lime, with sugar and rum.

One anonymous traveller, who called himself 'ex-settler,' ruefully remarked that 'in travelling through the country, you will see every inn, tavern and beer shop filled at all hours with drunken, brawling fellows; and the quantity of ardent spirits consumed by them will truly astonish you.' It was not unknown, according to one traveller, for unscrupulous tavern-keepers to encourage certain customers to pile up debts 'anticipating the day when they should be enriched by the possession of another good farm.'

Yonge Street boasted more taverns than any other road in the province, a dubious honour perhaps, but a result of the proliferation of traffic to Lake Simcoe and beyond. As well, the state of the road almost warranted their number. Built under the supervision of Lieutenant-Governor Simcoe as a military route to Lake Huron, Yonge Street opened in 1796. It was named after British Secretary of War Sir George Yonge, and was for many years little more than a rutted trail an ox-cart in width and dotted with tree stumps. In wet weather Yonge Street was all but impassable – 'a slough of despond,' as one writer put it.

In time, increased traffic brought demands for improvements, and gradually Yonge Street became less difficult to traverse as the stumps and boulders were removed. This latter effort was assisted by local tipplers, for the Stump Act of 1800 required a convicted drunk to remove a stump from the road. The system must have been effective and the drunks numerous, for John Goldie, who travelled Yonge Street in 1819, remarked that it was 'the best road that I have seen in Upper Canada, and since I left York there have been more waggons travelling this road than all those that I have seen since I left Montreal.'

Six years later, Lewis Bapp was advertising a twice-weekly stage run along the thirty-three miles between York and Holland Landing in a 'Light Covered Waggon' with at least three stops along the way. Before long other entrepreneurs, including William Weller, were operating stages on what one owner called 'one of the most pleasant Stage Routes in the Canadas.'

Passengers may have felt that 'pleasant' was a misnomer. In the early years of the nineteenth century, Yonge Street was in such terrible condition that coaches were forced to avoid it entirely as they headed north from York, detouring first to Parliament Street, then north to a point where they followed a farm trail to Bloor Street at the head of (the present) Jarvis Street. Where Bloor met Yonge Street the Red Lion Inn offered a welcoming respite before the coaches lurched northwards towards the next tavern.

Adding to the woes of long-suffering travellers were the detested toll-gates, the first two of which made their appearance at Yorkville and Hogg's Hollow in the early 1830s. In time, more were added, to the dismay of the settlers for whom Yonge Street provided the only reasonable access to the markets at York. 'Running the toll-gate' was considered great sport as long as it was successful, but trouble was sure to ensue when it was not.

Toll-gate keepers leased their toll-gates by the year, paying sums that ranged (in 1868) from $455 at an outlying gate, to $5,000 or more for the gate at Yorkville. W.H.G. Kingston, who travelled through Upper Canada at about that time, described the toll-gates as

> very convenient, especially in preserving the health of the keepers in winter. The house is of two stories, and in the top one is a small window, from which the custos can look out; a broad shed extends across the road, and the gate slides in grooves like a portcullis, the keeper having a winch inside his house to raise and lower it. He has also a ladle, with a long stick, to receive his toll, and a small hole to pass it through. Thus, instead of having at night to descend into the cold, or even open a window, he looks through the glass when a traveller appears, pokes out his ladle through the hole, and raising his gate, lets him pass.

Funds raised by toll-gates eventually helped to improve the state of the road and, in 1833, a one-mile stretch of Yonge Street became the first macadamized road in British North America. By 1850 this work had been completed as far as Holland Landing.

Stages heading north from Toronto might have made their first stop at a single-storey log building on the north-west corner of what is now Avenue Road and Bloor Street. Called the Tecumseh Wigwam, it was built in 1820 and catered to young men with some pretensions and a good thirst. During the 1850s its host was George King, and the hostelry gained some fame of a different sort. King's son, one of a band of robbers, murdered a stage-coach driver and was hanged at Cayuga. In spite of this dubious notoriety the Tecumseh Wigwam continued in business until it was destroyed in the 1880s.

By 1862, north-bound stages could also stop at a popular spot located where Yonge Street crossed a concession road now known as St Clair Avenue. Irish innkeeper Michael O'Halloran, formerly of the Cove of Cork at Scott and Wellington streets, had just completed construction of a twelve-room inn on the south-west corner of St Clair and Yonge. O'Halloran was a man of many talents. He was innkeeper, tailor, and owner of a thriving livery business. In addition, he was the recognized North American hurling champion (hurling being a popular Irish sport). He operated an athletic field south of his inn for football and hurling. O'Halloran retired from the innkeeping business in 1864, but his hostelry continued in operation through the century.

Across the road from O'Halloran's inn was a farm where deer were kept. This farm was owned by Agnes Heath who had settled there with her son, Charles, shortly after her husband died in the service of the East India Company. The Heaths' deer soon became part of the inn's entertainment as animals learned to come at mealtimes to the corner of the farm, where guests at O'Halloran's enjoyed watching and feeding them. As a result, in time the

The Tecumseh Wigwam, Bloor and Avenue Road, the present site of the Park Plaza Hotel

Michael O'Halloran's hotel, St Clair and Yonge streets, advertised its own football field.

Montgomery's tavern, on Yonge above Eglinton, was razed after the rebellion of 1837.

area became known as Deer Park.

A short distance north of O'Halloran's Hotel was another of Yonge Street's ubiquitous watering holes, a tavern called the Sickle and Sheath, owned by John Montgomery and better known locally as Montgomery's tavern. It stood on the west side of the road, just above present-day Eglinton Avenue at Montgomery. It was central to the skirmish that resulted in the defeat, in 1837, of William Lyon Mackenzie and his ill-fated rebels.

Mackenzie and the rebels from York County met at the tavern, a two-storey frame structure built in 1830. There they planned an assault on Toronto and the defeat of the government under Sir Francis Bond Head. Head, long on arrogance and short on common sense, had earlier dispatched the troops of the garrison to quell revolt in Lower Canada, leaving Toronto unprotected and ripe for violence.

But the violence was short-lived, thanks to the rebels' poor planning, inadequate weapons, and lack of military expertise, and to the eventual arrival of the loyal militia – nine hundred strong and equipped with several small cannon. The rebellion ended almost as soon as it began. Mackenzie and his men fled in all directions, and the governor, to set an example, ordered that Montgomery's tavern be razed. This was done, but not before the building was thoroughly searched, with disastrous results for the rebels. During the search, Mackenzie's carpet-bag was found. In his frantic rush to escape he had left it behind. Inside were his records and the names of his supporters – a list that simplified the task of a vengeful government in its search for rebels.

While John Montgomery owned the tavern, it had been leased only a week before the rebellion by John Linfoot, although Montgomery still kept a room there. Linfoot, a Tory, wasted no time in self-righteously proclaiming his blamelessness. On 14 December 1837, he gave his side of the story, stating under oath that:

> On Monday the 4th inst. a number of armed men came to the Tavern of which I had no

The Jolly Miller in its prime

previous information ... Shortly after the first party arrived W.L. Mackenzie came into the house and took me by the collar and desired me to show him a room up stairs. He then took some persons into the room and placed a guard over them ... I took Mrs Linfoot over to Snider's for safety and when I returned I saw Col. Moody in the house wounded in the right side below the ribs. Mackenzie addressed those present and said among other things that 'those who had not arms should take pipes in their mouths as they could take the city with pipes as well as with fire arms' ... Some person whose name I did not know told Mackenzie that they might have been in Toronto if they had not got so bad a General. Mackenzie told him to take his gun and go home.

John Montgomery was sentenced to hang for the part he played in the rebellion. He heard his sentence and then announced to the chief justice: 'You think you can send me to the gallows, but I tell you that when you're all frizzling with the devil, I'll be keeping tavern on Yonge Street.' Montgomery was pardoned in 1845 and, true to his word, returned to Yonge Street where he built another two-storey hotel, just south of the original. Eventually he leased this enterprise to his son, William. John Montgomery continued in the hotel business, opening the Franklin House in downtown Toronto in 1855 and, four years later, the Robinson House on Bay Street.

Heading north from Montgomery's tavern, through the mud and mire of Yonge Street, travellers next faced the toll-gate at the south end of Hogg's Hollow and, immediately afterwards, the treacherous hill beyond it. Until 1835 Yonge Street branched to the east at that point and then continued up Old Yonge Street. The

The Golden Lion, Yonge and Sheppard. Its life-sized carving of a lion was a landmark.

reverse of the trip, the descent into the valley en route to Toronto, was particularly harrowing, and frequently tree branches were tied to wagon wheels to help prevent the wagons from tipping over. Sliding down the slippery slope was a hair-raising experience for passengers, with nothing to recommend it but the presence of another tavern when they finally reached the bottom.

There has been a tavern at the foot of the hill for almost as long as there has been a Yonge Street. According to Patricia Hart in *Pioneering in North York*, a widow by the name of Vallière kept a wayside inn there during the War of 1812, providing 'food, drink, and lodging for the ragged soldier-farmers returning to and from the battle area as well as men with supplies going north to the Upper Lakes.'

Other taverns were built there in later years. The best known of these was the York Mills Hotel, built in the late 1850s and known today as the Jolly Miller (just south of York Mills, on the east side of Yonge Street). A series of unfortunate renovations has destroyed any claim to architectural interest that the Jolly Miller might have had. It was originally a pleasant brick structure with a central gable and a verandah sheltering the entrance below.

The hotel changed hands several times in its early years. In the 1860s, William Lennox, an Irishman and Worshipful Master of the Orange Lodge, became the first of its several innkeepers with Orange leanings. By 1866, M. Stewart, Proprietor, was advertising 'Best Attention Paid to Travellers;. Good Stbling and Attentive Hostlers.' Stewart too was an Irishman, and during his tenure the York Mills Hotel became a meeting place for the Orange Lodge in the days when that organization was central to the social, political, and religious life of the province. Every year on 12 July, the loyal Orangemen with banners flying sallied forth to celebrate 'the glorious twelfth' in towns and cities throughout Ontario. Every year the parades, which culminated in celebratory dinners at hostelries such as the York Mills Hotel, grew bigger. Every year the rhetoric became more agitated during the bombastic after-dinner speeches. Newspapers did their best to stir emotions; bigotry was rampant.

'The difference between William and James is identical with the difference between Protestant and Roman Catholic,'

The Bird in Hand: first one, then two

intoned the *York Herald* on 17 July 1863, 'and their difference is as that between Truth and Error – the Infallible Truth of Scripture and Fallible human popery! in one word, the difference between Christ and Antichrist.'

Two years later, the same newspaper reported that there were 'from eight to ten thousand Orangemen in the [12 July] procession in Toronto.' The Orange Order had been a powerful force in Ontario since the arrival in the 1830s of large numbers of Protestant Irish and Anglican English, all of whom rabidly supported the Tory establishment. They were involved in election rioting in Toronto in 1841 and remained part of the political scene for many more years. By 1851, fully one-third of Toronto's citizens were of Irish origin.

Upper Canadians, whether Orangemen or not, needed few excuses for stopping at any tavern along the way. One early ditty summed up the situation by listing five reasons why men drink:

Good wine, a friend, or being dry;
Or lest you should be by-and-by;
Or any other reason why.

If travellers refrained from stopping at the taverns immediately north of York Mills, they were sure to come to a halt at the Golden Lion. This inn was known for its dances, which attracted young people from as far away as Toronto.

The Golden Lion, an impressive frame structure, stood on the south-west corner of Yonge Street and Sheppard Avenue. A life-sized carving of a lion over the main entrance made the place a landmark. The inn was built in 1825 by Thomas Sheppard, a pioneer in the area. The Sheppards actively supported Mackenzie in the 1837 Rebellion, and it was at the Golden Lion that the rebel leader obtained a horse when he fled from Montgomery's tavern with the loyalists in hot pursuit.

The Sheppards were a musical family. They held band practices at their inn and,

Passengers enjoy a Richmond Hill stop, a break from bone-jarring stage-coach travel.

in time, built a dance hall over the driving sheds to accommodate the enthusiastic young people who came from far and near. Everyone sang a little number that went:

Here am I
On my way to Zion
I find my sons
In the Golden Lion.

North of the Golden Lion, at the south-west corner of Finch Avenue and Yonge Street, stood a seventeen-room, two-storey brick inn, built at about the same time as the Golden Lion but patronized by a different clientele. Its owner, James Davis, after attending a meeting of the first Temperance Society of the Township of York in 1831, returned to his hotel and dumped all his beer, whisky, and rum into the garden. The place then became known as the Temperance Inn.

A short distance north of the Temperance Inn, on the east side of Yonge Street, stood John Montgomery's first tavern, the Bird in Hand. Built in 1820 by John and his father, Alexander, the two-storey frame building became two buildings seven years later, following a heated disagreement between father and son. From top to bottom and front to back the building was cut in half, with John retaining the southern half as an inn. It would be pleasant to think that the two structures were then called 'Two in the Bush,' but if they were no record of it exists.

When John Montgomery decided to move to his tavern at Yonge north of Eglinton, he leased his half of the Bird in Hand to John Finch, and for years it was a popular stopping place for travellers, thanks to the good food served there. In 1847 Finch built another hotel at the north-east corner of Finch Avenue and Yonge Street, calling it Finch's Hotel. That same year, Thomas Steele became the proprietor of a tavern at the north-west corner of what is now the intersection of Yonge Street and Steeles Avenue. Like Sheppard and Finch avenues, Steeles Avenue was named for an innkeeper, a reminder even today of the importance of

Daniel Soules's Thornhill hostelry, 8038 Yonge Street, later the Temperance Hotel

these establishments to settlers in pioneer communities.

Business was brisk at most of the better inns and taverns on Yonge Street. In September 1836, one writer reported that in a single day more than two hundred teams stopped to water at a trough in front of a tavern in Thornhill. This might well have been Soules Inn, a sturdy brick building still standing at 8038 Yonge Street.

The hotel was built by Daniel Soules, who purchased the property in 1827 on the lot next to one settled by David Soules as early as 1798. The relationship of the two men is unknown, but several Souleses – Peter, George, Achrah, John, and Susannah – all appear on the title over several years, suggesting that Daniel sold the property in bits and pieces to his children. He also sold part of it to Benjamin Thorne, after whom Thornhill was named.

For the better part of a century the building was known variously as the Mansion House, the Royal, the Thornhill, and – briefly – as Mrs Christian's Temperance Hotel. Mrs Christian's foray into hotel-keeping lasted only from November 1871 to October of the following year. Perhaps the name discouraged customers.

Another popular hotel in Thornhill was the Queen's, an establishment run for many years by Henry Lemon, an Englishman. He too played host to the local Orangemen on 'the glorious twelfth,' an event reported with its usual lack of restraint by the *York Herald* on 15 July 1859. Introduced by the heading 'Orange Procession,' it concluded:

every Protestant has cause for gratitude that the great William was successful in this struggle, for he delivered us from the thraldom of a narrow-minded and bigoted king, and gave to us the liberty we now enjoy ... the company adjourned to dinner which was provided by Mr Shields in a beautiful grove, and by Mr Lemmon at his hotel.

Whatever the food served by Mr Lemon at his hotel, the meal was sure to be accompanied by liquid refreshment, with toasts offered to everyone and everything imaginable. By the end of the evening, the good health of everybody (except, possibly, the celebrants) should have been assured. Toasting was a tradition carried on with great enthusiasm by Canadians throughout much of the nineteenth century, and the success of a banquet was measured by the number and variety of toasts given. Toasts were a challenge to the banqueters' imagination, and they manfully rose to meet it.

One occasion that inspired particular inventiveness was the annual St Andrew's Day banquet celebrated with gusto across the province. Plumer Burley's hotel in Ancaster was the scene of one such event on which loyal Scots gathered to raise their glasses in toasts. As T. Roy Woodhouse recorded in *Ancaster's Heritage*:

After the excellent dinner, they drank 'The King' standing, to thunderous applause. Dr Willison and lawyer William Notman sang Auld Lang Syne. The toast to 'St Andrew' drew great cheering. 'The King and the Royal Family' brought three times three cheers. Then followed 'The Navy and Army of old England' and 'Earl Grey and His Majesty's Ministers,' and 'Our English and Irish friends.' Then there was a short recess to await the return of several who had gone out to the back. Then came a toast to 'Sir John Colborne and the Province of Upper Canada' during which a couple of the younger Scots unaccountably slid under the table; then 'Lord Aylmer and the Province of Lower Canada,' with a couple more sliders. The final toast to 'Lady Colborne and the Fair of Upper Canada' was a relief to many because nine 'bottoms-up' toasts were too many if you were foolish enough to fill your glass each time. But it was a glorious St Andrew's Day.

When the coaches lurched into Oak Ridges there was an available connection westward to Bolton through Springhill (now King City) and Nobleton. The Bolton *Enterprise* of 6 September 1889 extolled the virtues of the trip as one that allowed the passenger to appreciate the 'fields of waving grain and the neat and substantial farm houses which are on both sides of you, evidencing the excellence of the land, its high state of cultivation and the consequent prosperity of the farmers.'

After surmounting a hill about two-thirds of the way between Bolton and Oak Ridges, Springhill appeared in view:

Across the Northern track [of the rail line] you arrive in front of Mr Hogan's hotel where you alight and are received by the genial proprietor and escorted into his well-kept house. Mrs Hogan, his good lady, will receive you kindly and prepare an excellent lunch while you are examining the famous Minnie Hogan (the finest bred mare in Canada), and Rys, her son, equal to his mother in breeding, and said to be not inferior to any blood stallion in Canada at the present time ... [After a tour of the village] you will be about ready to start home in the cool of the evening, and when your horse is brought out to you by John, at the hotel, you will meet in him one of the best fellows you have met in some time and every inch a gentleman.

The reader is assured that he will leave Hogan's with his buggy filled with apples from their orchard, which Porter, the Hogans' son, 'who would be a pride to any father and mother,' had obligingly loaded in the buggy.

Agnes Hogan was the daughter of hotel-keeper Isaac Dennis and thereby the fortunate recipient of the inn her father built, which provided a living for her and her husband, John Hogan, for the next

John and Agnes Hogan's King City inn had a private race track.

fifty years. The inn, which stands at the intersection of Keele and the King Sideroad, became known throughout King Township as Hogan's at Four Corners. Attached to the building were stables with a ballroom above. A track on the property provided the arena for innkeeper John Hogan to test the speed of the racehorses that were his great interest, one of which was mentioned in his will. At his death in 1899, Hogan left his son, Robert Porter, his weigh scales, ten dollars a month, and 'my grey horse Frank Ellis.' Hogan also instructed in his will that after his death the sale of the hotel be considered.

That sale took place a year after Hogan's death. George Phillips of Kleinburg became the proprietor. At Prohibition the hotel closed and became for many years a private residence. It is now open for business again and restored to a state of elegance no doubt undreamed of when shoppers and travelling salesmen were met at the railway station down the road and taken by buggy to the door of Hogan's.

The Northern Railway, which came into use in 1853, running straight up the main street of Springhill and on to Aurora, was the first to be opened in Upper Canada. Travellers now had an alternative to the difficult journey up Yonge Street, and before long the taverns became fewer. In villages bypassed by the railway, the taverns that remained served mainly as watering holes for the local people. But two substantial hotels, the Marksman's Inn and the

The welcoming door of Hogan's Inn

Royal, remained in business in Holland Landing even after the coaches stopped running.

Holland Landing was the end of the coach line from Toronto and the site of the link with travel across Lake Simcoe. There had been an inn there since 1821, when the enterprising Peter Robinson established the Red Mills in Holland Landing and, soon afterwards, being a man not to miss an opportunity, built a tavern. A brother of John Beverley Robinson, he was at the time serving in the Upper Canadian Assembly and running a profitable mercantile business in nearby Newmarket.

By 1823, Robinson was assisting with the settlement of a group of southern Irish immigrants near Almonte in the Ottawa Valley, and two years later he led another group to Peterborough, which took its name from him. His tavern in Holland Landing was called Phelps Inn, and even twenty years after it was built it seemed to be the only civilized stopping place for miles around. Sir Richard Bonnycastle, who was there in 1841, urged travellers to, 'Get over ... to Phelps' Inn on Yonge Street as fast as you can,' this in spite of the fact that he found Holland Landing itself an abominable place,

> the seat of fever and ague, of black flies, sand flies, mosquitoes, and water snakes ... I recollect ... being so intolerably stung that, although I thought myself mosquito-proof, I was obliged to get the poor host's kind daughter, who could scarcely lift her head for ague, to make me a green gauze veil, without which I could not have proceeded.

The Marksman's Inn, a pleasant brick hotel at 18244 Yonge Street in Holland Landing, was owned in the middle years of the nineteenth century by James McClure, an Irishman who advertised in 1866 that he offered 'Good accommodation for Travellers.' The same words were used in the same directory (*Mitchell's General Directory for the City of Toronto and Gazetteer for the Counties of York and Peel*) to advertise a competitor, the Royal Hotel, a short distance away, leaving travellers new to the place presumably tossing a coin. The Royal was owned until the 1890s by the Sheppard family, first John, an Englishman who listed himself as 'Hotel Keeper and Carpenter,' and after his death in 1877 by other family members.

Throughout Ontario, hotels like these were springing up at mid-century, particularly in towns where the railway brought increased prosperity. As always, they welcomed not only travellers but also townspeople and farmers from the surrounding countryside. And, as always, liquor flowed freely. The happy customers might have called it 'whisky'; or, just as likely, 'stagger juice,' 'tangle leg,' 'nose paint,' or 'dead-and-gone'; there were as many euphemisms for liquor as there were establishments to drink it in. In some places the really potent whisky made in backwoods distilleries was fondly referred to as 'forty-rod stuff,' liquor so strong that after a few healthy swigs no one could hope to walk more than the length of a field – a distance of forty rods.

Uxbridge was founded by Pennsylvania Germans and Quakers, and from earliest times, when John Plank built the first tavern there, business and drinking flourished. By mid-century there were eight taverns in Uxbridge Township and, in the free-and-easy spirit of the times, people as young as fifteen years were allowed to drink in them.

Joseph Bascom, a tanner, arrived in town in 1834 and thirteen years later purchased one hundred acres on which much of Uxbridge grew. When Bascomb died in 1875, he was survived by a wife, five sons, and six daughters, a sizeable family by anyone's standards but even more surprising considering that the prolific Mr Bascom had been predeceased by three wives and five other children. One of the surviving sons, John, became a hotel-keeper in Uxbridge. After his first hotel burned, John Bascom operated a thriving establishment called the Commercial Hotel. Built in the early 1860s, the Commercial had already seen a series of owners, among them John Fralick and his wife, Elizabeth Bascom, a sister of John and daughter of the prolific Joseph.

Thomas Fogg purchased the Commercial in 1872. As a new owner, Fogg decided to thrust himself on public attention with an event that was reported with appropriate enthusiasm by the Uxbridge *Journal* of 11 April 1872:

FORMAL OPENING OF THE COMMERCIAL HOTEL
This event took place on the evening of the 23rd inst. under the most auspicious circumstances. It is known to some that a short time ago this valuable property was purchased by Thomas Fogg, Esq. of Markham and after giving the establishment a thorough overhauling in re-painting, re-papering and otherwise putting it through a cleansing has leased the premises to 'mine host', also from Markham, Mr E. Milliken, whose reputation as a caterer to the travelling community and others is well known and needs no eg'onium from us.

About eighty gentlemen showed up for the feast and then, 'ample justice having been done to the viands ... [the guests] ... proceeded to give the usual loyal and patriotic toasts, which were responded to with enthusiasm ... The singing of "God Save the Queen" wound up a pleasant and harmonious evening's entertainment.'

Only two years after John Fogg launched his new enterprise, the hotel, for some reason, changed hands again. Perhaps the hospitable host, Edwin Milliken, a youthful twenty-four when he leased the Commercial, lacked the experience necessary to operate the business.

Today the Commercial Hotel has a new lease on life. It has been restored, moved from its original location on Brock Street to 37 Main Street North, and now, as the Hobby Horse Arms, operates as a dining establishment, thanks to far-sighted owners and financial assistance from the Ontario Heritage Foundation.

South-east of Uxbridge, in the hamlet of Ashburn, the Wilson House was a favourite overnight stop for farmers taking grain to Whitby harbour. Built by Alexander Wilson in 1869, it was operated by him and his son until it was sold ten years later, a transaction noted in the *Whitby Chronicle* of 9 January 1879:

The Wilson House, Ashburn, is about coming into possession of Mr Alex Barclay who will always be ready with a warm welcome to receive his friends and treat his guests with good old style hospitality.

That hospitality, at hotels like the Wilson House, usually centred on the bar and, as one old-timer recalled, treating was a feature of each evening:

Drinking bouts for the whole night were then very common. Usually a party of boon companions – say eight or ten of them –

The Commercial Hotel, newly restored at 37 Main Street North, Uxbridge

would assemble in the sitting room of the hotel, next the bar, and someone would at once 'stand treat' all round. This having been partaken of, one of the number would sing a song and then someone else would provide a drink all round. Probably a story would follow, succeeded by another drink; then another song and another treat, as a matter of course, and so the song, story and glass passed around until everyone had treated.

Then it was the landlord's turn to collect his money, which he did when his patrons were in no condition to count their change. These drinking bouts 'were so common that one was usually going on at one of the hotels every night of the week,' no doubt excepting Sunday.

Not far from Ashburn, in a quiet village called Whitevale, the Whitevale Hotel was the centre of what, for the middle years of the nineteenth century, was a thriving industrial community. Built by Thomas Burton about 1859, it served the village under a series of owners until, after several disastrous fires, the fortunes of Whitevale declined. An item in the *Pickering News* of 10 February 1882 suggested that business had declined to a point at which it didn't take much to create news in Whitevale: 'The enterprising proprietor of the hotel in Whitevale, has placed a lamp on the street in front,' it reported. The addition of a lamp may have lured new customers to the

Greenwood, where a modest inn adopted an impressive name: the British Arms Hotel

hotel, but generally speaking a small hotel like this survived by virtue of being the only one in town.

Nearby, in the appealing village of Greenwood, the British Arms Hotel was by 1870 one of two hostelries serving a population of about five hundred people. This establishment's grandiloquent name was belied by its modest appearance, for it is a simple frame structure, set a few steps back from the main street. At the west end of the building a separate door led into the taproom. The British Arms boasted a spring in the basement. Water was piped to a trough at the front, where horses were watered. Perhaps, on occasion, patrons inside drank the water as well, sometimes to their sorrow. One newspaper of the day reported the death of a man whose demise was the direct result of 'drinking cold water in a tavern.'

It was, of course, rarely the water that caused problems in taverns. The liquor was not only cheap but of poor quality, particularly in the early days when local stills were licensed and innkeepers usually had their own source of supply. As one traveller put it, much of the liquor was made from 'frosty potatoes, hemlock, pumpkins and black mouldy rye.' By the 1820s whisky of better quality became available thanks to better distilling methods and more distilleries. These were built to meet the demand of farmers, who preferred to take grain to a distillery rather than have it rot on the field. The cheapest way to transport grain was as whisky. Canada's growth from colony to nation was the result, in large part, of the income on customs duties from alcoholic beverages. In the words of Merrill

Thomas Burton's Inn, Whitevale

Denison, a biographer of the Molson family (which, along with its brewing interests, was for many years Canada's largest distiller), 'Canada had to drink herself to nationhood.'

The social problems that accompanied all this were legion. In virtually every issue, newspapers reported with tight-lipped disapproval the deaths, brawls, and fires that resulted with dismaying frequency from the use and abuse of liquor. On 3 December 1861, the *Bruce Herald* reported

> a shocking case of addiction to the excessive use of intoxicating liquors ... revealed at an inquest at Newcastle. The wife of a beer-house keeper being in liquor, fell down stairs last week and died from the effects of the injuries sustained. The husband of the deceased told the coroner that the night before the accident she drank four gallons of beer out of a bucket after she had gone to bed.

Then as now the double standard was evident in society's attitude to drunkenness. In *Macnab's Phenomena of Drunkenness* the subject was solemnly, if unscientifically, discussed and reprinted in the Niagara *Gleaner* of 28 July 1827:

> Female drunkards are very subject to hysterical

effections. There is a delicacy of fibre in women and a susceptibility of mind which makes them feel more acutely than the other sex all internal influences. Hence their whole system is affected with hysterics, and other varieties of nervous weakness. These afflictions are not always traced to the true cause which is often neither more nor less than dram drinking. When a woman's nose becomes crimsoned at the point, her eyes somewhat red, and more watery than before, and her lips fuller and less firm and intellectual in the expression, we may suspect that something wrong is going on.

John A. Macdonald, in a ditty he used to sing with D'Arcy McGee, put it more succinctly:

Oh a drunken man is a terrible curse
But a drunken woman is twice as worse.

Perhaps it is fitting that a woman should have the last word on the subject. In reply to a suggestion in an earlier letter to the *Upper Canada Gazette*, one irate reader voiced her solution to the problem of male drunkards. Signing herself 'A Female,' she wrote on 21 September 1799 suggesting a tax on drunkenness and referring to men who 'resort to those receptacles of idleness, taverns.' She suggested the following system of fines:

For getting drunk in the morning, £30 per annum; twice a day, £40; three times a day, morning, noon and evening, £50; every alternate day, £20; once a week if not on Sunday, £15; on Sunday, £60; for beating his wife once a day, £200; twice a day, morning and evening, £400; every alternate day, £100; once a week if not on Sundays, £80; on Sunday £500; coming home from the tavern drunk and beating his wife into a fit of hysterics, consumption or giving her a pair of black eyes, £700; Getting drunk and being in consequence confined to his bed a week or two, £1000.

The Governor's Road

JAMES FULTON.
Richmond Hill, Markham, Nov. 13th, 1829. 287з

Stray Ox and Steer.

Broke into the inclosure of the Subscriber, a LARGE OX, blind of the off eye, with seven wrinkles on his horn, a yellowish Red and White colour; also a RED STEER with him, nearly three years old; with a brindle face, and part white under his breast. The owner or owners are requested to prove property, pay charges, and take the animals away.

SALT RHEUM.—This inveterate disease, which has long baffled the art of the most experienced physicians, has, at length, found a sovereign remedy in Dr. La Grange's genuine ointment. Few cutaneous diseases are met with more reluctance by the physician, which he is so universally unsuccessful. This stood the test of experience, and justly obparalleled celebrity. It immediately removes a healthy action to the vessels of the skin, poles and smoothness. Numerous recommight be obtained of its superior efficacy.

deed for cash, or if one half or one third of the purchase money is paid down. Immediate possession can be given, and, for further particulars appply to PHILIP CODY.
Toronto, Nov. 16th, 1829. 287z.

WHERE IS WILLIAM SUTHERLAND?

THE Subscriber is desirous of ascertaining the place of abode of Mr. William Sutherland and family. They lived in or near Glengarry, about the time of the last war, and were originally from the parish of Kindonan, Sutherlandshire. Address a letter to the Subscriber, at Niagara, care of Messrs. Chrysler, Merchants.
N. B. Mrs. Sutherland's maiden name was Catharine Macpherson.
DANIEL MACPHERSON.
Niagara, 17th Nov. 1829. 2873.

Boarding.

THE Subscriber can furnish Boarding, Lodging, &c. for six steady mechanics, reasonable, on Dundas Street, between Mr. Willmot's Tavern and four doors from Mr. Bird's Tavern, in the house lately occupied by Mr. George Hutchison, Plaisterer.
JAMES PARKER.
Nov. 18. 87.

STRAYED, on the 10th October last, into the premises of ANDREW BIGHAM, on lot No. 12, in the first concession of ETOBICOKE, A LIGHT IRON-GREY HORSE, rising five or six years of age.—The owner is requested to prove property, pay charges, and take him away.
Nov. 17. 873.

SAWYER & LABOURERS WANTED.

WANTED by the subscriber, a Sawyer who understands his business, and two men who understand Chopping; to whom liberal encouragement will be given. Apply to JAMES STEPHENS.

THE SUBSCRIBERS have just received direct from London, a general assortment of
Hosiery,
Black and Colored Gros-de-Naples,
Figured Norwich Crapes,
Black Silk and Cotton Velvets,
Sewing Silks,
Lace Thread Edgings,
Worked Insertions, and Scollop Muslins,
Red and Bell Cotton,
Geo. the 4th Regulation Swords, Belts, and Sashes,
J. C. GODWIN & Co.

WILLIAM KENT.
Stoney Creek, Nov. 13, 1829. 87z

NEWMARKET MAIL STAGE.

WILLIAM GARBUTT, having taken the contract for carrying His Majesty's Mails between York and Newmarket, for the next four years, respectfully informs the public that THE MAIL STAGE will start from Joseph Bloor's Hotel, York, on Mondays and Thursdays, at 12 o'clock, noon, and arrive at nine o'clock, the same evening in Newmarket;—and will leave Mr. Barber's Tavern, Newmarket, for York, on Wednesdays and Saturdays, at in the morning, and arrive in York at 2 P. M. on the same day.
York, March 30th, 1829. 254z.

NEW ARRANGEMENT OF STAGES

Between York and the Carrying Place at the head of the Bay of Quintie.

WEDES IRON.

WILLIAM BUDDEN,
Point a' Callierre.
August 10, 1829. 274z

LOOKING GLASSES.

J. R. ARMSTRONG.

YORK FURNACE.

F. R. DUTCHER continues his FURNACE in complete operation, where can be had, at short notice,
Castings of any description from one to thirty cwt:
Also on hand a general assortment of STOVES, HOLLOW WARE, PLOUGH CASTINGS and PLOUGHS.

THEODORE BURLEY,
SMITH AND *Brass Founder:*
Yonge Street, next door to Judge Macaulay.

PETER PATERSON, *Agent.*

CHAPTER SEVEN

The Governor's Road

TEMPERANCE

'We were so happy till father drank rum,
Then all our sorrow and trouble begun;
Mother grew paler and wept every day,
Baby and I were too hungry to play.
Slowly they faded, and one summer's night,
Found their dear faces all silent and white;
Then with big tears slowly dropping I said:
"Father's a drunkard and Mother is dead."'

Anonymous, 1870s

HEART-RENDING doggerel such as this was used as ammunition in the never-ending war that temperance advocates waged against 'fiery rum.' Their opponents ridiculed temperance societies as consisting only of 'old men and maidens, widows and wives,' but those urging a change could be excused for their zeal. Evidence of alcohol abuse and its attendant social problems was everywhere to be found.

Liquor was so much a part of life, both in the backwoods of Canada and on the frontier of the United States, that some of the first temperance societies advocated merely cutting back on consumption. There were a variety of approaches to the problem. Total-abstinence societies demanded that liquor be used only for medicinal purposes in cases of 'bodily infirmity.' Other temperance societies allowed wine or beer while prohibiting hard liquor. A temperance group in Morristown, New Jersey, pledged merely to drink no more than 'a pint of liquor in one day.'

In 1828, the first temperance society in Upper Canada was formed in Bastard Township, and shortly thereafter similar organizations sprang up across the province. Temperance meetings were widely advertised in sympathetic newspapers. They usually consisted of a volatile sermon followed by either a heated debate on temperance versus total abstinence or some rousing songs. The atmosphere of the meetings was intense, and the resulting excitement brought out many who may have come simply for diversion, a change from a mundane daily life. Various groups were targeted – men, women, young people, blacks, and soldiers – with each approached differently. Nor were children forgotten. Many of them earnestly memorized verses that would, it was hoped, keep them forever on the straight and narrow.

This little band
Do with our hand
The pledge now sign,
To drink no wine,
Nor brandy red
To turn our head,
Nor whisky hot,
That makes the sot
Nor fiery rum
To turn our home,

Into a hell,
Where none could dwell,
Whence peace would fly,
Where hope would die,
And love expire,
Mid such a fire:
So here we pledge perpetual hate
To all that can intoxicate.

To prevent backsliding from the pledge some societies – the Royal Canadian Rifle Regiment Temperance Society of Niagara was one such – urged members to be their brother's policemen and 'communicate any infringement' of the rules to a committee. The committee would then 'advise, remonstrate and admonish the offending member' and 'report all the circumstances to the Society at its next meeting for final decision.'

Both Canadians and Americans were taking tentative steps towards a temperance movement at about the same time and at about the same pace. Canadians who objected to the whole idea grumbled that it was all due to insidious influences from south of the border. Colonel Thomas Talbot, no mean tippler himself, complained of the 'damned cold water drinking societies' that, in his opinion, were tinged with 'Yankeeism.' He was right. Certainly when it came to church support for the movement, those churches that had strong connections with the United States (American Presbyterians, Methodists, Baptists, and Quakers) were solidly in favour, while the Church of England clergy tended to be opposed. This approach to temperance had elements of class bias, as well. James S. Buckingham, a temperance advocate, after addressing a total-abstinence society in Toronto, noted tersely in his journal that there was very little interest in temperance among 'the higher classes of society, and the Episcopal clergy.'

On the whole, though, innkeepers who sold liquor didn't have to worry about losing customers to their temperance competitors. They even found humour in the situation. The formation of a Total Abstinence Society in Peterborough in 1840 prompted innkeepers there to request that their former patrons would 'have the honesty to abstain from leaving their Tavern Bills unpaid, and thus prove that tho' inimical to ardent liquors, they possess a quantum stuff of the proper spirit.' Some innkeepers went so far as to advocate 'Intemperance Societies.' One wily host – Irish innkeeper Thomas Montgomery – in order to ensure that no potential customer escaped temptation, cut a short-cut to the local mill, a path that ran directly past his taproom door.

Montgomery had emigrated from Ireland with his parents in 1812 at the age of twenty-two. On his arrival in Quebec, he put his worldly possessions on his back and trekked through the wilderness to Chatham, a distance of nearly 750 miles. Here he operated as a merchant and, later, as a surveyor in Peel County.

In 1830 Thomas Montgomery settled in Etobicoke with his wife, Margaret, and infant son, William, and started to build his inn. This was a two-storey limestone structure, laid out in a plan standard for inns of this size. The taproom was on the main floor and ran the full length of the building. A separate door opened to the inn yard. This was an obligatory feature, allowing guests at the inn to be undisturbed by the comings and goings of local patrons. A hall ran the full depth of the inn as well, dividing the main floor in half. Across the hall from the taproom were two rooms, the inn parlour and the dining-room. The second floor, once again divided by a hall, contained six rooms, for use by both family and paying guests.

In October 1832, Montgomery paid £7.10.0 for his first licence to operate as an innkeeper and 'to retail spiritous liquors.' His own records show, however, that he had already been in business for more than a year, unlicensed and unencumbered by legal niceties. Surveyor David Gibson wrote in June 1831 that he 'came to T. Montgomery tavern on Dundas Street.' By 1838, business was brisk enough to warrant an

Thomas Montgomery's inn, 4709 Dundas West. The path ran temptingly near its door.

expansion, and Montgomery more than doubled the size of his inn, adding a two-storey east wing. This included a new taproom, a kitchen, and pantries on the main floor, additional sleeping accommodations on the second floor, and a ballroom. Present research indicates that there was originally a verandah on the building.

Thomas Montgomery was a member of the Loyal Orange Lodge, which met regularly at his inn. Township council meetings were held in the ballroom, as were magistrates' courts, with prisoners confined in the basement.

The last tavern licence issued to Thomas Montgomery was in 1856. After that he concentrated mainly on farming. Whether this change had anything to do with the death of forty-seven-year-old Margaret Montgomery in 1855 is unclear. That unfortunate soul had been predeceased by five of her seven children. The five died at five days, twelve days, two months, five months, and eleven years. Of the two remaining sons, Robert died at the age of twenty-seven, and William lived until his ninetieth year.

In his account books, Thomas Montgomery kept track only of those who owed money. Presumably those who were not regular customers paid cash, and the regulars kept a running account. This accepted practice made operations difficult for an innkeeper. Customers ran up as many as fifteen or twenty dinners before settling the account and, of course, a certain amount of time was expended collecting debts. Montgomery had his share of bad accounts. On the other hand his own record of bill paying was so poor that on many occasions he found himself in court. He was even charged with arson and threatening his competitors, the other tavern-keepers in the area. His papers reveal him as an uneducated but hard-nosed businessman, frequently disorganized in his affairs.

Although shrewdly non-temperance innkeepers like Montgomery were more typical of the breed, the temperance (or abstinence) movement gradually gained support, and temperance taverns and inns opened in hundreds of places throughout the province. They attracted patrons who knew that, within their walls, a traveller could avoid the noise and rowdyism that was so often a part of the regular tavern scene and hear only the clink of ice in a pitcher filled with pure water.

In the village of Port Credit one innkeeper carried the temperance idea to a contradictory extreme by establishing a temperance inn for sailors. He was James Wilcox, himself a sailor. Known as the Wilcox Inn, it was mentioned in the *Colonial Advocate* of 28 April 1831 in a request for tenders to build a bridge across the nearby creek. The present pleasant frame building, built in 1850, replaced the earlier structure. For a few years the hostelry accommodated sailors and other visitors until, in 1855, the arrival of the railway caused the decline of the port. Wilcox converted the building to a two-family residence and continued living there and working as a sailor on Lake Ontario. His inn, beautifully restored, stands at 32 Front Street.

The area boasts other historic (though not necessarily temperance) establishments. Not far from the Wilcox Inn, at the mouth of the Credit River, an inn had been built as early as 1798 as part of a scheme suggested by Lieutenant-Governor Simcoe, who saw the importance of establishing government-owned inns between Newark (Niagara-on-the-Lake) and York. The first of these, the King's Head Inn, was built at the south end of Burlington Beach in 1794 and operated until 10 May 1813, when cannon shot from two American schooners set it ablaze. Its Port Credit neighbour, built in 1798, stood on the east bank of the river, south of today's Lakeshore Road. That primitive inn was first leased by William Allan, a Scottish emigrant who made a fortune as a merchant in York and rose to become the financial genius of the Family Compact. Allan himself never operated the inn. He in turn leased it to a series of innkeepers who ran it for him and operated a ferry across the mouth of the Credit. In 1805 the government, perhaps dissatisfied with an absentee owner, leased the inn to a man who would run it himself. That innkeeper was Thomas Ingersoll, a man whose main claim to fame was as the father of Laura Secord. Until his death five years later, he welcomed to that early inn the first settlers in the area that is now Mississauga.

In the 1830s, Russell Bush, a young American, settled nearby and, as did so many others, tackled a variety of enterprises. His most ambitious was the sizeable stage-coach stop he ran at what is now 822 Clarkson Road.

Along with operating the inn and the farm (with the help of his wife, Mary, their three children, and two servants), Russell Bush served as a fence-viewer and poundkeeper for Toronto Township. As poundkeeper he had to ensure that hogs did not run wild in any village. Those that did were captured and sold, with half the fine going to the informant and the rest (minus Bush's fee) into township coffers. As fence-viewer, he had to ensure that all township fences were 'five foot high and staked or locked.'

As it did for James Wilcox, the coming of the railroad in 1855 soon brought an end to the traffic that had always passed in front of Bush's Inn. Bush then sold the inn and all his property to Edward Sutherland, a farmer, who called it Woodburn.

Today's Lakeshore Road follows the old Mississauga trail that led westward from York. It and the Governor's Road were the first roads in the area. The latter (Dundas

James Wilcox's temperance inn for sailors, 32 Front Street, Port Credit

Street) was Ontario's first 'road,' commissioned by Simcoe mainly for military reasons but also as an incentive to settlement and a deterrent to American expansionist policies. The Governor's Road, originally little more than a narrow trail, was blazed and cut by 1796, but it was years before it was of much use to anyone. Its name was coined by disdainful settlers as a term of derision.

But by the 1820s, stages were rumbling along the Governor's Road and, in 1833, William Weller's line began to carry passengers westward towards Oakville with connections to feeder routes leading north. On the gravel road that led to Streetsville, stages stopped at John Crozier's Cold Spring House, a handsome Georgian building; its name alludes to Mullett Creek, a gentle stream that meanders along behind and below the inn.

Conflicting records make it impossible to determine exactly when Crozier started as an innkeeper. An Irishman, he arrived in Upper Canada in 1834 and in short order found himself embroiled in the political upheavals of the day. Crozier was a Tory and loyally joined the local militia under Captain William McGrath, son of another Irish immigrant, the influential Reverend William McGrath of nearby Erindale.

With the excitement of the 1837 Rebellion behind him, Crozier settled down to farming pursuits. He operated the toll-gate for a while, living in a two-storey frame house with his wife, Jane, a small daughter,

John Crozier's Cold Spring House, 4034 Mississauga Road North

and ten servants, all but one of them Irish. Such a large staff suggests that Crozier was already operating a sizeable inn; however, his name did not appear on the title, so it would seem that he was either renting the building or acting as proprietor for Peter McDougall, who had built the inn in 1830. After 1865, township minutes provide ample evidence that John Crozier was indeed keeping tavern at Cold Spring House.

The Brampton *Conservator* of 8 August 1907 reported that John Crozier, 'who had reached the wonderful age of 95 years and who has been fairly active until a short time ago, is confined to his bed and is under the doctor's care.' The paper went on to mention Lord Strathcona, 'who, at 97 years of age is performing the duties of Canadian High Commissioner in London. Careful diet is said to be the secret of the High Commissioner's health and age. The same, no doubt, applies to Peel's sturdy nonagenarians.' A few weeks later, on 22 September, the same paper carried the following obituary notice:

Crozier. At Streetsville, on Thursday, September 5, 1907, John Crozier, aged 96.

For many years in Streetsville a fine redbrick hotel known as the Franklin House, at 263 Queen Street, provided accommodation for travellers; now restored, it is once

John Lennon's good liquor, cigars, and food graced the Franklin House, Streetsville.

Front door, the Franklin House

more open to the public. John Lennon, the owner, advertised the opening of his establishment (previously the home of Bennet Franklin, a Streetsville lumber merchant) in the Brampton *Conservator* on 16 March 1877. He promised that the bar would be 'well supplied with pure and genuine good liquor and cigars and the table amply provided for.'

For a time magistrate's court was held in Franklin House. A month after Lennon took over, the *Conservator* reported:

> A magistrate's Court sat on Monday at the Franklin House. If a moral is to be abstracted from beleaguerant feuds, it is that he who gets the best of the fight, is most certain to come in for the worst of the law.

Lennon later sold Franklin House to popular innkeeper Thomas Campbell. During Campbell's time the hostelry housed three dentists, a market, other merchants, and a tonsorial artist.

Only a year after John Lennon advertised his 'pure and genuine good liquor,' the Canada Temperance Act, generally known as the Scott Act (after Richard William Scott, Secretary of State), was enacted. Arguments about prohibition and temperance had been raging for more than fifty years before the Scott Act. Previous attempts to deal with the liquor problem, such as the Dunkin Act of 1864, had introduced the principle of local option; but it, like other legal approaches, led only to the discovery by the drinking public of increasingly creative ways to flout the law.

It took little intelligence on the part of determined drinkers to find loopholes in the Scott Act. Although it prohibited the sale of liquor in any county whose residents voted it into law, it lacked restrictions regarding where or by whom any liquor brought in from another county could be consumed. In effect, as long as it was not purchased in a 'dry' county, liquor could be quaffed in the middle of the town square, if that seemed desirable. It could be given to anyone – even children – quite legally, but it could not be legally sold.

Newspaper stories of liquor abuse continued unabated. On 7 August 1884, the *Bruce Herald* disapprovingly reported an incident in Milton, where the Scott Act had been in force for two years.

WHISKEY'S WORK

... three men on a drunk locked themselves in a third story room in the Temperance Hotel. They sat in a window which faces Main Street and drank whiskey from a bottle and indulged in horseplay for the benefit of the passers-by ... throwing a bottle which they had emptied at Mr David Hamberry who happened to be below them ...

Much earlier, a pair of entries in the *Halton Journal* of Milton indicated a possible motive for one John Shillingshaw's personal battle with whisky:

June 13, 1856. I, John Shillingshaw, hereby request all Grocers and Innkeepers to refrain from selling me any liquor, of any description, as I have abstained from drinking any more.

February 27, 1857. BIRTHS. at Milton, on the 24th inst ... the wife of John Shillingshaw of a son.

Although Halton County was the first to take a step towards prohibition (thereby acquiring the name of the 'banner county'), its residents coped admirably with the restraints imposed by the Scott Act by developing a frequent and prolonged need of spirits for medicinal purposes. There were five druggists in the county who had been granted special Spirit Licences under the act. They were required by the government to furnish lists of those customers to whom they had sold liquor, as well as the names of the prescribing physicians, the amounts purchased, and the purpose for which the liquor was required. Georgetown's Reverend J. Halling stands out in the list because his purchase of one bottle of wine was for sacramental purposes. The hundreds of others all stated their needs as 'medicinal.' Since pharmacists could legally supply only ten ounces of liquor per prescription, some names appeared more than once on the list.

In Trafalgar Township a temperance society had been formed as early as 1830, and in 1843 the first 'Temperance Hall' in the province was erected to serve Oakville's temperate citizens. Nowhere, however, did the residents of Halton County cope more imaginatively with the Scott Act than in Oakville. Most of the townspeople appeared to suffer from some unknown malady, the cure for which was everyone's favourite remedy. In a ten-day period from 17 to 27 November 1883, more than 125 people bought 'medicine' from druggist C.W. Pearce, all of it prescribed by Doctors

Barnet Griggs's Halfway House, 1475 Lakeshore Road East, Oakville

Front door, the Halfway House

Sutherland, Urquhart, or Williams. One customer whose name appeared with regularity was Peter McDougald, a colourful mayor of Oakville whose dependence on 'medicine' resulted in his death only five months later. The unfortunate McDougald died from 'congestion of the liver caused by exposure and whiskey' a few days after searchers found him 'hanging by the feet head down fast and nearly dead.'

Earlier that same year the business district of Oakville had been destroyed in a disastrous fire that originated in Pearce's drugstore. Historian Hazel Mathews in *Oakville and the Sixteen* quotes one newspaper report that read: 'The entire village of Oakville ... was destroyed by fire today ... the village fire department got drunk on two barrels of whiskey rolled out of a drug store in which the fire started.' If this account was, as Mathews claimed, an 'inventive' one, it was probably because Halton, the first county in Ontario to go 'dry,' was an object of derision to those opposed to prohibition. Many were just waiting for the opportunity to ridicule the whole idea. And yet it seems entirely possible (if not probable) that tired, thirsty firefighters might have 'rescued' a quantity of whisky from Pearce's drugstore. Whisky wasn't likely to be found anywhere else in town.

Although a temperance group was functioning in Trafalgar Township as early as 1830, it is unlikely that it interfered with the hospitality offered by Barnet Griggs, a Yankee innkeeper who had for many years been operating the Halfway House just east of Oakville (1475 Lakeshore Road East). Griggs and his wife, Nancy, had left the United States in 1811 bringing with them (according to one enduring legend) a grandfather clock securely strapped to the side of one of their horses.

By word of mouth, travellers learned that Griggs's house was a good place to stay. He was still living in a one-storey frame house in 1828, but increased traffic along the Lakeshore Road suggested to his shrewd Yankee mind that a two-storey establishment was in order. By 1833 stages were changing horses at the Halfway House and continued to do so for many years. Today it is a private home.

Not long after Barnet Griggs enlarged his family home and became an innkeeper, he purchased a house at 29 Navy Street in Oakville from his son-in-law, John Moore. The year was 1840, and Moore, along with his wife, Sally, and infant son, Barnet Griggs Moore, had been living in the house for only a short time. Moore was a loyal supporter of the government and as such was one of the men who patriotically torched Mackenzie's supply ship, the *Caroline*, during 'the troubles' of 1837. Griggs leased the house, then a small two-storey structure, but soon realized that its proximity to the lake meant business in the form of passengers going to and from the steamships that docked at the foot of the street.

Griggs enlarged the house and leased it to Jesse Belyea, who advertised in 1853 that his Frontier House would provide the best accommodation in Oakville. The hostelry soon became known as the Steamboat Hotel, operating under that name until it reverted to a private home in 1860. The new owner, lawyer Robert Appelbe, found the house spacious enough for his family of six children, but by 1916 the need for that space had gone and so, when a neighbour proposed buying part of it, the northerly end of the building was sawn off and moved around the corner to a lot on King Street. The house standing by Navy Street today is what was left, the asymmetrical façade a reminder that the south half was built by John Moore, the north part by Barnet Griggs.

The demise of the Steamboat Hotel may have been hastened by the construction, in 1855, of the Canadian Hotel, a much larger hostelry a few doors to the north. Its arrival on the scene coincided with the arrival of the railroad, and it met with immediate success. Its popularity notwithstanding, the hotel changed hands frequently. In 1881, it was owned by two women. As a neighbour, George Sumner, wrote in his journal at the time, 'The town is pretty quiet were it not for the Canadian Hotel. They keep up a continual noise – most disreputable for those who profess to be ladies.'

George Sumner's father, William Johnson Sumner, was a well-known innkeeper with a flair for promotion – and at least a professed interest in temperance. Son of a Loyalist who had fought with Wolfe at Quebec, he kept tavern on Dundas Street (Governor's Road) in the 1820s. Sumner's ads showed a creative and irrepressible sense of humour. The first issue of the *Gore Gazette*, on 3 March 1827, contained the following announcement: 'The new broom sweeps clean, but the old broom knows the corners best. Grove Inn, 35 Miles from York.' In the *Canadian Freeman* of 9 November 1827, Sumner gleefully announced that he was operating 'that old and well established House,'

> The Grove Inn
>
> for the use of which he pays three hundred and fifty dollars a year! ... no credit will be given on Liquors, and tipplers and drunkards are sincerely requested to shun it, as a genuine Christian would the Devil.

Sumner was still on this tack four years later when, in the same paper, on 30 October 1831, he declared:

> all gamblers, tipplers, grog-bruisers, drunkards, and such-like idle and useless characters, are warned against calling on him, as he does not in the least degree want their custom and will take it as a particular mark of their esteem, if they will always pass his House without noticing it – they are informed there is no room for them
>
> In the Grove Inn

A few years later Sumner bought the Oakville House, which was one of the best-known hostelries in the area. Built in 1827, Oakville House survived for more than 150 years until it was demolished in 1984.

Adam Fergusson, who greeted every new experience with enthusiasm, stopped at Sumner's tavern in 1833. He mentioned that the host 'stood high in favour wth Dr D—— [Dunlop; the Canada Company's William 'Tiger' Dunlop of Goderich], and a few lines from him secured me an extra welcome.' Not surprisingly. Any friend of 'The Tiger's' would likely be greeted with pleasure by the many settlers who so enjoyed Dunlop's irreverent wit and abiding sense of fun. Not much wonder that he and Sumner liked each other. On this trip, Fergusson went on to Guelph, while his fellow passengers proceeded to Hamilton, a journey that would take them all night.

Hamilton was a few miles off the Governor's Road and did not really come into its own until the 1840s, although Fergusson had been there previously in 1831, as had Patrick Shirreff during his tour in 1835. Shirreff had difficulty finding a place to stay. He had almost given up hope of finding anything when the barkeeper at one establishment said he would let Shirreff and his companion sleep on a makeshift bed on the floor: 'Mr C—— and I were soon stretched side by side, and soon afterwards some individuals, similarly situated, were admitted to share our bed. On awakening next morning I missed Mr C—— from my side, who was lying in a distant corner of the room; and he afterwards told me, that disliking the company which joined us, he slipped from bed so soon as he could do so unnoticed.'

Writing under the pseudonym 'Rubio,' one traveller described Hamilton in 1842 as 'a very thriving, well situated but drunken town at the head of Lake Ontario, containing about 12,000 inhabitants. Everything appeared rough, prosperous, cheap and abundant; those who abstained from ardent spirits were good-looking and healthy.' Robert Godley, in 1844, described Hamilton as 'one mass of rubbish and dirt.' There he found an inn and spent the night in 'a dirty bedroom without any window, where I managed to sleep pretty well in spite of the fleas.'

Burlington, on the other hand, came in for praise from inveterate traveller Joseph Pickering who, passing through in 1830, called it 'perhaps as beautiful and romantic a situation as any in the interior of America.' Halstead's Temperance Inn was situated in this romantic spot overlooking Burlington Bay (at 2429 Lakeshore Road). On 24 October 1848, Halstead sent out invitations to a ball.

> Sir:
>
> The Pleasure of your Company and Partner are respectfully requested to attend a Ball and Supper, to be held at E.B. Halstead's Inn, Port Nelson, on Thursday, the 2nd of November next.
>
> Stewards:
>
> Wm Trimble — John Roberts
>
> Joseph McCarty — Robert Miller
>
> Dancing to commence at 7 O'clock, P.M.
>
> Tickets, 7s. 6d.

Halstead's Inn, 2429 Lakeshore Road, Burlington, was welcoming guests in 1848.

Halstead, an American, had run the inn from about 1840 with the help of his wife, Sarah. In 1851 the census listed the Halsteads as being parents of five children and residing in a two-storey frame house designated as a tavern. Also living there was Joseph McCarty, a teamster, obviously the man who had served as a steward at the ball and supper four years earlier. The building stayed in the family until 1879. The Halstead Inn, one of the few remaining inns in the area, has been restored by its present owners.

In the early years of the last century, before Hamilton was founded, the nearby villages of Ancaster and Dundas were important centres. As early as 1797, Jean Baptiste Rousseau built a hotel in Ancaster, about two years after he and his family had arrived in the area. Rousseau, a fifth-generation Canadian, became the driving force in the growth of what soon became a lusty little pioneer settlement. In short order he acquired the local mills, a brewery, a distillery, a blacksmith's shop, and a store. As the local assessor, tax collector, and magistrate, Rousseau was a busy man.

Rousseau's first hotel was a log building that he replaced with a larger frame structure in 1809. He called it the Union Hotel. Within a few years a tragic episode in Canadian history was played out within its walls. Here the Bloody Assizes took place – the trial of a number of turncoat citizens who, because of their actions during the War of 1812, were tried and convicted of treason. Authorities had decided to hold the trial at Ancaster because it was a safe distance from the frontier, and because the Union Hotel was large enough to hold the number of people involved. Among those tried in absentia was Abraham Markle, an American who had kept tavern in Ancaster and who, ironically, owned Ancaster's Union Mills, which he and other investors had recently purchased from Rousseau. Prisoners at the trial were housed at the Union Mills in a temporary jail.

In 1814, on a fine June day, fifteen farmers stood to hear their sentence:

> You are to be hanged by the neck, but not until you are dead, for you must be cut down while alive and your entrails taken out and burned before your faces, your head then to be cut off and your bodies divided into four quarters and your heads and quarters to be at the King's disposal.

Seven of these men received reprieves, but eight of the unfortunate souls were brought by wagon to hastily erected scaffolds. The wagons, each carrying four prisoners, were brought underneath the waiting nooses. The wagons were then driven off, leaving the victims to strangle. Afterwards, their heads were displayed on

ANCASTER HOTEL,
TO RENT.
THE above well known and excellent Hotel will be re-let on the 12th of October next, the lease of the present incumbent (Mr. Burley) expiring on that day. The proprietor thinks it unnecessary to speak of the superior advantages of this property—as it is well known to be one of the best Inns in Upper Canada. For particulars apply to the proprietor at Ancaster.
GEORGE ROUSSEAU.
Ancaster, 14th May, 1828. 12

Gore Gazette, 31 May 1828

pikes so that, in the words of Chief Justice Thomas Scott, the impression of the executions on the public would be both 'striking and lasting.' Abraham Markle was more fortunate. He and twenty others were tried in absentia and convicted. Markle's property was confiscated, and he fled to the United States, leaving his family in Newark. He died in obscurity.

Jean Baptiste Rousseau had died of natural causes during the first year of the war while serving at Niagara as an Indian interpreter for the British army. He was fifty-four years old. For three years after his death Rousseau's widow, Margaret, ran the hotel, and then for several years it was operated by their son, George. In 1827, a new owner took over and politely announced the change on 1 March in the *Gore Gazette*:

> ANCASTER HOTEL. Plumer Burley informs his friends and the public that he has taken the House formerly occupied by Mr George Rousseaux, in the village of Ancaster, which he has fitted up in complete order for the reception of Travellers, and hopes the public will favor him with a share of their patronage.

A year later the ambitious Burley had started running a stage-coach line between Ancaster and York. Leaving Ancaster at 4:00 AM each Monday, Wednesday, and Friday, it arrived at York an exhausting eleven hours later. The return trip was made the following day.

In 1832 George Rousseau, the son of Jean Baptiste and Margaret, built a small stone building at Wilson and Academy streets (380 Wilson), across the street from the site of its predecessors. He called it the Union Hotel. Rousseau leased it for several years to his son-in-law, J.T. Roy. When Roy died his wife, Rousseau's daughter, Margaret, ran the hostelry, of which she became the owner upon her father's death in 1851. Three years later she remarried. The lucky man this time was John Crann, a gentleman who acquired, in short order, a wife, a hotel, and a run of bad luck. Even in an age

John Crann's Union Hotel, Ancaster

when disastrous fires frequently wreaked havoc on the country's main streets, Mr Crann's buildings seemed to fall victim to more than their share of trouble.

In 1865, Crann leased the Union Hotel to a man named Phillipo. The following year, Crann purchased Kemp's Hotel, also in Ancaster. It was destroyed by fire two years later. On 6 January 1878, Margaret Rousseau Crann died, and that same month the stables of the Cranns' Union Hotel were set on fire. On August 1 the stables again caught fire and burned to the ground. Eight days later the hotel itself was also destroyed by fire, leaving only its stone walls standing. Before very long, John Crann rebuilt the hotel, utilizing the original walls and doubling the size of the building. And so, only nine months after the stone building had been all but destroyed by fire, a new Union Hotel arose from the ashes, its façade resplendent with a two-storey verandah and lacy bargeboard on the gable. The new proprietor, Crann's son-in-law, Edward Henderson, proudly celebrated the opening by holding a 'grand banquet and gala ball' on 2 May 1879.

Ancaster was the centre of commerce and industry for the Gore District, until neighbouring Dundas forged ahead after the completion of the Desjardins Canal. From the early 1800s it is evident that Ancaster boasted many taverns in addition to Rousseau's, all of them doing a brisk business. In a speech at the Ancaster Union Chapel on 23 October 1829, John Rolph, an advocate of temperance societies, claimed that eleven of thirteen recent deaths in the

The Elgin House, Dundas

area could be directly or indirectly attributed to alcohol abuse. Although a temperance society was formed in Ancaster that year, the battle was, as always, an uphill one.

Artist Daniel Fowler, who travelled west from Hamilton in 1843, was happy to find a macadamized road and remarked that the district had 'all that the most fastidious need desire in the way of scenery and improvement.' Even so, the trip took time. In Dundas, next door to Ancaster, the main streets were lined with 'drink emporiums and groggeries,' causing travellers to claim that, while the trip from Hamilton to Galt took four days, two of those days were needed to get through Dundas.

In 1837 the Desjardins Canal opened; and in time to share the prosperity that the canal would bring, the Elgin House (96 King Street West) opened as well. Its builder was a hard-working, ambitious man named William McDonnell who started his working life as a peddler, first on foot and then on horseback. For more than ten years, McDonnell plodded along backwoods trails, where he was greeted with pleasure by the settlers in the remote reaches of the township. He carried with him not only an amazing array of goods but an equally welcome fund of news for lonely people starved for information about their neighbours and the outside world.

It was hardly surprising, then, that when he opened his spanking new Elgin House in 1837 it was well patronized, for the farmers around Dundas knew McDonnell well and had undoubtedly heard of his new venture from the three peddlers who were by that time working for him. He had also been leasing the Farmer's Inn since 1831. His wife operated that inn for him.

When the Elgin House opened on St Andrew's Day, 30 November 1837, the guest speaker at the opening banquet was none other than John Rolph, a Dundas doctor and the gentleman who had so eloquently urged the formation of a temperance society in Ancaster in 1829. But by this time Rolph was more concerned with politics. Just one week after his speech at the Elgin House, John Rolph, physician, barrister, and friend of William Lyon Mackenzie, was fleeing for his life in the aftermath of the débâcle at Montgomery's tavern. After a sojourn in the United States, Rolph returned and, in 1843, established a medical school in Toronto. His contributions to medical education in the province were unsurpassed in his time.

From Dundas and Ancaster the Governor's Road headed west through Brantford, Paris, and Woodstock. One popular stopping place was a hostelry at 40 Dundas Street in Paris. The town, founded by Yankee Hiram Capron, was named for the plaster-of-paris deposits located there. Consummate traveller W.H.G. Kingston called Paris 'the prettiest town we have yet seen in Canada.' The inn now operates as a tea room.

The Six Nations Indians, led by Joseph Brant, were granted almost 700,000 acres of land by the Grand River in 1785 as a reward for their service to the British Crown during the American Revolutionary War. The settlement became known as Brant's Ford. An innkeeper named Foster was not far behind Brant and his settlers. Moses Mott, travelling to Poughkeepsie in 1810, stopped at an inn on the banks of the Grand.

> We crossed the Grand River which we had to ford, for there was no ferry boat. A man rode a pony through as a guide and the teams followed, the water coming up to the horses' sides some of the way through. We put up at a tavern just below where we crossed, kept by a man named Foster.

Another log house that served for a time as an inn was built at the same location shortly after Mott's visit. It is believed to have been standing by the Grand River on the road to Burford in 1820. The builder is unknown. The dressed log inn originally had a central chimney, evidence of its early construction date. The building, thirty-six by twenty-seven feet, had a gambrel roof (a curved roof, so named for its resemblance to the shape of a horse's hind leg), six-over-six double sash windows, and the customary two doors that indicated it was a tavern. By 1836 it was being enlarged and 'modernized' by its then owner, William D'Aubigny.

D'Aubigny came to Upper Canada in 1835 to join his friend Major James Winniett, who sent him to Samuel Street near Chippawa with a letter of introduction. D'Aubigny got two hundred acres on the Grand River, which included the log building, and proceeded to clear the land for a farm. He put on a new roof and removed the central chimney, replacing it with a hall and staircase leading to a loft. He was gone by 1843, remembered only for nearby d'Aubigny Creek named after him.

The simple little inn was purchased in 1855 by James and Thomas Robson, who remained there for the next thirty years. In 1974, the building was moved to Wentworth Heritage Village, just north of the village of Rockton, on Highway 52 North. Alterations to the windows and the interior have enhanced the charm of one of the few log inns still extant.

Taverns dotted the roads throughout the area and in the towns were even more in evidence. By 1854, there were fifty-three taverns in Brantford, which had a population of less than four thousand. The revenue inspector for the town had collect-

The road to Goderich

ed £397.10 for tavern and shop licences and issued licences of only £2.10 to temperance establishments. Clearly, the cause had not made much headway in Brantford.

Throughout the province, however, temperance forces continued to fight the good fight. Attempts were made to legislate reforms (in 1860, a law was passed allowing no more than one tavern for every 250 people), and temperance newspapers continued the attempt to instil guilt in their readers with constant reminders of the evils of drink. The *York Herald* of 9 February 1872, for instance, carried an item called 'The Bar and the Road':

A Bar to Respectability
A Bar to Honour
A Bar to Happiness
A Bar to Domestic Felicity
A Bar to Heaven.
and
The Road to Degradation
The Road to Vice
The Road to Gamblers' Hell
The Road to the Brothel
The Road to Poverty
The Road to Wretchedness
The Road to Robbery
The Road to Murder
The Road to Prison
The Road to the Gallows
The Road to Hell

The Governor's Road led on to London. Seemingly built in the middle of nowhere, London had been the capital of its district since 1826. Judicial and administrative offices were located in a fortress-like stone court-house that towered above the few frame buildings that made up the remainder of the village. Lieutenant-Governor Simcoe had chosen this site at the forks of the Thames because he felt its remote location made it safe from possible American invasion.

Taverns were among the first structures to be built in London, of course, and they flourished thanks to the town's growing commercial importance and the arrival in 1838 of three regiments of British soldiers. London had all the aspects of a boom town. By 1844 a new jail was deemed a necessity because the first lock-up, housed in dank, medieval quarters in the court-house basement, was badly overcrowded. That year a grand jury reported on the dreadful conditions in the jail, the result according to an item in the *St Thomas Standard* of 30 May 1844, of overcrowding caused by

> the alarming increase in crime in the town [London] and surrounding neighborhood ... One great cause of which ... may be ... attributed to the number of petty beer shops and houses of ill-fame, in some of which from evidence before them, the most unheard of and brutal scenes of immorality have been practised, the continuance and spread of which must very shortly place the morals of the whole community in the greatest danger.

Most of London's early frame buildings were destroyed the following year when the 'Great Fire' of 1845 wiped out three-quarters of the village. Their replacements, wisely built of brick or stone, changed the appearance of London, as did the arrival of the Great Western Railway in 1853. With the railway came prosperity and more hotels and taverns to meet the needs of a population that by then was near the ten thousand mark. The Western Hotel, still standing at the south-west corner of Richmond and Fullarton streets, was among the first of these hostelries to capitalize on London's booming economy. In the ensuing years that hotel became part of the background for the Donnelly massacre, a horrifying event that has been called 'Canada's own Greek Tragedy.' The brutal murder of five members of the Donnelly family became the most infamous unsolved murder in Canadian history.

The Western Hotel was built in 1853, the same year the railway arrived. Although the hotel accommodated passengers from the train, it also served as the terminus of a stage line that ran from London through the town of Lucan to Goderich, sixty miles away. (The Goderich trip could be a slow one if the whim of the driver led to stops at the local inns, for there were thirteen of them on the first twelve miles of the road.) It would be many years before rail service was extensive enough to make the stage lines unprofitable. In fact, by 1869, such was the demand for their services that there were two rival lines operating on the road to Goderich.

One of these lines was run from 1873 to 1878 by the energetic, rowdy, tough, and touchy Donnelly family. They were known and feared throughout Biddulph Township and beyond. At one time or other most of the boys in the family had worked as drivers for other stage lines, and once they started in business for themselves they achieved considerable success, offering dependable and prompt service. The exuberant Donnelly brothers were affable, courteous, and hard-working. 'A more obliging people never lived,' remarked one customer. And if the opposing coach line suffered a surprising number of accidents when the competition got tough, the customers didn't worry – they benefited from the resulting lower fares.

Lucan, located on Highway 4 north of London, was a tough little frontier town with two sizeable hotels, the Queen's and the Central, to handle the many passengers who clambered down from the crowded coaches. The Central Hotel is still in business today.

Most of the people who lived in Lucan and in the surrounding countryside had come from Ireland, and it was a factional feud begun years before in Tipperary that culminated, on 4 February 1880, in the death of James Donnelly, his wife, their son Tom, and a young niece, Bridget Donnelly. They were clubbed and hacked to death and their small farmhouse set afire. Their

A Lucan tavern, where the Peace Society imbibed before bringing death to the Donnellys

charred remains were found in the smoking ruins. Another son, John, died two hours later in nearby Whalen's Corners when the same vigilantes (they called themselves the Biddulph Peace Society) gunned him down at the door of his brother's home.

Once more the London jail was filled to capacity as thirteen accused men awaited a preliminary examination. Of these, only eight were committed for trial and, in spite of two eyewitnesses to the murders, the defendants were eventually acquitted. At their first trial in September 1880, the jury disagreed, but a second trial held the following January returned a directed verdict of 'not guilty' – this in spite of seemingly overwhelming evidence against the accused. The jury, however, was reflecting the public sentiment about the affair, at least in that part of the country. The jubilant men were carried from the London court-house on the shoulders of their supporters and welcomed back to Lucan (which was still caught up in internecine rivalry) as conquering heroes.

Of James and Johannah Donnelly's seven sons, two had died violently before the massacre, so by the 1880s only three of their sons were left. A married sister, Jennie, lived in St Thomas. Gradually the surviving sons left the district, and in time all entered the hotel business: Patrick first in Thorold, where he acquired the Mansion House Hotel, and later in St Catharines, where he ran a tavern; Will in Bothwell and then in Appin, where he purchased the St Nicholas Hotel. Bob, after a few years away, eventually returned to Lucan and, in 1901, purchased the Western Hotel there. He died in Lucan ten years later.

The Donnelly massacre was indeed a tragedy. And while no one in the family could qualify for sainthood, there were few

The Western Hotel (far right), London

in that warring township who would have. On the day the final verdict of acquittal was given, a bitter Bob Donnelly strode into the barroom of London's Western Hotel, in happier days the terminal of his family's coach line. To the patrons discussing the case there he cried, 'I want all of you murderers to come and have something.' No one accepted his offer.

According to an old Irish saying, 'God invented whisky to keep the Irish from ruling the world.' Unquestionably whisky played a part in the Donnelly tragedy. The members of the 'Peace Society' had quaffed copious amounts of usquebaugh, 'the water of life,' before embarking on their mission of death. It was one of the worst massacres in the country's history, and it provided additional fuel to the temperance fire.

Long before the tragic events in Lucan, however, it was evident that a significant portion of the public favoured some form of temperance reform. Even John A. Macdonald, whose fondness for a drink was legendary, had actually been moved to sign the pledge. On 23 July 1862, the *Montreal Star* reported that at a meeting of the temperance society in Kingston, Macdonald, then joint premier (with Etienne-Paschal Taché) of the Province of Canada, had been initiated into the order. In a brief address to the crowd he explained his reasons for becoming a Son of Temperance. He had for some time been 'fully convinced of the evils of the drinking customs of society, and had come to a determination to renounce them ... ' The paper went on to quote Macdonald as saying that 'he had no political object in view by taking the present course.' Perhaps not. But as he remarked on another occasion: 'I do know a thing or two about politics.'

The Roads to the Bay

CHAPTER EIGHT

The Roads to the Bay

TAVERN FOOD

'... the proverb of "God sending meat and the devil cooks" never was so fully illustrated as in this country; for, with a superabundance of the raw material, the manufactured article of a good dinner is hardly to be found in a public-house in the province.'

William 'Tiger' Dunlop, *Statistical Sketches of Upper Canada*, 1832

PIONEER A.M. Stephens was one of a party of men cutting a trail through dense bush from Mount Forest to Owen Sound in the winter of 1842. Their meals, prepared by the camp cook, consisted of bread and salt pork – and usually all of it was frozen before it reached them. Ten days and forty miles after they began, they found themselves lost – in the middle of nowhere, knee-deep in snow, and nearly out of food. After a cold and hungry night they sent their foreman to try for a sighting of Georgian Bay. A welcome gunshot soon announced that they had reached the bay and civilization in the form of three log buildings. Closer scrutiny revealed that they had found the rainbow's end – and a pot of gold – for one of the three log buildings was an inn.

Stephens and his men undoubtedly found whisky to warm them when they reached that welcome inn, but finding a good meal may well have been a different matter. Meals in those early backwoods hostelries ranged from adequate to abysmal. Travellers suggested that it was necessary to be ravenous in order to appreciate the food placed in front of them. Such was the case at Hall's Tavern, between Horning Mills and Mono Mills, an establishment known as 'Starvation Hall' to at least one disgusted patron, George Snider. An agent for the Toronto–Sydenham Road, Snider wrote that he preferred living alone in the bush to enduring the vermin at Hall's and the scanty food served there.

Country inns such as Hall's were typical of many throughout the province and often induced culture shock in travellers accustomed to a refined table. Thomas Need, travelling in the Cobourg area in 1838, described in *Six Years in the Bush* a scene faced by many an unwary visitor when a meal was announced. After a general rush to the table,

> the work of destruction commenced – plates rattled, cups and saucers flew about, and knives and forks found their way indifferently into their owners' mouths or the various dishes on the table ... The company was of a motley description, Yankees and emigrants, washed and unwashed ... At the top of the table, enveloped in sundry great coats, sat a large unshaved backwoods settler, just dismounted from his waggon: – opposite to him, with his hat on, an amusing contrast – a little, prim, puritanical store-keeper, with well-brushed clothes, sleek countenance, and

straight greasy hair ... The post of honour at this meal was occupied by our despotic host in person, who dealt out a 'Benjamin's mess' to each hungry expectant: – puddings and creams succeeded the substantials, which were conveyed to the mouths of the different guests with frightful rapidity, on the blades of sharp dirty knives. I ventured to ask for a spoon, a request which only drew from 'Miss' a disdainful toss of the head, accompanied by the exclamation of 'my! if the man be'ent wanting a spoon now!'

Yet the difficulties faced by innkeepers were many. The arrival of the stage-coach often brought surprises, not all of them pleasant. Seldom did the woman of the house know how many people she would have to feed and at what meal. Edward Talbot, travelling in the London District in 1824, recalled with wry humour that, after obtaining lodging and requesting a meal, the ingredients of that meal were

still in a very awkward state for mastication. The bread, for instance, was yet in the flour bag, the chickens were feeding at the barn door; the tea was in the grocer's canister, and the cream in the cow's udder ... but ... before the lapse of an hour all were smoking on the table in prime condition.

Improvisation was the order of the day. One traveller overheard an exasperated wife demanding of her husband just what he expected her to feed their nine unexpected breakfast guests. 'Eggs and ham, summat of that dried venison and pumpkin pie,' he suggested. And there was always the staple 'salt pork fried, hot potatoes, doughnuts made of strips of dough twisted into corkscrew forms and fried in fat ... ' Whatever was served, there was a strong possibility that it would emerge swimming in a pool of grease.

At Fergus, where the Garafraxa Road began, Hugh Black's tavern offered food for both soul and body. Church services were held there on occasion, with worshippers and patrons seated uncomfortably on the floor, since innkeeper Black had little in the way of furniture. But because a few of the floor boards were missing, diners could sit with their legs dangling through the holes. The floor in front of them served as a table.

From Fergus, the Garafraxa Road (now Highway 6) led north to Georgian Bay, and before long the communities of Arthur, Mount Forest, and Durham, grew up along its length, with numerous taverns interspersed between them. At the village of Chatsworth, the Garafraxa Road joined the Toronto–Sydenham Road, the terminus for both roads being the burgeoning community of Sydenham, a few miles to the north. (Later Sydenham was renamed Owen Sound after Sir Edward Campbell Rich Owen, who had charted Georgian Bay in 1815.)

Built in fits and starts during the early 1840s as an inducement to settlement, the Garafraxa Road was soon handling an ever-increasing influx of optimistic pioneers taking advantage of free fifty-acre land grants in the Queen's Bush. By mid-century the wife of an innkeeper on the Garafraxa claimed that within one week she had served meals to two thousand of these hardy souls. A missionary travelling the road at the time mentioned that he had passed eighteen or twenty log taverns, one every two or three miles. Certainly pioneer James Cochrane of Derby Township had no complaints on that score. He fondly recalled that the proprietors were, as a rule,

the most generous and good-hearted men that I have ever met. As to numbers, after one hour's drive, on a cold winter's day, you did not think that one [tavern] every 3 or 4 miles was too many.

By 1853 all the lots in the remote village of Sydenham had been sold, and its future looked promising. Even Toronto's *Daily Leader* grudgingly allowed on 14 September 1853 that although there were twenty-five acres of marsh on the south of the bay, Sydenham boasted 'one of the best harbours in America. In point of capacity, it

West of Owen Sound, in Springmount, the spartan Jones Falls Tavern

Door, Jones Falls Tavern

might contain the fleets of the world.'

A scant ten years passed between the welcome discovery of the lone log tavern at Sydenham and the construction nearby of the Jones Falls Tavern. Samuel Ayres Jones bought his land and considerable adjacent acreage near the falls of the Pottawahamie from surveyor Charles Rankin in 1849. Jones built a mill and, when it was working to capacity, looked to the next order of business: he built a tavern. The two-storey frame inn, which was completed in the mid-1850s, is located west of Owen Sound on the road that runs west from Meaford on Georgian Bay across the base of the Bruce Peninsula to Southampton on Lake Huron. Then known as the Southampton Road, it is now Highway 21. The community too changed its name, from Jones Falls to Springmount, and so the inn followed

The addition to William Spencer's first inn, Hepworth

suit and became the Springmount Inn.

For many years the Springmount Inn was popular with people from Owen Sound, for it was an easy drive from town, and William Brown, for many years the proprietor, kept a good house. The old inn made headlines in the Owen Sound *Advertiser* of 26 March 1917 when the widow of innkeeper Brown was found

> dead in her room in the old Springmount Inn under circumstances that would seem to point to foul play ... When found Mrs Brown was half kneeling against the bed in her room with her face upon the edge of the mattress ... Blood was sprinkled over the bed clothing and the furniture was upset and the general appearance of the room would indicate that there had been a scuffle ... The widow had lived alone for many years in one end of the old inn, the other end being occupied until re-

Window detail, Spencer House, Hepworth

cently by a horse trader who has moved to town ... Mrs Brown was known in the neighbourhood as 'Beauty Brown' ... At one time she was proprietor of the old Springmount Inn.

A coroner's jury determined that Mrs Brown (who had outlived her husband by thirty-eight years) had not been the victim of foul play but had died of a stroke. The following year a local farmer purchased the inn and moved it across the road to use as a barn. It stands there today perched on a high stone foundation.

An eccentric Yankee named Nathaniel Harriman was one of the first innkeepers on the Garafraxa Road. He settled in the area in 1839. After living for sixteen years in a small log house, he built a splendid stone building, which he operated as an inn, calling it Rockford Castle. A night's lodging cost twenty-five cents, and breakfast, typical of that served in most good inns, consisted of beef steaks, cold meats, potatoes, bread, eggs, tea, and coffee. Harriman reputedly built himself a coffin, which he kept on the premises and used for his afternoon nap. Eccentricity, of course, was often good for business.

The village of Hepworth owes its existence to an innkeeper. Located south of Wiarton on the Bruce Peninsula, this remote community developed on land ceded to the government by the Saugeen Indian Council of 1854. Two years later lots were put up for sale but, as most were sold to speculators, development was slow. In 1862, William Spencer, a young Englishman living in Oshawa, saw an ad for bush land near Owen Sound, purchased two hundred acres in Amabel Township, Grey County, and set off with his wife, his two children, and his brother-in-law on a journey of more than two hundred miles. Three years later, having established a successful farm, Spencer was elected as a councillor from his municipality. Walking the twelve miles home from a meeting in Wiarton, he passed the present site of Hepworth, decided that the dearth of inns was insupportable and, since the spot on which he stood seemed as good a place as any for a halfway house, he built one. The community grew up around it.

As William Spencer prospered, he was able to build and move into a bigger inn nearby. By 1889 the population of Hepworth had soared to 310, at which time, not surprisingly, the only hotel was Spencer's. Five years later business warranted another addition; the present Victorian building at 513 Spencer Street is that expanded hostelry. It is now used as a store.

Of Spencer House and its proprietor a publication of the day boasted that:

The dining room is always supplied with the best that can be procured, the bed rooms are large, airy and well furnished, and commodious sample rooms are at the disposal of commercial men. First-class stable accommodation is available for horses, and nothing is omitted that is necessary to give the best of accommodation to the travelling public. As a citizen Mr Spencer is one of the most enterprising, ever in the front rank with those who assist any legitimate business enterprise that is likely to result in benefit to the community, and never behind in the cause of charity.

William Spencer, it seems certain, was a paid-up subscriber to the publication.

Spencer House may indeed have provided 'the best that can be procured' in its dining-room, but such was not the case in all such establishments; certainly not half a century earlier when the irrepressible William 'Tiger' Dunlop felt compelled to warn those who would venture on a tour of the colonies just what they might encounter in the way of food. In *Statistical Sketches of Upper Canada: by a Backwoodsman,* Dunlop obligingly provided 'recipes':

To Dress a Beef Steak

Cut the steak about a quarter of an inch thick, wash it well in a tub of water, wringing it from time to time after the manner of a dish-clout; put a pound of fresh butter in a frying-pan (hog's-lard will do, but butter is more esteemed) and when it boils, put in the steak, turning and peppering it for about a quarter of an hour; then put it in a deep dish, and pour the oil over it; till it floats, and so serve it.

To Boil Green Peas
Put them in a large pot full of water, boil them till they burst. Pour off one half of the water, leaving about as much as will cover them; then add about the size of your two fists of butter, and stir the whole round with a handful of black pepper. Serve in a wash-hand basin.

To Pickle Cucumbers
Select, for this purpose, cucumbers the size of a man's foot, – if beginning to grow yellow, so much the better; split them in four, and put them into an earthen vessel – then cover them with whiskey. The juices of the cucumber, mixing with the alcohol, will run into the acetous fermentation, so you make vinegar and pickles both at once; and the pickles will have that bilious, Calcutta-looking complexion, and slobbery, slimy consistence, so much admired ...

To Make Butter Toast
Soak the toasted bread in warm milk and water; get ready a quantity of melted butter and dip the bread in it; then place the slices stratum super stratum in a deep dish, and pour the remainder of the melted butter over them.

How poultry is dressed, so as to deprive it of all taste and flavour, and give it much the appearance of an Egyptian mummy, I am not sufficiently skilled in Transatlantic cookery to determine; unless it be, by first boiling it to rags and then baking it to a chip in the oven.

Anna Jameson was inclined to agree with Dunlop's assessment of the food: 'Pork – morning, noon and night, – swimming in its own grease,' she wailed. 'No wonder I am thin; I have been starved – starved upon pritters [potatoes] and pork, and that disgusting specimen of unleavened bread ... cakes in the pan.'

The ever-present salt pork was a staple in virtually every tavern in the province. As for the rest of the meal, clearly the offerings of the landlord's table varied between succulent and inedible with a leaning in the latter direction. A low point was reached for William Lewis Baby and a friend named Felin, travellers on the road near Chatham in the 1830s, when they stopped for a meal that became an unforgettable experience. The fare was pancakes, and

the fragrant odor arising from the hot iron, as it permeated the surrounding atmosphere of this rural retreat, acted like a charm, for in an instant a bevy of young urchins, followed by a half-starved cat and cur, came rushing in seeking what they could devour. The youngest, a yearling I should judge, was clad in nature's garb (with the exception that a cloth was substituted in place of a fig leaf) and clung tightly to its mother's skirts ... I expected that some mishap would befall the little scamp and my expectations were shortly afterwards fully realized. Felin's sudden appearance at the door caused the good lady to quickly turn around, in doing which she switched the little brat plump into the batter. You are mistaken if you think this untoward event disconcerted her in the least. She simply seized the imp by the nape of the neck and swashed the batter from its naked limbs into the trough whence it came, and proceeded with her culinary art as if nothing had happened. There was a grave consultation held outside of the hut immediately after that between Felin and myself. He was for total abstinence, and so was I if I could, but couldn't. It proved that hunger was an uncompromising foe, and proved the victor. (*Sic semper Tyrannus.*)

But John Howison of Edinburgh, in *Sketches of Upper Canada*, took a less jaundiced view of the fare when he wrote in 1821 of a visit to a log tavern:

This tavern ... had a sign swinging before the door, so covered with gilt and emblematic paintings, that it probably cost more than the house itself ... there we found a table amply furnished with tea, beef-steaks, cucumbers, potatoes, honey, onions, eggs etc. During this

Early days at Lawrence Hartleib's hotel, Chepstow

delectable repast, we were attended by the hostess, who poured out the tea as often as we required it, and having done so, seated herself in the door-way, and read a book (which I afterwards found to be *Miss Edgeworth's Tales of Fashionable Life*).

That same year, John Duncan was writing *Travels through Parts of the United States and Canada*, in which he related surprisingly pleasant memories of Canadian food and

a crackling fire of pine logs ... festoons of sliced apples for winter pies, hung round it to dry ... hot steaks, fried bacon and potatoes ... tea and toast.

Tavern food, in spite of the fact that it was most often served floating in grease, could look particularly appealing after a hard night in a coach. A glass of gin and bitters helped to whet the appetite. Thomas Fowler, a Britisher writing in 1832, described a journey by stage in which the stop for breakfast was the only good thing to be said for the trip:

the gentlemen went to the bar and had a glass of bitters to cheer their drooping spirits after the fatigue of so unpleasant a night. In the course of an hour we were shown into a large room where the breakfast was set ... tea and coffee, cold beef, pork ham and potatoes, with plenty of bread, butter, crackers and eggs.

Even Anna Jameson, who was revolted by the grease, on another occasion and in a better frame of mind identified the 'travellers' fare in Canada – venison steaks and fried fish, coffee, hot cakes, cheese and whiskey punch.'

In spite of the sometimes indifferent quality of the food served, early inns and taverns continued to be well patronized. Some patrons, of course, were singularly uninterested in the food. The *Huron Signal* of 11 February 1848 cautioned that

numbers of persons instead of meeting to discuss the business of the township came there apparently with no other aim than that of getting drunk ...

One tavern frequently used for such township meetings was in Chepstow, a quiet village north of the Durham Road – an

Hartleib's Hotel, now the King Edward, Chepstow

east-west artery that bisected both the Garafraxa and Sydenham roads. Chepstow was first called Phelan's Dam after Irish immigrants John and Bridget Phelan, but the loyal Phelan, his heart still in Ireland, wanted the village called Emmett, to honour an Irish patriot. He petitioned the government requesting a change of name, but before the application could be approved bureaucracy intervened in the form of an English clerk who chose the name Chepstow, after the home of Earl Strongbow, an Englishman who had invaded Ireland.

Irish quarrels, however, would have held little interest for Chepstow innkeeper Lawrence Hartleib, owner of Hartleib's Hotel, a thriving establishment and the location for many years of various community meetings. Hartleib purchased the property in 1871, and by 1885 the tavern was regularly being used for Court of Revision meetings. County council meetings also took place there, and in 1890 the hotel served as a polling place during elections.

Minutes of the Court of Revision held at Hartleib's indicate that social assistance was an interest of the county councillors. On 28 May 1899 they granted $5 to James McNeil for keeping an indigent girl for a month. Later that same court granted 'That Mary Taylor who had lost her husband by death should be granted a rebate of $13.10 as she was in straightened circumstances.'

Beer cooled in the cellar beneath Henry Heuther's Crystal Springs Brewery, Neustadt.

Today Hartleib's, now called the King Edward Hotel, is still drawing appreciative customers from miles around. Its exterior appearance has changed little since Lawrence Hartleib's day, but the brew dispensed inside is no longer a local product, as it once was. The *Bruce Herald* of 8 January 1891 raised this sensitive topic in its Chepstow news with a searching question: 'our genial hotel keeper has been requested by his numerous customers to secure the celebrated Formosa beer. What's the matter with Chepstow beer?'

The people responsible for Formosa's competing brew were virtually all German or Alsatian immigrants. Naturally, they knew about beer and breweries for, as historian Norman Robertson remarked in his *History of the County of Bruce*:

> A German settlement without a brewery would be incomplete. This need was supplied to Formosa in 1869 ... In a purely German settlement lager beer is partaken of as one of the ordinary and necessary things of life ... every Sunday morning after hearing mass the hotels were filled by the churchgoers having a quiet mug before starting the drive back to the farm; and, strange as it may seem, the license operators did not think it advisable to enforce the law there in regard to prohibited hours.

Formosa's beer did not have a monopoly in the neighbourhood. Chepstow obviously

Travellers on the Durham Road welcomed a stop at Priceville's Commercial Hotel.

made its own and, at nearby Neustadt, an industrious Henry Heuther was busily brewing beer and hauling it by wagon to appreciative customers throughout the district.

Neustadt ('new town' in German) was an exclusively German settlement. Immigration from Germany to this area of Grey County began in the mid-1850s, and soon these settlers had chosen the rich lands in the south-western part of Normandy Township. An 1865 directory described Neustadt as having 'a Flouring Mill, Sawmill, Flax-Mill, Brewery, Tannery, Post Office, 3 stores, 3 Hotels, 2 blacksmith shops ... ' The population was three hundred and growing. The brewery 'was built in 1859, a stone building – Heuther, Henry, Proprietor; who reports his operations extending every year.'

Heuther's Crystal Spring Brewery was housed in a long, low stone structure with, at one end of the building, a sizeable inn, the Royal Hotel, run independently from the brewery. Damaged by fire in 1869, the brewery was rebuilt with stone brought to the site by local farmers. It was built on a natural rock foundation, its vaults, hewn out of rock, serving as cooling rooms for the beer. Underground pipes brought spring water from across the road. Horses, stabled in Heuther's barns behind the brewery, were used to haul the beer to local inns.

Henry Heuther died at age sixty-seven,

Satisfied patrons at ease in front of the Commercial Hotel, Priceville

his passing noted by the *Bruce Herald* on 30 January 1896: 'Though lacking the ruggedness of the typical German he considered the Fatherland set the model for everything.' Heuther left an estate of $15,800, a healthy amount for the day. His brewery and hotel were valued at $10,000.

Irish innkeeper Hugh Bell was only thirty-eight years old when he died, yet he was able to leave his second wife, Catherine, a comfortable seven thousand dollars. Included in the estate was the fine two-storey stone structure he had built in the village of Dunkeld in 1868. It served as an inn, post office, and store. It still stands at the north-west corner of concession 4 and Bruce County road 3.

On 19 February 1874, the Orangeville *Sun* announced Bell's untimely death:

> Mr Hugh Bell, a prominent citizen of Dunkeld, County Bruce, and well known in Brampton and Orangeville died on the 2nd inst. By his enterprise and energy he had accumulated considerable property, and was yet in the prime of his life when his sudden death occurred.

Bell was survived by his widow, aged twenty-seven, and two children, Jane and James, products of his first marriage. Several children born to Catherine had all died young.

From the brewing communities of Formosa, Chepstow, and Neustadt near Walkerton, the Durham Road led west to Lake Huron and east to Barrie on Lake Simcoe. It was one of a network of secondary roads crossing the Garafraxa Road at Durham and the Sydenham Road at Flesherton. Between these communities was the quiet village of Priceville, in Artemesia Township, Grey County, a convenient halfway

The Cataract Inn, where John Hawkins served the town's seventy-five thirsty residents

stop for the stage-coaches travelling between these two points.

Though quiet, the village supported six inns with no difficulty. One of these hostelries was built by Alexander Brown, a man who had a curious set of standards. He disapproved of the serving of spiritous liquors so he rented the inn to a proprietor who had no such qualms, thereby pacifying his conscience and deriving some income at the same time.

Across the road from the site of Brown's inn stands the Commercial, a building constructed of local white brick with red-brick trim, an attractive combination of materials seen in most of the other buildings on the old main street (which curves off from and runs parallel to the present Highway 4). The property was part of a block of one

The Horseshoe Inn, once the Cataract

thousand acres held by the government and gradually put on the market when the Durham Road was built. The patent for the site of the Commercial was granted to Archibald McArthur in 1862. McArthur is listed as proprietor of the Wellington Hotel in 1865. That same year McArthur sold the land for $299. Three years later the same plot sold for $1,300. This sizeable jump in purchase price would indicate that the inn was probably built during those three years. In 1879 Thomas Atkinson became the owner, paying $2,300.

Atkinson ran the inn with his wife, Sarah. He died intestate in 1888, and the letters of administration contained the following statement by his widow, Sarah Ruth Atkinson:

> All the household furniture and effects in the Hotel of which the said Thomas Atkinson was proprietor at the time of his death, were and are my own property and did not belong in any way to the deceased.

Sarah later married Archie Butter. The hotel remained in her name until 1910.

The Sydenham Road led north-west from Toronto (following the present Highway 10) through Caledon, Orangeville, Jelly's Corners (Shelburne), Flesherton, and on to where it joined the Garafraxa Road at Chatsworth. In the Caledon Hills, scene of a brief and disappointing gold rush in 1818, Richard Church, a hotel-keeper from Cooksville, discovered a ghost town called Gleniffer where, thirty years earlier, eager fortune hunters had flocked in search of gold near the Credit River. A new village grew up there called Church's Falls and, later, Cataract.

By 1866, Cataract was home to a grand total of seventy-five people, thirty-seven of whom petitioned that year 'Praying for a licence to be granted to John Hawkins to keep a hotel in the township, known as the Cataract House.' Hawkins was granted his licence and opened his doors to a thirsty public. He wouldn't have wanted it any other way – penalties in Peel County for selling without a licence ranged from, for the first offence, '$20–$50 plus costs. Second offence hard labour in the county jail for three months. Third offence hard labour in the county jail for six months.' The county councillors meant business.

In 1871 Joseph Silk followed Hawkins as proprietor of Cataract House. He was succeeded in the 1880s by a Mrs Glen, who renamed it, unfortunately, the Dewdrop Inn. Today it is proudly called the Horseshoe Inn, and is still popular and well known for the hospitality to be found there.

From Caledon, the Syndenham Road led through Mono Mills, where innkeeper John Kidd's bid for immortality was carried out after his death in 1892. His teenage wife (she was about eighty years younger than he) followed his instructions to the letter and had his body placed in a glass-topped coffin, which was then interred in a tomb near the old road into the village.

After Mono Mills the Sydenham Road continued to Orangeville, a town laid out in 1843 by Orange Lawrence. What Lawrence didn't own in Orangeville, Jesse Ketchum did. A son of the Toronto educator and philanthropist of the same name, Jesse had inherited a great deal of Orangeville property from his uncle, the bristly, devout, and eccentric Seneca Ketchum, who died in 1850. Orange Lawrence owned most of the land south of Broadway, while the land to the north was owned and laid out by Jesse Ketchum. The fine stone inn at the corner of East Broadway and Second Street, now a restaurant called Greystones, was owned by Ketchum and run for many years by an Irishman, James Graham. On 10 December 1874, the Orangeville *Sun* reported that Graham, although he had been an innkeeper there for many years, was fined twenty dollars and costs for operating without a licence, the rules in Dufferin County being similar to those in neighbouring Peel.

Jesse Ketchum never ran the inn himself. No doubt he was fully occupied administering his holdings and managing a family that consisted of fifteen children – five by his

In Orangeville, on the Sydenham Road, the Greystones stood on Jesse Ketchum's land.

first wife, Elizabeth Wilson, and ten by his second wife, Mary Colvin. He died at the age of fifty-four in Michigan, where, according to the *Elora Observer* of 16 October 1874, 'he was taking mineral waters for his health.'

From Orangeville the Sydenham Road, important both to the military and to the settlers, led through Shelburne and Dundalk to Flesherton. The road had just been surveyed when, in 1849, Aaron Munshaw decided to move from Thornhill to Flesherton, where fifty-acre lots were available for the taking, just as long as settlement duties were met. Munshaw was then in his early fifties. His wife, Mary, was not much younger, and the youngest of their six children was only five, so their journey up the newly opened Sydenham Road was a difficult one. It was little more than a trail then; but, fifteen years later, the Sydenham had been gravelled, and thus in 1865 Smith's *Gazeteer and Directory of the County of Grey* could extol its virtues: the road was 'cleared out to a great breadth, and as straight as an arrow; a splendid drive in sleighing, or in good weather anytime.'

The Munshaws settled at Artemesia Corners (later named Flesherton after W.K. Flesher, a county warden). It was an inspired choice. Not only could they cater to travellers along the Sydenham Road but, in due course, the Durham Road also went by their door, and so the Munshaws, happily situated at the crossroads, drew customers from all directions.

For a few years the Munshaws lived in a one-storey log house, but by 1864 they were able to build a larger building. The substantial two-storey brick structure was called Flesherton House or Munshaw House. It had two large dormitory-style rooms for sleeping and, at the north end of the building, two rooms for use as sample rooms by travelling salesmen. Here the salesmen could display their goods to the residents of Flesherton while at the same time providing the local citizens with a welcome diversion. Innkeepers willingly offered space to salesmen, who in the course of selling their wares also attracted customers to the bar.

These itinerant vendors of everything from shoes to fancy goods travelled many roads and paddled many streams in search of customers. Their place of work and their home were the same – one of the province's welcoming hostelries. One mobile merchant, calling himself 'a guerilla,' wrote of his life as a travelling salesman, calling his treatise *Notes on the Road.* This work was an attempt, he said, to 'record the sober realities of a commercial traveller's every day life.' To anyone contemplating this line of work he offered, in a 'sadder but wiser' vein, a few words of advice:

How many scores of times I have heard a novice express his admiration of a guerilla's life, and paint with his own imaginative fancy the jolly times he would have, the sights he would see and the tales he would hear. Verily, young man, thy dreams of the same are pleasant. Continue to indulge in the soothing delusion; but for the sake of romance, never undertake the sober reality.

He then obligingly proceeded to paint the reality as he saw it:

– Tough customers and still tougher grub.
– Fried pork for breakfast, boiled pork to dinner, and pork cold for supper ... Pork! pork! universal pork! thy fragrance seems to linger around the dining-room of every country tavern.
– Feather beds made of straw, crowned with an almost invisible pillow (called such by courtesy) and lined with two sheets; the dampness of which gave me a nightly attack of ague.

Even worse was a mattress stuffed with corn-leaves:

... if one's body was moved ever so fractional a part of an inch, the rustling sound that proceeded from this novel stuffing would have awoke the Seven Sleepers.

And, of course, there was the ever-present insect population:

... there was ... before morning a bug stained floor and a blood marked wall. The sacrifice of insect life was immense. The piled up carcasses of the slain attested the vigilant night watch of the unfortunate.

Finally, for washing, 'a lump of that useful compound called yellow soap,' was accompanied by 'a towel ... this eight by six inch rag ... and that unique object tacked to the wall which does service for a looking-glass.'

But the life of a commercial traveller was not all fleas and pork. There were adventures for the taking. On one occasion, a number of salesmen were

splashing through the mud and mire on the road between Arthur and Mount Forest. The inclemency of the weather was a sufficient excuse for the speed with which the party were hurring onward independent of visions of a good hot supper and cosy rooms at friend Wilson's. Nothing unusual occurred till they arrived at the toll-gate near their destination, and through which the first team dashed at full speed, the other three following suit.

The toll-gate keeper, deprived of his fare, followed the guerillas to their inn. They managed to induce him to partake of the wares of the host until he fell to the floor. They said he 'took his tippling well.'

In spite of his denials, the 'guerilla's' memoirs showed that he had, for the most part, enjoyed his travels through the bush.

The Sing brothers' hotel on the stage run between Singhampton and Jelly's Corners.

It was a way of life chosen, he admitted, because, 'I like elbow room.'

The host behind the bar of a nineteenth-century inn was, with few exceptions, an Irishman or a Yankee. In each case the atmosphere was the same – democratic. Such must have been the situation at the Exchange Hotel in the village of Singhampton. It had been built by a man named Josiah Sing, the son of an Irish father and an American mother, so it seems likely that the establishment would be operated along egalitarian lines.

In Ireland, Cyrus Richmond Sing's ancestors spelled their name Synge, as did Irish playwright J.M. Synge, but in Upper Canada the spelling became Sing, probably because so much Canadian spelling was phonetic. Edward and Elizabeth Synge, grandparents of Cyrus, were linen weavers, a family tradition that their descendants continued in Upper Canada. Edward and Elizabeth eventually came to Ontario, but they were preceded by their eldest son, Joseph, who made the crossing in 1816. He settled in Bloomfield, Prince Edward County, and combined teaching with preaching and travelling the saddle-bag circuit. Joseph married Sarah, daughter of Cyrus Richmond, a United Empire Loyalist from New York State. According to her descendants, Sarah was 'fair and good to look upon,' and her friends persuaded her that the young, serious Quaker with a gift for oratory 'was a fine young man with no bad habits and she would have a home of her own.' After their marriage the couple moved to Pickering Township just east of York, where Joseph took up his two-hundred-acre farm.

Sarah Sing produced children, while Joseph produced debts. According to family tradition, 'he traded 100 of his 200 acres

... When Joseph sold the remaining acres she refused to sign away her dowerage.' By this time, Sarah had lost twin daughters, another daughter, and Gersham, one of twin sons. She took her remaining children – son Cyrus and two daughters – and moved to the village of Duffin's Creek (now Pickering), where she supported them all by her weaving. Another son, seven-year-old Joseph, went with his father to live on fifty acres of bush land in Brock Township, where Joseph, Senior, intended to teach and preach. Later, undernourished from a diet of salt pork and potatoes, young Joseph was taken in by relatives, who raised him and called him Josiah.

In 1848 Cyrus Sing, then in his mid-twenties, settled in Osprey Township at a point between the Saugeen, Beaver, and Nottawasaga rivers where the potential for mills was excellent. He wrote to his brother, Josiah, urging him to come, and so Josiah, by then seventeen, trekked up Yonge Street from Newmarket, with his small white dog for company. Within a year or two the two young men were able to send for their mother and sisters, who joined them at the site of Meaford. The brothers bought a carding machine and moved it overland in winter to the Nottawasaga River and then by schooner to Meaford. Later, as business expanded, the Sings added a fulling mill and a sawmill.

In 1852 the Sings moved to Mad River Mills, where they ran mills, a store, and the post office. The postal station took their name – Singhampton. They laid out the townsite and, in the mid-1860s, built the spacious Exchange House to serve passengers and merchants on the Collingwood run.

Cyrus returned to Meaford in 1857 and became the town's first mayor and warden of Grey County. Josiah and Cyrus brought their parents to Singhampton, but the couple who had separated back in Pickering were not about to change the situation at that late date. Crotchety old Joseph lived, hermit-like, in a small log house by a swamp. Later he moved to a house in town provided for him by the loyal Josiah. Sarah lived with the family and was later remembered as a short lady of five-foot-two inches and weighing 210 pounds.

A stage line was operating between Singhampton and Jelly's Corners (Shelburne) by the mid-1860s when the Exchange House was built. After stopping at one of the five taverns in Jelly's Corners a passenger could connect with the line east to Cookstown operated by Dan McCallum, a man famous for his small but carefully trimmed white beard. At Rosemont, a convenient halfway point between the two towns, the coach was sure to stop at Thomas Henderson's two-storey frame Globe Hotel.

The 1866 directory for Simcoe County, with the usual enthusiasm shown by such journals, called Rosemont a 'post village rapidly increasing in importance ... in the midst of one of the finest agricultural districts of the County.' The population then was 140. Irishman Thomas Henderson of the Globe Hotel had paid Alfred Coulson of Toronto $1,300 for the property in 1859, a sizeable amount of money for one acre, so the hotel may already have been on the site. Business was so good that competition, in the form of two new inns, soon developed. By 1886 the population had reached 275, and Thomas Henderson

British Canadian Hotel

MELANCTHON, C. W.

WM. JELLY,.........Proprietor.

THE ABOVE HOTEL, SITUATE AT the terminus of the Owen Sound & Sydenham Gravel Road in Melancthon having been fitted up regardless of expense, possesses every-thing necessary for the convenience and comfort of travaelers and guests. The Bar is well supplied with the choicest Liquors, and the Table with all the delicacies of the Season.

☞ Excellent Stabling, and a careful hostler always in attendance.

Melanthon, No.v 26, 1864. 42-tf.

Orangeville *Sun*, 15 February 1866

The Globe Hotel in Rosemont, run successfully by Thomas and Elizabeth Henderson

was forced to contend with rival innkeepers George McCarthy and William Reid. By 9 April 1891, the Shelburne *Economist* noted sardonically: 'We are blessed (?) with what few places of the same size as Rosemont can boast of – three licensed hotels.'

Rivalry was fierce. According to local legend, the Globe possessed the only water pump in the village, so when a fire broke out at a tavern across the road, the proprietor's wife made the most of the opportunity. She chose to protect her water supply and sat by her pump, shot-gun at the ready, to ensure that the competition did indeed burn to the ground.

It is unlikely that the aggressive spouse was Thomas Henderson's wife, Elizabeth, for that couple seemed to be community-minded, though perhaps inclined to nepotism. The Orangeville *Sun* of 3 March 1870 suggested something of the sort when it reported the following local event:

> Shooting Match
>
> Company met at the Drill Shed on Feb 18 to compete for a valuable silver cup presented

Doorway, the Globe Hotel

by Mr T Henderson of the Globe Hotel and a number of other prizes. Although the day was stormy, quite a number of Volunteers turned out, and competition was keen. The cup, however, was finally carried off by Mr R. Henderson and Mr W. Henderson of Stanton obtained second prize.

After presenting his trophy, Henderson no doubt took advantage of the day of the competition to sell some of his wares. Perhaps he took similar advantage of the famous Fenian scare in 1866. A local Paul Revere rode through town shouting that the Catholics of Adjala Township were about to attack. The turn-out was swift. Protestants hastily congregated at Rosemont ready to meet the attack in the name of King Billy. But nothing happened. The rumour was unfounded, and the stalwart Protestants, undoubtedly disappointed, headed for home.

Perhaps three inns were too many for the small community. Liquor, the panacea of the hard-working settler, created problems here as elsewhere. Rosemont's reporter in the *Economist* of 18 September 1890 described the situation:

We would like to know where our once quiet little village is drifting. The air is full of wars and rumours of wars, and if such conduct continues we shall have to organize a corps of police to maintain law and order ... Friday night of last week was one of the wildest nights that has ever been experienced here. All through the night could be heard the sounds of brawling and fighting.

Thomas Henderson died in 1891 at the age of seventy. He was in business to the end, having been granted a renewal of his tavern licence five months before his death. As the *Economist's* faithful reporter noted, 'A large concourse of people followed his remains to their last resting place at St Luke's ... The bereaved family have our deepest sympathy.'

The road from Shelburne through Rosemont led to Cookstown, where it met another north-south artery, now Highway 27. Not far to the north was the village of Thornton, where passengers were welcomed by an innkeeper who, in spite of a Scottish-sounding name, had come from Ireland. Andrew Stewart was the proprietor of the Bee Hive Hotel (now the Village Inn), an impressive brick structure built in 1858. Thornton's population of one hundred – and the travelling public, as well – beat a path to his door.

Within eight years, however, Stewart decided to sell. The *Examiner and County of Simcoe Advocate* of 4 January 1866 announced that the Bee Hive was up for sale: 'part of the north half of lot 1 in the 7th concession of the township of Innisfil [the poetic name for Ireland, presumably the choice of the many Irish residents of the township] ... on which property there is erected a dwelling house and driving shed, now used as a tavern by Andrew Stewart of Thornton which property will be sold at auction at the Town of Barrie on 30 December 1865.' The notice was quickly followed by a postponement to 13 January 1866. Apparently further postponements came into play, for Andrew Stewart was still listed as a hotelkeeper in the 1871 census. He was then sixty and assisted by his wife, Annabella, and his children, Alexander, John Andrew, and Mary. Elsewhere Stewart was identified as a carpenter, and his son Alexander as a farrier (a blacksmith and horse doctor). In Thornton, as elsewhere, innkeepers were men of many talents.

Whether a jack-of-all trades or a will-o'-the-wisp, the average innkeeper had a hand in a multitude of activities. This was one reason why succulent meals might be low on his list of priorities. Good cooks were scarce, supplies were limited, and refrigeration was, particularly in the summer months, virtually non-existent. The frustrated traveller penning a nightly journal while trying to digest yet another meal of greasy salt pork might have felt fortunate that at least the host had not put tainted meat on the table. It is to be hoped that few innkeepers felt it necessary to follow the

Andrew Stewart's Bee Hive Hotel, Thornton; later the Queen's; then the Village Inn

instructions that appeared in the Niagara *Gleaner* on 31 December 1825:

Meat tainted to an extreme degree may be speedily restored by washing it in cold water and afterwards in strong cammomile tea; after which it may be sprinkled with salt and used the following day; or if steeped and well washed in beer, it will make a pure and sweet soup, even after being fly blown.

Entrance, the Village Inn

The Huron Road

Subscriber.

JAMES FULTON.

Richmond Hill, Markham, Nov. 13th, 1829. 2873

Stray Ox and Steer.

Broke into the inclosure of the Subscriber, a LARGE OX, blind of the off eye, with seven wrinkles on his horn, a yellowish Red and White colour; also a RED STEER with him, nearly three years old; with a brindle face, and part white under his breast. The owner or owners are requested to prove property, pay charges, and take the animals away.

...deed for cash, or if one half or one third of the purchase money is paid down. Immediate possession can be given, and, for further particulars apply to PHILIP CODY.

Toronto, Nov. 16th, 1829. 287z.

WHERE IS WILLIAM SUTHERLAND?

THE Subscriber is desirous of ascertaining the place of abode of Mr. William Sutherland and family. They lived in or near Glengarry, about the time of the last war, and were originally from the parish of Kindonan, Sutherlandshire. Address a letter to the Subscriber, at Niagara, care of Messrs. Chrysler, Merchants.

N. B. Mrs. Sutherland's maiden name was Catharine Macpherson.

DANIEL MACPHERSON.

Niagara, 17th Nov. 1829. 2873.

Boarding.

THE Subscriber can furnish Boarding, Lodging, &c. for six steady mechanics, reasonable, on Dundas Street, between Mr. Willmot's Tavern and four doors from Mr. Bird's Tavern, in the house lately occupied by Mr. George Hutchison, Plaisterer.

JAMES PARKER.

Nov. 18. 87.

STRAYED, on the 10th October last, into the premises of ANDREW BIGHAM, on lot No. 12, in the first concession of ETOBICOKE, A LIGHT IRON-GREY HORSE, rising five or six years of age.—The owner is requested to prove property, pay charges, and take him away.

Nov. 17. 873.

SAWYER & LABOURERS WANTED.

WANTED by the subscriber, a Sawyer who understands his business, and two men who understand Chopping; to whom liberal encouragement will be given.

Also; TO LET, for one or more years, the SALT WORKS of the Subscriber. For further particulars, apply to the subscriber, on the premises.

WILLIAM KENT.

Stoney Creek, Nov. 13, 1829. 87z

THE SUBSCRIBERS have just received direct from London, a general assortment of Hosiery, Black and Colored Gros-de-Naples, Figured Norwich Crapes, Black Silk and Cotton Velvets, Sewing Silks, Lace Thread Edgings, Worked Insertions, and Scollop Muslins, Red and Bell Cotton, Geo. the 4th Regulation Swords, Belts, and Sashes, ...ware and Cutlery, ...eral Stock of Saddlery: also an extensive a... of England Cloths, &c. &c.

J. C. GODWIN & Co.

NEWMARKET MAIL STAGE.

WILLIAM GARBUTT, having taken the contract for carrying His Majesty's Mails between York and Newmarket, for the next four years, respectfully informs the public that THE MAIL STAGE will start from Joseph Bloor's Hotel, York, on Mondays and Thursdays, at 12 o'clock, noon, and arrive at nine o'clock, the same evening in Newmarket;—and will leave Mr. Barber's Tavern, Newmarket, for York, on Wednesdays and Saturdays, at ... in the morning, and arrive in York at 2 P. M. on the same days.

Price for passengers conveyed between York and Newmarket, six shillings and three pence currency, and in proportion for shorter distances. Packages carried on this route at moderate rates.

Mr. BARBER will accommodate passengers arriving with the Mail Stage at Newmarket; and they may be comfortably conveyed to the Holland Landing, or in other directions if required.

York, March 30th, 1829. 254z.

NEW ARRANGEMENT OF STAGES

Between York and the Carrying Place at the head of the Bay of Quintie.

THE Public are respectfully informed that a Mail Stage will run regularly twice a week between York and the Carrying Place; leaving York every Monday and Thursday at 12 o'clock, noon, and arriving at the Carrying Place on Tuesdays and Fridays at 2 o'clock, P. M. Will leave the Carrying Place every Tuesday and Friday at 9 o'clock A. M. and arrive at York on Wednesdays and Saturdays, at 12 o'clock noon. There will also a Stage leave Cobourg every Monday at 10 o'clock A. M. and arrive at the Carrying Place the same day, and leave the Carrying Place every Saturday at 9 o'clock, A. M. and arrive at Cobourg the same day.

The above arrangements are in connexion with the Steam Boats *Sir James Kempt* and *Toronto*, so that Travellers going the route will find a pleasant and speedy conveyance between Kingston and York, as the line is now fitted up in good order with good carriages, good horses and careful drivers.

Every attention will be given to render passengers comfortable while on the line, and the drivers instructed to stop at the best hotels on the route.

All baggage at the risk of the owners.

Extras furnished to any part of the country.

The Stage Books will be kept at Mr. Bradley's Steamboat Hotel.

SALT RHEUM.

—This inveterate disease, which has long baffled the art of the most experienced physicians, has, at length, found a sovereign remedy in Dr. La Grange's genuine ointment. Few cutaneous diseases are met with more reluctance by the physician, which he is so adversely unsuccessful. This ... stood the test of experience, and justly obtained unparalleled celebrity. It immediately removes ... a healthy action to the vessels of the skin ...

PETER PATERSON, Agent.

SWEDES IRON.

...ing from the Ship *General Wolfe*, direct from ...NBURGH, ... ASSORTED SWEDES IRON.

WILLIAM BUDDEN, *Point a' Callicre.*

August 18, 1829. 274z

LOOKING GLASSES.

...ived by the subscriber, a large and elegant ... of Looking Glasses; German Plate; a va... and the prices remarkably low.

J. R. ARMSTRONG.

YORK FURNACE.

F. R. DUTCHER continues his FURNACE in complete operation, where can be had, at short notice,

Castings of any description from one to thirty cwt:

Also on hand a general assortment of STOVES, HOLLOW WARE, PLOUGH CASTINGS and PLOUGHS.

R. D. having erected a first rate Lathe for ... is ready to complete any order at short notice.

THEODORE BURLEY,

SMITH AND *Brass Founder:*

Yonge Street, next door to Judge Macaulay.

...ASTINGS for Mill work, &c. &c. done on ...est notice. ...White and Blacksmith's work done to order. ...hest prices, in CASH, will be paid for old ...and tin.

CHAPTER NINE

The Huron Road

INNS AS ESSENTIALS TO SETTLEMENT

'We were about sixty miles within the depth of the primeval forest. The moonlight only served to show the falling flakes of snow. All around was silence, and the winds slept even in the branches. We halted, where, by a strange glare reflected from the ground, we seemed in the spacious court of a college, solemn with overshadowing trees.'

The Autobiography of John Galt, Vol. 2, 1833

JOHN GALT was a poet, a humanist, an adventurer, and a businessman. His physical stature – six foot three – made him a giant for the times. His vision and compassion were of like size, encompassing the settlement of two million acres of land in Upper Canada. (Some thought his ego was just as large.) His ambition was simple: he planned to 'benefit the world.'

As a romantic and adventurous young man, Galt travelled the Mediterranean with fellow poet Lord Byron. He wrote prodigiously – novels, plays, essays, and a biography of Byron. A childhood spent in the Scottish port of Greenock, a point of departure for the destitute emigrating to Canada, had left him sensitive to the plight both of the tenant farmers displaced by the trend to large-scale sheep and cattle farming in Scotland and of the wretched victims of the Industrial Revolution. Galt expressed his compassion in a practical manner: he founded the Canada Company. Thus he benefited his world by relocating nearly a hundred thousand impoverished British workers to the wilderness of Upper Canada.

The Canada Company began in 1814 when Galt was asked by the Canadian government to act as an agent for those settlers making claims for losses sustained during the War of 1812. The project appealed to his compassionate nature. He began to pressure the Colonial Office in England, but the immediate response was negative. Funds were not available. But there was one revenue-producing resource – the vast acreage in Upper Canada held as clergy and Crown reserves. The sale of these lands could take care of the war-loss claims.

Years of negotiations between the Colonial Secretary, Lord Bathurst, and the colonial government concluded with the formation of the Canada Company. The clergy and Crown reserves would be purchased for one million pounds over a sixteen-year period with funds raised in England through the sale of shares. Holdings consisted of scattered Crown lands and one million acres in a block called the Huron Tract, which fronted on Lake Huron and formed a triangle with its eastern point in what became the city of Guelph.

The scheme promised to satisfy every-

Near Guelph: corduroy roads promised a head-cracking journey.

one: investors would make money on the sale or leasing of lands; emigrants would find a challenging but better life; and, for the government of Upper Canada, there was all that lovely money. Britain also approved because the influx of British settlers meant that there would be a better balance in Canada's population, which was two-thirds American and, the British feared, of questionable loyalty.

But this seemingly perfect scheme had imperfections. Management of the Canada Company lay in the hands of its directors in England, and distances made communication difficult. The directors were looking for a reasonably quick return on their investment, while the impoverished settlers were still struggling to make a subsistence living. A hard-working John Galt was trying to oversee it all, without the assistance of even an administrative clerk. He was also, unfortunately, hampered by an overbearing manner, and before long he managed to offend both the governing elite in Canada and the company directors in England. And so in 1829, after only three years, a disheartened Galt was relieved of his duties and returned to England. Yet he and his associates had, in those brief years, managed to settle fifty thousand emigrants, opened twenty-one townships in the Huron Tract, and founded the communities of Guelph, Goderich, and Stratford. It was no mean accomplishment.

Guelph was the first Canada Company town. On 23 April 1827, a party led by John Galt trekked through the bush from Galt (named after the commissioner by an admirer) to a selected maple tree that marked the site of the future town. It was left to Galt to fell the tree, an event that stirred the commissioner's poetic soul. 'To me at least,' he rhapsodized, 'the moment was impressive, and the silence of the woods that echoed to the sound was as the sigh of the solemn genius of the woods departing forever ... The tree fell with a crash of accumulated thunder, as if ancient nature were alarmed at the entrance of social man into her innocent solitudes with his sorrows, his follies and his crimes.'

The next day work began on the 160 lots that had been spoken for and the promised public buildings. The stump of that felled tree remained for years as a symbol of civic pride and the focal point of a street plan that resembled an outstretched left hand with the stump at the base of the palm.

The town's name remained a point of dispute between Galt and the directors. Galt had chosen to call it Guelph to honour the royal family, Hanoverians who were descended from the Guelfs, one of the great political factions of medieval Germany and Italy. The directors wanted it named after Viscount Goderich, a man then influential in colonial affairs. For a while Galt referred to the town in all communications as Guelph, while the directors stubbornly referred to it as Goderich. Galt won that round and then gave the name Goderich to the second Canada Company town. These annoying frictions were not forgotten in England.

The first building erected in Guelph was a market house, the second an all-purpose log building called the Priory. It served as a school, a store, and, of course, an inn. This hostelry in the Priory was the first of many – later in the century there were twenty-two inns within a one-mile radius of the downtown area (Macdonell Street was known as 'Whisky Street').

Guelph also produced an innkeeper of international reputation – if only in his own mind. Like Galt, he was a poet. Of sorts.

In the innkeeping trade, to be an eccentric was rarely bad for business. It was no wonder, then, that James Gay was a success. He owned two hostelries and rented and operated still another. He was the proprietor of the Bullfrog Inn, 414–16 Eramosa Road, and the self-styled Poet Laureate of Canada. Born in Bratton, Devonshire, he came to Canada in time to be listed in the 1828 census along with John Galt. He was then twenty-one. His first establishment, Gay's Inn, was a frame structure, but by the late 1850s he had prospered enough to build a substantial stone inn. He named it the Bullfrog.

James Gay had a flair for showmanship. He distributed his poetry to the citizens of Guelph as he wandered the streets playing his flute and greeting bemused passers-by with a cheery, 'Nice day; good day; James Gay; here today; soon away!'

No one could accuse James Gay of being unduly modest. In later years he privately published his collected works so as not to conceal his talent from a waiting world. One copy went to Alfred, Lord Tennyson, along with this immortal letter:

DEDICATION

To Dr C.L. Alfred Tennyson
Poet Laureate of England, Baron etc. etc.

Dear Sir,
Now Longfellow is gone there are only two of us left. There ought to be no rivalry between us two.

A poet's mind is clear and bright,
No room for hatred, malice or spite.

To my brother poet I affectionately dedicate these original verses, not before printed. Other verses from my pen, when so inspired, have been numerously printed in Canadian and American papers:

Giving a few outlines of my fellow man,
As nigh as I can see or understand.

Almost the first poetry I can remember is the beautiful line –

'Satan finds some mischef still for idle hands

to do.' and similar sentiments likewise occur in my own poems –

Up, up with your flag, let it wave where it will:
A natural born poet his mind can't keep still.

I do not know whether a Baron or a Poet Laureate gets any wages in England. In Canada there is no pay.

Ambition is a great thing, if this I must say;
This has been proved by the poet James Gay;
He feels like Lord Beaconsfield, and best left alone;
Respects every man and yet cares for none.

It is a solemn thing to think that I am the link connecting two great countries.

I hope when I am gone another may raise up.

I believe you have one boy, dear Sir, and I read in the papers the other day as he had been play-acting somewheres. I once exhibited a two-headed colt myself at several fairs, ten cents admission, and know something about play-acting and the like.

DON'T YOU LET HIM.

I hope to be in England sometime during the present year, if spared, and shall not fail to call round, if not too far from my lodging for a man nigh upon seventy-four, which dear Sir, is the age of

Yours alway,
James Gay
(this day)

Poet Laureate of Canada
and Master of all Poets.
Royal City of Guelph, Ontario.

As an afterthought, Gay added:

Then you can Publish
These poems and send
Them Through England
And no mistake you will
Find they will sell like
Hot Cakes.

While James Gay hoped to make poetic history with an alliance with Tennyson, the next innkeeper at the Bullfrog succeeded in becoming a footnote in Canadian medical history when he had bladder stones removed – the first and quite likely the last such operation to take place in a tavern. The date was 20 April 1878, and the patient was innkeeper William Hood, who had purchased the Bullfrog from James and Elizabeth Gay in 1860. The surgeon referred to his patient as 'a man of 63, weighing 300 pounds and a hard drinker.'

Dr Abraham Groves of Fergus told the story in his memoirs *All in the Day's Work.* Groves was a friend of Dr (later Sir) William Osler and a graduate of the Toronto School of Medicine. His career, while less spectacular than Osler's, was none the less impressive. Most of his operations took place in the patient's home on the kitchen table. He wrote for medical journals, his first papers being on the subject of an ovariotomy he had performed successfully although he had never before seen an open abdomen. Five years after he performed the bladder-stone operation in the Bullfrog Inn, Groves performed the first successful appendectomy in Canada. He wrote enthusiastically of his sterile techniques and of the importance of flushing out the abdomen with gallons of boiled water. Before each operation Dr Groves would shoo the family from the kitchen, and then, he reported, 'I boils me tools' – this before doing so was an established practice.

Before Groves agreed to operate on the innkeeper, Hood had consulted several doctors, all of whom had refused to treat him because of his age, weight, and condition. Dr Groves decided to proceed by cutting into the bladder just above the pubic bone. The success of the bladder-stone operation at the Bullfrog Inn put Hood back tending bar – no doubt as his own best customer.

Between the Guelph block and the Canada Company's one-million-acre Huron Tract lay Waterloo Township with its predominantly German-speaking population. The

The Bullfrog Inn, Guelph, where innkeeper James Gay dispensed spirits and bad poetry

area had become a haven for settlers from Germany and the Netherlands who had emigrated first to Pennsylvania and then, not satisfied with conditions there, made the move to Upper Canada. Other German settlers, who left their homeland to escape the religious persecution that followed the Napoleonic Wars, also found their way to Waterloo Township and took up farming in the area. These settlements around Kitchener still retain their German-speaking character.

Petersburg, seven miles west of Kitchener, is named after John Peter Wilker of Wallersdorf, Germany – an indomitable settler who arrived in York in the middle of a cholera epidemic and got his first job digging graves for cholera victims. On the

The Blue Moon, 'one of the great roadhouses'

Classical detailing: the Blue Moon, Petersburg

south-east corner of Petersburg's crossroads stands a building that has been called one of the last of the great Georgian road houses. It is the Blue Moon Inn, built and operated by innkeeper John Ernst. Ernst began business with a store on the site of the Blue Moon. By the 1851 census he was listed as an innkeeper. That and a mortgage taken out two years previously suggest that his handsome hotel was built about mid-century.

When settlement was under way at Kitchener and Guelph and James Gay was writing his immortal poetry, John Galt turned his attention west to the one million acres of Canada Company land that lay between what is now Perth County and Lake Huron. To settle families throughout the Huron Tract it was necessary to launch a massive and hazardous project – the construction of a road through more than sixty miles of forest. There were other dangers, but the forest was the major enemy – an unbroken sea of massive trees, many of them eighty feet tall and ten feet in diameter. Their towering height kept the undergrowth in constant darkness. It was impossible to walk on the ground, for it lay hidden under piles of dead and fallen trees and an untouched cover of vines. As sun rarely reached the undergrowth, the forest was continuously damp, and mosquitoes were a constant torment.

The men were subject to severe attacks of ague. Injuries were frequent, since many new arrivals had never before handled an axe. But the road had to be built. Galt employed as workers those same men who were trying to pay for their land. The Canada Company had allotted an insufficient three thousand pounds for the venture, and so when the money ran out Galt gave the settlers options on more land. They had no other way of making money until they could clear their acreage and grow crops. The directors also sent instructions regarding the location of bridges and the layout of townships but, logical as these seemed in faraway England, they were frequently unsuitable on the spot.

In the end, the completion of the road was due mainly to a man who made one million acres of forest his back yard. Dr William 'Tiger' Dunlop was the Canada Company's Warden of Woods and Forests. Like Galt, he was a giant, a hulking man with shoulders two and a half feet broad, calves like tree stumps, and skin like leather after years spent in the bush. His hair and beard were a flaming red. A descendant of Robert the Bruce, a physician, and a writer, Dunlop was an original. Fearless and adventurous, he lived life to the hilt, approaching every situation with a zany, irreverent, and irrepressible sense of humour.

Tiger Dunlop's personal eccentricities were many. His constant companions were the 'Twelve Apostles' – a dozen one-gallon bottles of whisky and brandy, carried in a handsome mahogany box with wheels and brass handles. He reportedly hated water, preferring to use it, boiled, to warm his whisky glass, then pouring it out to make room for the more jovial liquid. William Dunlop had earned his nickname 'Tiger' in India when he allegedly repelled an attacking tiger by throwing snuff in its face, a ploy that stunned the animal long enough for Dunlop to kill it.

Enthusiastic, intelligent, and larger than life, Dunlop was a natural backwoodsman. Before setting out to build the Huron Road, he wrote to his sister, 'I am now preparing to make a dive into the woods, and shall not emerge, most probably, until midsummer.' For the next three months he and his party hunted, fished, and slept in this uncharted wilderness. When they emerged they had surveyed the million-acre tract, planned roads and bridges, and marked concession lines. Dunlop had prepared the tract for settlement. He had encouraged the sick men working on the road and slogged through the forest swinging his axe with them. The Huron Road was completed during the summer of 1828.

Tiger Dunlop was a kind man, but not one to be trifled with. When Canada Company directors became concerned with the amount of money Galt was spending on the settlers, they sent over one Thomas Smith to check the accounts. Officious and self-important, Smith made one major error – he decided to monitor Tiger Dunlop's work in the bush. He didn't know his man. Heading into the woods, Dunlop filled the credulous accountant's mind with terrifying tales of wolves. He caused Smith's horse to bolt and then, when certain that his victim was thoroughly lost, galloped through the woods crying: 'The wolves! the wolves! Ride for your life, man!' He finally 'rescued' Smith, but a gleeful Dunlop continued to subject the clerk to further torment. Tiger had dropped one of his many snuff-boxes in a river. He rescued the treasure, but since his clothes were soaking, the red-haired, bearded giant had to pitch camp naked. That sight plus the mosquitoes and the hard work were enough to finish the effete Londoner – and a delighted Dunlop was spared from further monitoring expeditions.

Tiger Dunlop and his men opened sixty miles of bush road, but settlement could not proceed without one remaining – and essential – ingredient. Inns, or as Galt referred to them 'houses of entertainment,' were a necessity. Settlers moving into the bush, their wagons laden with possessions, needed stopping places where they could find food, supplies, directions, and, most of all, encouragement and advice. So innkeepers had to be found, and they had to be reliable. The selection of these key people fell to the third giant of the Huron Tract, Anthony Van Egmond. He chose first Sebastian Fryfogel, second, Andrew Seebach, and filled the third post himself. These three men were so important to the success of the settlements that they received a subsidy from the Canada Company. Knowing that business would be slow for a while, Fryfogel was given fifty dollars per month, and Seebach received seventy dollars. Van Egmond took no subsidy.

Van Egmond, like Galt and Dunlop, was more than six feet tall. Born in the Netherlands, he fought in the Napoleonic Wars in which, according to legend, he lost both his ears and therefore always wore a skull-cap. After the wars, he and his family emigrated to Pennsylvania, but they found that the many black rocks scattered across their fields made the land there unsuitable for farming. (They later learned that the lumps were coal. They had been located on the Pennsylvania coal fields.) Hearing of good land in Waterloo County, Van Egmond headed north, where, in due course, he met John Galt, who appointed him honorary agent for the Canada Company and asked him to seek out strong and dedicated men to run inns along the Huron Road. The men Van Egmond selected were, like himself, German-speaking settlers: Fryfogel a Swiss, and Seebach a Bavarian immigrant. Van Egmond felt German-speaking men would be reliable and businesslike.

Sebastian Fryfogel was born in Gelter-

Giant of the backwoods: 'Tiger' Dunlop

Fryfogel's Tavern: a decaying reminder of our disappearing architectural heritage

kinden, Switzerland, in 1791. His parents, Jakob and Elisabeth Freyvogel, had emigrated to Pennsylvania in 1806. (The family name, meaning 'bird in flight,' has a variety of spellings, some differentiating between city and country branches. Sebastian used the anglicized form.) While in Pennsylvania Sebastian married Mary Eby. In 1827 they and their five children moved to Waterloo County, where they met Anthony Van Egmond, who convinced Fryfogel to become an innkeeper on the proposed Huron Road. It took Fryfogel eleven days to move his family to the site chosen for the first stopping place, a spot just east of the present village of Shakespeare.

In John McDonald's 1828 survey of the Huron Tract, he noted that Fryfogel was 'a building.' He made reference to a stream he named Tavern Brook on the property, a fortunate designation, as it dates the first log inn and indicates that the family was sheltered for its first winter in the bush. It was a lonely, difficult winter and required of the Fryfogels a rugged stoicism. Settlers were not yet moving along the road, but the Fryfogels were busy with their growing family (it eventually numbered twelve, although one son died as an infant and another later of accidental poisoning), all of whom existed somehow in a log house measuring eighteen by twenty-four feet.

The building's one large room had a fireplace at one end, while about six feet from the other end a retaining log defined the communal sleeping area, which was filled with branches and straw and concealed by a curtain. A table and chairs stood in the middle of the room.

Patrick Shirreff, travelling west through the Huron Tract in 1833, described his night's lodging in an 'inn' not unlike Fryfogel's. Conditions were, in any event, primitive:

> We were conducted to a shanty thirty or forty yards from the tavern, consisting of one apartment, containing three beds, one of which was already occupied, another was destined for our waggoner, and the third for my friend and self. This hovel did not contain a seat, or any kind of furniture, except the fore-mentioned beds, and the door was without a fastening; the roof was of bark, and the rays of the moon shone through it and the sides of the building, which bore a stronger resemblance to a bird-cage than a human habitation. The beds were boughs of trees, put together in the manner of a camp stool, with a netting of bark connecting the frame-work ... [they] felt as rough and hard as the corduroy roads over which we had travelled in the course of the day.

Travellers had to adapt to conditions on the Huron Road or go hungry. Meals were often little more than some kind of mash. Worse still, a traveller could arrive and find no food at all, since the innkeeper had to travel many difficult miles to procure his supplies. Even salt pork was an unexpected luxury.

Yet Fryfogel managed to run a good house. Each year he obtained a renewal of his licence as an innkeeper. By 1843 the inspector's only complaint concerned the lack of a privy at Fryfogel's; nor, he said, was there a sign announcing the sale of spiritous liquors. Fortunately for the guests, both were in place within months. Another visitor, in the person of Thomas Mercer Jones, son-in-law of Archdeacon John Strachan and one of Galt's two successors as Commissioner of the Canada Company, dropped by to inspect the tavern. The night he was there the Fryfogels' ninth child, Nancy, was born. Jones presented the baby with a future town lot in nearby Stratford. She claimed it on her twenty-first birthday.

Travel along the Huron Road in 1830 was hazardous for many reasons, not the least of which were bears and wolves. Yet these perils didn't deter a courageous Mary Strickland from trudging the sixty miles from Guelph to Goderich carrying her baby. Her husband, Samuel Strickland, a brother of writers Susanna Moodie and Catharine Parr Traill, had been moved to Goderich after a term spent as manager of the Guelph operations for the Canada Company. It was intended that Mary join her husband later, but she was anxious to be with him, so she hired a wagon and driver and set out with her baby and a servant. After the wagon overturned twice in the

Samuel Strickland

first few miles on the stump-ridden road, the party decided to walk; and this they did, covering the sixty miles in six days. En route they spent a night at Fryfogel's. Samuel Strickland recorded his wife's travails:

During the afternoon of the second day, when within six miles of Trifogle's tavern, their intended resting place for the night, they were overtaken by a man who was going in the same direction, who very politely – as my wife thought – offered to carry her baby part of the way. She was, of course, very glad to avail herself of his kind offer; nor did she perceive, till after he had got possession of the bairn, that he was intoxicated. She immediately demanded back her little treasure, but no inducement could persuade him to relinquish it, and he set off with the infant as fast as he could. In vain the poor mother besought him to stop – in vain she sobbed and cried. On he went, followed by my Mary, who found great difficulty in keeping up with him, which she did at first, till, at length, exhausted by the unusual fatigue, maternal anxiety, and the roughness of the road, she lost sight of him about a mile from the tavern. He had walked off with his little burden.

She was now dreadfully alarmed, for night was fast coming on, and she did not know whether she was on the right track or not. Fortunately, a light through the trees extricated her from this dilemma: her only uneasiness was now for her child. She was soon, however, relieved from this uncertainty; for, on entering the house [Fryfogel's], there sat the man with the baby on his knee ... He at once restored the child to her mother's arms, observing, 'that he hoped she would give him the price of a quart of whiskey for his trouble, for the child was main heavy, God bless her.'

The red brick building that stands today near Shakespeare is Fryfogel's second tavern. It served not only as an inn but as a community hall, since Sebastian Fryfogel, who held a number of municipal positions in the 1840s and 1850s, had his office on the first floor while, on the second floor, the ballroom provided space for meetings. Fryfogel had gradually accumulated sizeable land holdings and had prospered. He was also a captain in the militia. A letter he wrote in that connection indicates that he was a literate man although, as English was his second language, the spelling was largely phonetic.

Fryburgh, June 15, 1847.

Sir:

As you are appointed ensign in mi company, i can inrol the mann mi selfe and you will attend on the 27th hear for to muster the mann

Yor Most truly
Sebastian Fryfogel,
Captain of the first company
4 Huron Reg.

Fryfogel died on 11 June 1873, at the age of eighty-two. On 13 June, the *Stratford Beacon* included an extensive obituary.

Death of Mr Fryfogel ... He was the first settler in what now comprises the County of Perth. He was the father of twelve children – five sons and seven daughters; many grandchildren and great-grandchildren and, we believe, leaves over 120 lineal descendants. He served as reeve of South Easthope for several years in the district council of Huron, Perth and Bruce and for the same township after Perth was set apart, and was elected one of the first wardens of the County. Circumstances compelled him to keep a tavern, his being the only house for miles where a person could stop at or get a meal. The few early settlers of the Huron tract now remaining will regret to hear of his death. He was a kind, hospitable man and respected by all who knew him.

When the Huron Road opened in 1828 there were twenty lonely, silent miles between Fryfogel's and the next stop, Seebach's Tavern (no longer standing), at the west end of Ellice Township. It was the second of the three Canada Company inns. Samuel Strickland spent a sleepless night there in the winter of 1831 en route to Goderich. He graphically described the place. In spite of the discomfort, he seemed almost to enjoy the antics of the Seebach children:

In regard to our sleeping we had some difficulty to arrange that important matter, since they had only two beds for our numerous party, and they were both in the same room. Under these circumstances undressing was out of the question. Luckily we had several horse-blankets and buffalo-robes, so that I was enabled to separate our dormitory by these fancy hangings. The teamster and myself contented ourselves with a shake-down before the fire, where five of our hostess's boys had already ensconced themselves for the night on a number of deer-skins.

About the middle of the night we were awakened by one of the Dutch boys tumbling into the fire in his sleep ... This little incident having thoroughly roused his brothers, they seemed determined to let no one sleep for the remainder of the night ... At length they became silent, and I had just fallen asleep when I was again awakened by a shriek from Mrs R——, who seemed to be in an agony of terror; and no wonder, poor woman! for these impish Dutch boys had slily crept under the lady's bed, and almost frightened her out of her wits by placing their shoulders under the mattress and, all lifting together, nearly succeeded in rolling her out of bed.

The third Canada Company tavern, located about twenty-two miles further along the Huron Road, in Hullett Township, was run by the generous and hospitable Anthony Van Egmond, who in time became the company's fiercest enemy. His life ended in tragedy when, disillusioned by what he saw as the company's lack of interest in the needy settlers, he chose to join the rebel cause and follow William Lyon Mackenzie. He was captured at the time of the rebellion and thrown in a damp cell. He died shortly thereafter.

In 1832, Stratford, the third Canada Company town, grew up between Fryfogel's and Seebach's outpost taverns. In almost no time an inn was built and given its name by Thomas Mercer Jones, who seemingly enjoyed visiting the inns along the Huron Road. He brought with him a gift for owner William Sargint – a sign bearing the portrait of William Shakespeare. That decided the name of the inn and led to the town's being named Stratford. The river, originally called the Little Thames, became the Avon.

Mrs Sargint made the Shakespeare Inn a popular place. 'A fine buxom-looking woman,' recalled one early customer; 'fair and good-natured, rosy and blue-eyed, free in her speech and fond of a joke.' She organized a school in the inn and welcomed the formidable Canon William Betteridge to her tavern to preach. Tiger Dunlop and Thomas Mercer Jones also appeared from time to time, but not to attend church services – although Betteridge so impressed Dunlop that the doctor praised him for 'a damned good sermon' and handed over a five-pound note.

Stratford grew steadily and, in 1856, the convergence of two railway lines on the town assured its prosperity. This also prompted the construction of several large hotels, one of which, the Albion, built that same year, is still standing, although much altered.

Further along the Huron Road, just east of Goderich, was a simple frame tavern known as the Rob Roy Inn. It was owned, of course, by a Scot, David Munro, who started in business in the 1840s when traffic along the road warranted more than those first taverns designated by the Canada Company. Munro was said to have served some of the best ale in the district, but before long he was finding it necessary vigorously to pursue those customers who had neglected to pay their bar bills. In the *Huron Signal* of 24 March 1848, he placed a warning:

NOTICE

All persons indebted to the subscriber either by Note or Book account, are requested to

David Munro's inn by the Huron Road, where Dunlop's body rested on its final journey

make payment on or before the first of May next; after that date all demands remaining unsettled, will be positively handed over to an Attorney for immediate collection.

David Munro.

Munro might well have considered posting the ditty (of which there were many versions), that gave a friendly warning to customers before they started to drink:

Gentlemen walk in and sit at your ease;
Pay for what you call for and call for what you please.
As trusting of late has been to my sorrow,
Pay today, and I'll trust you tomorrow.

It was in 1861, after David Munro died, that the family finally received title to the land on which the tavern stood (lot 3, Maitland Concession, Huron County) at the corner of Highway 8 and the Mill Road. David Munro, who had for years been gradually paying the Canada Company for the land, didn't live to enjoy the day when the property finally became his. But his wife, Ann, and their son, James, carried on the business, as did other family members who worked as blacksmiths and harness-makers.

The deed that gave the Munros title to their land stated that one Louisa Dunlop had advanced twenty-seven pounds 'On behalf of the heirs at law of the late David Munro to enable them to come into possession of the title to said property.' This was a woman who could well afford the money. Louisa Dunlop was by that time a wealthy woman – the widow of Captain

Robert Dunlop and sister-in-law of the indomitable Dr William 'Tiger' Dunlop.

Louisa McColl had come to Goderich as a housekeeper for the bachelor Dunlop brothers, at the request of friends at home in Scotland who felt the men needed a 'respectable Scotch-body' to look after them. She was all that and more. An astute businesswoman, she eventually became their manager and, in time, the wife of Robert Dunlop. The brothers led unsettled, unstructured lives, particularly 'the Tiger' who, as Warden of the Canada Company, spent much of his time enjoying the demands and challenges of life in the backwoods.

The story of Louisa's marriage to Robert Dunlop is the stuff of legend. After she had been with them for some time, the brothers decided that it would be seemly if one of them married the lady. Tiger produced a coin, which was to decide the matter after three tosses, the loser to marry Louisa. The coin came up heads on each throw, and Robert gave up his carefree bachelorhood. Only later did he discover that his wily brother had been up to his usual tricks – Tiger had used a two-headed coin. Many thought, however, that Robert was the winner. Louisa cared for both brothers and managed Gairbraid, their log 'castle' in Goderich.

'Tiger' Dunlop was a giant of a man, and the legends that grew about him were of like size, for his exploits were many. Serving as a doctor in 1813, he rescued men who had fallen in battle at Lundy's Lane, carrying them on his back out of firing range. He directed the affairs of the Canada Company in Goderich and supervised settlement there. Later he became a founder of the Mechanics' Institute, wrote a highly successful book entitled *Statistical Sketches of Upper Canada* (1832), was elected a Member of Parliament, and finally became superintendent of the Lachine Canal. He took great delight in shocking the genteel citizens of York by appearing from the backwoods, unshaven, uncivilized, and covered (as always) with snuff.

Dunlop, more than most, enjoyed a joke. He loved animals too. According to W.H. Graham, a Dunlop biographer, one young horse at Gairbraid 'gave evidence of the effect of the environment' there. 'Given a shilling between his teeth he would trot down to the Crown and Anchor and lay it on the bar for a drink.'

It is quite likely that his will gave Tiger Dunlop more pleasure than anything. In it he left his house and lands to 'my good friend and sister-in-law, Louisa Dunlop,' and then went on to needle the rest of the family:

> I leave my silver tankard to the eldest son of old John, as the representative of the family. I would have left it to old John himself, but he would melt it down to make temperance medals, and that would be sacrilege – however, I leave my big horn snuff-box to him; he can only make temperance horn spoons out of that.
> I leave my sister Jenny my Bible ... and when she knows as much of the spirit of it as she does of the letter, she will be another guise Christian than she is.
> ... I leave my brother Alan my big silver snuff-box, as I am informed he is rather a decent Christian, with a swag belly and a jolly face.
> I leave Parson Chevasse (Magg's husband) the snuff-box I got from the Sarnia Militia, as a small token of gratitude for the service he has done the family in taking a sister that no man of taste would have done.
> I leave John Caddle a silver teapot, to the end that he may drink tea therefrom to comfort him under the affliction of a slatternly wife.
> ... I give my silver cup, with a sovereign in it, to my sister Janet Graham Dunlop, because she is an old maid and pious, and therefore will necessarily take to horning. And also my Gramma's snuff mull, as it looks decent to see an old woman taking snuff.

Tiger Dunlop died in Montreal in 1848 at the age of fifty-six. His faithful Lou travelled there to be with him at the end and then accompanied his body back to Goderich for burial beside his brother. It was necessary to leave the casket at Sir Allan

MacNab's grave plot in Hamilton until the weather became cold enough to travel the rest of the distance. Once winter arrived, they were able to continue on their slow, sad journey. On their final night, Dunlop's coffin rested at Munro's Inn. Lou went on to Goderich to make arrangements for the funeral, while a family friend stood guard over the coffin. On the following day, the school children in Goderich were given a holiday so they too could watch the Tiger's last trip to his beloved Gairbraid and a grave on the hillside by Lake Huron.

Goderich, the second Canada Company town was, like Guelph, a planned community. As one contemporary writer put it, it was 'the pet and youngest darling of the Canada Company,' which saw it as a natural harbour of future importance. It was linked by the Huron Road to communities in the east and by the London Road to the south. Situated on a breathtaking site on the cliffs overlooking Lake Huron, it was laid out with an octagonal central market square and broad avenues leading, spoke-like, from it.

In spite of the beauty of its plan, Goderich was a town of extremes. Patrick Shirreff noted in 1833 that the Canada Company was 'very unpopular at Goderich although Dr Dunlop is a favourite amongst the settlers, who are of the poorest class, and seemingly without industry or energy of any kind.' This perceived lack of industry was the result of a situation that seemingly had no solution. The settlers were heavily indebted to the Canada Company. Some had been unable to read or understand the leases or land-purchase agreements they had signed. These became an increasing burden if there was no quick return on their land. Many were faced with losing their investment.

On the other hand the representatives of the company, who were gradually forming closer ties with the powerful Family Compact, were living conspicuously well. Thomas Mercer Jones, who had replaced John Galt as one of a team running the Canada Company's operations, moved to Goderich seven years after his 1832 marriage to Elizabeth Mary Strachan, daughter of Archdeacon (later Bishop) John Strachan, one of Upper Canada's most powerful figures. Keeping up with the Jones family wasn't easy. They arrived in town with twenty-one wagonloads of possessions. Elizabeth, then about twenty-five years old, held lavish parties and dressed her two young sons in velvet. They were followed about town by a liveried footman. This ostentation was tempered by the general knowledge that Jones's mistress had just moved out to make way for his wife.

One of the spokes of the wheel in Goderich is South Street. Part of the building now standing at number 35 dates from 1850, when Jacob Seegmiller built the rear portion to accommodate his harness-making enterprises. This German entrepreneur had been trading in hides and whisky on the Huron Road since shortly after it opened. Later he established a farm and operated two tanneries and the sizeable British Exchange Hotel in Goderich. Seegmiller shrewdly developed auxiliary businesses that employed several members of his large family. They worked as teamsters, tavern-keepers, and harness-makers. When he died at the age of seventy-two, Jacob Seegmiller left a respectable estate of almost

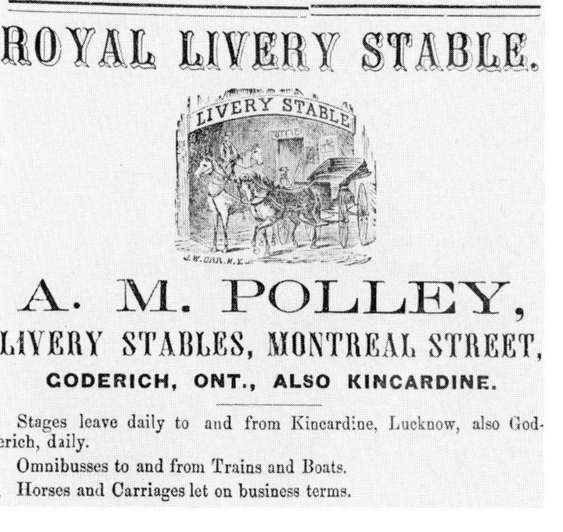

Huron County Directory, 1869–70

Polley's Livery Stable, now a theatre

ten thousand dollars and, in addition, extensive land holdings.

Seegmiller had disposed of his harness-making shop on South Street in the 1860s. It was bought by Albert Polley, who added the front section, built of Maitland River stone to blend with the original Seegmiller building. Polley also ran a livery and had the contract for mail delivery. In 1978 the Livery and Hack Stable, long since converted to housing automobiles instead of horses, looked like a candidate for demolition. The Goderich Performing Arts Foundation launched various projects to enable the old livery to start life again as a theatre, a role it fills successfully today.

The Canadian wilderness lured many well-educated men, who came in search of fortune and adventure. Such was the case with the members of the aristocratic van Tuylls of the Netherlands.

Carel Lodewijk van Tuyll, heir to a

Beauty in the most practical of buildings: Bayfield's Little Inn

Verandah, the Little Inn

sizeable fortune, began about 1830 to buy thousands of acres in and around Goderich and adjacent townships. He also purchased 1,500 acres on either side of the Bayfield River. The land was selected for van Tuyll by Admiral Henry Bayfield, a friend and brilliant naval surveyor, who at the time was charting Lake Huron.

Until the advent of the railways in mid-century, Bayfield was poised to outrank Goderich in importance. It was a shipping centre for farmers, and wagons were often lined up a mile or so from the harbour waiting to unload their produce. Bayfield had grist mills and sawmills, eight stores, four manufacturing establishments, a French seminary, and a dozen or so hotels, one of which still graces the corner of Main and Catherine Streets.

The first building there was a log house built by John Cronan, who in 1842 purchased the property from the aristocratic Viscount Gildermeester, Baron de Tuyle de Serooskerken. A small hotel was built by a carpenter, Donald Fraser, after Fraser bought from Cronan in 1847. Fraser owned the business for fifteen years, and then the property passed to Thomas Mossop, who, along with his partner, Richard Bailey, had been hired to dredge the Bayfield River. Finally Bailey, a ship's carpenter, bought out Mossop in 1870 and extended the building, calling it the Commercial Hotel.

The local papers loyally followed Bailey's progress, noting in 1881: 'The Commercial Hotel is being renovated and more added'; in 1888: 'Mr Bailey has completed extensive improvements and can accommodate lots of Yankees and Britishers'; in 1891: 'R. Bailey, Commercial Hotel, proposes erecting a handsome verandah which will add greatly to the appearance of the House.' A Goderich firm, Buchanan Brothers, did the ornate work, creating two storeys of Victorian elegance. The verandah lasted for more than half a century, but in 1945 dry rot forced its removal by innkeeper George Little (who renamed his establishment the Little Inn). Recent owners have replaced the verandah, taking care to study early photographs of the original. The present parlour was the taproom, and the dining-room served as a bakery at one stage as well as a popular location for dances.

One such gala was described by the Bayfield reporter for the *Huron Signal* of 2 June 1863. Clearly the Queen's birthday brought forth a surge of chauvinistic fervour from the unidentified reporter. The day ended at the Little Inn, then called Mossop's Commercial Hotel.

> Bayfield, as you are aware, is one of the most picturesque places on the banks of Lake Huron. The various and tortuous windings and the many rills of the Bayfield River through glens and ravines and the more noble expanse of Lake Huron together with a day when the heat of the sun was tempered by genial breezes, were sufficient to attract the most callous of nature's admirers and offer a limner a sketch that would vie with Niagara and revelling in its delight would lose his soul in fancy porticals. Such is Bayfield and its glories. But all these beauties were largely enhanced on Monday last by the presence of the ladies from all parts of Stanley, Hay, Goderich and other townships ... In the evening a large and pleasant quadrille party took place in Mossop's hall where Beauty reigned supreme and the fair votaries of the 'mazy danse' with their many partners 'Tripped the light fantastic' until rosy Sol smiled upon their joyous faces.

It is hard to relate that ecstatic description of the beauties of Bayfield with one that appeared ten years later in the *Huron Expositor*. On 8 August 1873, the Bayfield reporter regretted that a reader had seen fit to describe the place as 'a small dilapidated-looking place of 120 inhabitants and containing no less than nine grog shops.' Four of those 'grog shops' remain in Bayfield today – the Little Inn; the former River Hotel on Emeric Street, Bayfield's oldest inn; Pollock's Hotel, now apartments; and the Albion, dating from 1842, which welcomed travellers at the opposite end of Main Street from the Commercial.

The name 'Albion,' which was given to countless hotels throughout the province, was the ancient and literary name for England. (The Scottish equivalent was Albany.) Bayfield's Albion Hotel began life as a store owned by Robert Reid, an Irish bricklayer. In 1857, after a large addition was made to the building, it opened its doors as an hotel. There followed the usual succession of proprietors seeking a greener field and a better stand.

Take, for instance, innkeeper George Castles. In 1861 he and his Irish wife, Jane, two children, and three Irish boarders occupied a frame and log inn – an exact description of the Commercial Hotel. One of his boarders there was Thomas Mossop,

The Albion Hotel, where Bayfield celebrants creatively toasted the night away

Front door, the Albion Hotel

who the following year purchased the Commercial. In 1889 George Castles purchased the Albion. He sold it in 1894 to Edward Elliot, who had been proprietor of the Wellington Arms in 1863, the Commercial Hotel in 1869, and the Temperance Hotel on Main Street in 1881. James Pollock ran the River Hotel and later the Royal Exchange. Innkeeper John Pollock of the Albion may have been his son. John married the daughter of innkeeper George Castles of the Commercial and the Albion ... Their movements are confusing, but proprietors were nothing if not itinerant.

One innkeeper who established himself at the Albion long enough to get a fine reputation was William McCann. The *Huron Signal* of 10 March 1875 reported an event that took place under his auspices – an event that was a roaring success if success can be measured by the number of toasts the creative participants managed to include:

> The annual dinner of the Stanley Branch Agricultural Society took place on Wednesday evening 24th ult. at McCann's Hotel ... the dinner was excellent and Mrs McCann deserves credit for the manner in which the good things were placed on the table.

The toasts proposed were to:

> The Queen ... the Army and the Navy coupled with the Volunteers of Canada, the Agricultural interests of Canada, the commercial interests of Canada, the mechanical interests of Canada, the interests of Bayfield and vicinity and the railways of Canada, the Branch Agricultural Society of Stanley and the general prosperity of the province ... [and] ... the health of the host and hostess.

It was, the group concluded, 'one of the most pleasant evenings of the kind which has yet occurred in Bayfield ... '

Niagara

JAMES FULTON.
Richmond Hill, Markham, Nov. 13th, 1829. 287

Stray Ox and Steer.

Broke into the inclosure of the Subscriber, a LARGE OX, blind of the off eye, with seven wrinkles on his horn, a yellowish Red and White colour; also a RED STEER with him, nearly three years old; with a brindle face, and part white under his breast. The owner or owners are requested to prove property, pay charges, and take the animals away.

...deed for cash, or if one half or one third of the purchase money is paid down. Immediate possession can be given, and, for further particulars apply to PHILIP CODY.
Toronto, Nov. 16th, 1829. 287z.

WHERE IS WILLIAM SUTHERLAND?

THE Subscriber is desirous of ascertaining the place of abode of Mr. William Sutherland and family. They lived in or near Glengarry, about the time of the last war, and were originally from the parish of Kindonan, Sutherlandshire. Address a letter to the Subscriber, at Niagara, care of Messrs. Chrysler, Merchants.
N. B. Mrs. Sutherland's maiden name was Catharine Macpherson.
DANIEL MACPHERSON.
Niagara, 17th Nov. 1829. 2873.

Boarding.

THE Subscriber can furnish Boarding, Lodging, &c. for six steady mechanics, reasonable, on Dundas Street, between Mr. Willmot's Tavern and four doors from Mr. Bird's Tavern, in the house lately occupied by Mr. George Hutchison, Plaisterer.
JAMES PARKER.
Nov. 18. 87.

STRAYED, on the 10th October last, into the premises of ANDREW BIGHAM, on lot No. 12, in the first concession of ETOBICOKE, A LIGHT IRON-GREY HORSE, rising five or six years of age.—The owner is requested to prove property, pay charges, and take him away.
Nov. 17. 873.

SAWYER & LABOURERS WANTED.

WANTED by the subscriber, a Sawyer who understands his business, and two men who understand Chopping; to whom liberal encouragement will be given. Apply to

SALT RHEUM.

—This inveterate disease, which has long baffled the art of the most experienced physicians, has, at length, found a sovereign remedy in Dr. La Grange's genuine ointment. Few cutaneous diseases are met with more reluctance by the physician, in which he is so adversally unsuccessful. This has stood the test of experience, and justly obtained unparalleled celebrity. It immediately removes ... gives a healthy action to the vessels of the skin ...

SWEDES IRON.

...ding from the Ship *General Wolfe*, direct from ...
...ASSORTED SWEDES IRON.
WILLIAM BUDDEN, *Point a' Callіere.*
August 18, 1829. 274-z

LOOKING GLASSES.

...eived by the subscriber, a large and elegant ...t of Looking Glasses; German Plate; a va... and the prices remarkably low.
J. R. ARMSTRONG.
...pt. 10th, 1829.

YORK FURNACE.

F. R. DUTCHER continues his FURNACE in complete operation, where can be had, at short notice,
Castings of any description from one to thirty cwt:
Also on hand a general assortment of STOVES, HOLLOW WARE, PLOUGH CASTINGS and PLOUGHS.
...R. D. having erected a first rate Lathe for ..., is ready to complete any order at short notice.

THEODORE BURLEY,
SMITH AND *Brass Founder:*
Yonge Street, next door to Judge Macaulay.
CASTINGS for Mill work, &c. &c. done on ... notice.
... White and Blacksmith's work done to order. ...hest prices, in CASH, will be paid for old ...

...PETER PATERSON, *Agent.*

Also; TO LET, for one or more years, the SAW WORKS of the Subscriber.
For further particulars, apply to the subscriber, on the premises.
Stoney Creek, Nov. 13, 1829. WILLIAM KENT. 87z

THE SUBSCRIBERS have just received direct from London, a general assortment of
Hosiery,
Black and Colored Gros-de-Naples,
Figured Norwich Crapes,
Black Silk and Cotton Velvets,
Sewing Silks,
Lace Thread Edgings,
Worked Insertions, and Scollop Muslins,
Reed and Ball Cotton,
Geo. the 4th Regulation Swords, Belts, and Sashes,
...ware and Cutlery,
...eral Stock of Saddlery: also an extensive ... of England Cloths, &c. &c.
J. C. GODWIN & Co.

NEWMARKET MAIL STAGE.

WILLIAM GARBUTT, having taken the contract for carrying His Majesty's Mails between York and Newmarket, for the next four years, respectfully informs the public that THE MAIL STAGE will start from Joseph Bloor's Hotel, York, on Mondays and Thursdays, at 12 o'clock, noon, and arrive at nine o'clock, the same evening in Newmarket;—and will leave Mr. Barber's Tavern, Newmarket, for York, on Wednesdays and Saturdays, at ... in the morning, and arrive in York at 2 P. M. on the same days.
Price for passengers conveyed between York and Newmarket, six shillings and three pence currency, and in proportion for shorter distances. Packages carried on the route at moderate rates.
Mr. BARBER will accommodate passengers arriving with the Mail Stage at Newmarket; and they may be comfortably conveyed to the Holland Landing, or in other directions if required.
York, March 30th, 1829. 254z.

NEW ARRANGEMENT OF STAGES

Between York and the Carrying Place at the head of the Bay of Quintie.

THE Public are respectfully informed that a Mail Stage will run regularly twice a week between York and the Carrying Place; leaving York every Monday and Thursday at 12 o'clock, noon, and arriving at the Carrying Place on Tuesdays and Fridays at 2 o'clock, P. M. Will leave the Carrying Place every Tuesday and Friday at ... o'clock A. M. and arrive at York on Wednesdays and Saturdays, at 12 o'clock noon. There will also a Stage leave Cobourg every Monday at 10 o'clock A. M. and arrive at the Carrying Place the same day, and leave the Carrying Place every Saturday at 9 o'clock, A. M. and arrive at Cobourg the same day.
The above arrangements are in connexion with the Steam Boats *Sir James Kempt* and *Toronto*, so that Travellers going the route will find a pleasant and speedy conveyance between Kingston and York, as the line is now fitted up in good order with good carriages, good horses and careful drivers.
Every attention will be given to render passengers comfortable while on the line, and the drivers instructed to stop at the best hotels on the route.
All baggage at the risk of the owners.
Extras furnished to any part of the country.
The Stage Books will be kept at Mr. Bradley's Steamboat Hotel.
*** The roads between Kingston and ...

CHAPTER TEN

Niagara

INNS AS MULTI-PURPOSE BUILDINGS

'Niagara! to thee
  My spectacles I turn!
I see thy waters boil,
  As if all —— did burn,
And Satan's imps, with ardour hot
Were thrusting wood beneath the pot.

  And then, Oh what a waste
Of water power is here!
  'Twould take ten thousand water-wheels,
And run them through the year!
Well might the Yankee say – "be still –
Oh what a place to build a mill."'

Author unknown

FOR VIRTUALLY everyone visiting Upper Canada in the nineteenth century a visit to Niagara Falls was *de rigueur.* The spectacle elicited paeans of praise from British travellers, who filled their journals with page after mind-numbing page of detailed description, as each writer tried to surpass the others in painting word pictures of the wonders of Niagara. By the time Alexander Graham Dunlop arrived at the falls in 1845 after visiting his 'Tiger Uncle' at Goderich, he found himself almost – but not quite – at a loss for newer and more mellifluous words. Niagara Falls, he stated, 'have been described, and painted, and sketched, a hundred times. Each description is a paltry failure, and every sketch a caricature – nor need I add to them.' He then proceeded to do just that, filling several pages with his impressions.

Horton Rhys, cheerful as ever, aptly summed up the situation after his trip to the falls in 1861. Anyone wanting to know about Niagara, he said, should

> send to all the circulating libraries in your ken, and get all the works that treat upon the subject, read them all at the same time, occasionally varying the monotony of the employment by placing a few of them upside down, or crosswise, and commence the last page first, and you will know as much of Niagara when you have gone mad or asleep over the occupation, as you did before you began it ...

In 1843, Captain (later Sir) James Edward Alexander was part of a merry group that travelled in three sleighs to Niagara from London. He, too, of course, kept a journal. With three brother officers from the garrison at London, two women friends, and three servants, Alexander embarked on the adventure, hoping to see the falls when they were, as he put it, 'encircled with a snowy mantle ... and after viewing the sublime cataract under this peculiar aspect, the parties proposed to participate for a short season in the gayeties of Toronto before returning to the "stumps and squirrels" of the back woods.' Life in the colonies, while never easy, was not without its compensations.

Snuggled down under buffalo, fox, and raccoon robes the happy party sped over the snow, their sleighs and horses festooned with bells, following the horn sounded by those in the lead. Two officers and one woman occupied each of the first two sleighs, while the three servants brought up the rear. After a brief stop at Ingersoll they went on to Brantford, a rough and rowdy town where they found accommodation of sorts at a small inn. They spent a restless night, however, thanks to an inebriated woman who stumbled into the parlour where the men had stretched out to sleep. She announced her presence by falling down a flight of stairs and then, noisily proceeding to make herself at home, proclaimed to the sleepy Captain Alexander and his friends, that she would 'talk with ye first and try your grog.' After liberally sampling some cognac she had spotted on the table, the woman eventually departed, taking the bottle with her, so that she could 'treat the boys.' The officers' servants pursued the intruder and eventually recovered the bottle 'from her lower garments.'

Through Hamilton and Stoney Creek to Forty-Mile Creek (Grimsby) where they spent their second night in 'a clean wayside inn,' the party continued along the snowy trail to Niagara Falls, which they reached three days after leaving London. There they were able to enjoy the finest in accommodation at the Clifton House, a magnificent three-storey structure that offered a superb view of the Horseshoe and American falls from its spacious galleries and the belvedere on the roof. Built in 1833, it was for many years the favourite resort of British visitors.

Alexander and his friends were enchanted by 'the great cataract ... in its winter garb' and, although he had seen the falls several years earlier 'in all the glories of autumn, its encircling woods happily spared by the remorseless hatchet,' Alexander wrote rapturously of the snowy scene that lay before them. 'The waters,' he claimed, 'were unchanged by the season, except that vast sheets of ice and icicles hung on their margin; but where the deep waves of sea-green water roll majestically over the steep, large pieces of descending ice were descried ever and anon on its bosom.' Alexander, a talented artist, was impressed enough to record all this in a hasty sketch, his charming drawing capturing perfectly a few awestruck visitors rooted to the spot, their minds already searching for words to describe adequately in their journals the scenic wonders of Niagara.

The Clifton House was only one of several hotels that over the years housed the thousands who made the pilgrimage to Niagara Falls. Forsyth's Pavilion Hotel, built in 1821, was among the first. It was destroyed by fire in 1839 but replaced by a much grander edifice, one that seated at least 100 people in its dining-room and had

Spellbound spectators at Niagara Falls

beds for 150. Also popular were the Cataract House and the International Hotel, both boasting 'river parlours' – extensive wings that stretched to the river bank, luxuriously furnished to ensure the guests' every comfort. Both the Clifton House and the Cataract House burned to the ground in 1898, a fate suffered by nearly all the nineteenth-century hotels at Niagara Falls.

Many travellers on their way to and from the falls spent time in the town of Niagara (now Niagara-on-the-Lake), a convenient twelve miles north. Fortunately, several of the early inns there have survived, adding to the unique atmosphere of this historic community. Originally called Newark and chosen as the capital of Upper Canada, it was settled by Loyalists who had served with Butler's Rangers. When the capital was moved to York, the name of the town was changed to Niagara. In 1900 it was given its present name to avoid confusion with Niagara Falls.

The Niagara frontier became a major battleground during the War of 1812. In May 1813, the Americans captured Fort George, and on 10 December of that year their retreating troops set fire to the nearby village of Niagara, leaving several hundred women and children homeless in the midst of a Canadian winter. The splendid examples of neoclassical and Georgian architecture seen at Niagara-on-the-Lake today were built following that disastrous fire.

Taverns and inns, of course, were quick to spring from the ashes. Among the first was a simple brick building at 55 Prideaux Street, built on the foundations of a house originally owned by Elizabeth Thompson, 'a colourful person of strong character.' Mrs Thompson claimed that her losses during the war included two houses and a stable, as well as (among other items) a loaf of sugar and a box of chocolate. Then as now, governments were not quick to act, and thus, when the twice-widowed Elizabeth Thompson died in 1825, her will referred to 'a certain sum of money now due me by His Majesty's Government for losses sustained during the late war with the United States of America.' She had lost title to her house through indebtedness two years earlier.

Mrs Thompson's property was bought by a lawyer, John Breakenridge, who, it seems likely, was the builder of the trim, tasteful red brick house that stands there today. Breakenridge was a man who had built 'several of the most elegant and tasty houses in town.' In 1826 Breakenridge sold the building to David Botsford, who operated it as a hotel for the next four years. Botsford called his inn the Promenade Tavern. Local legend has it that the name derived from women of questionable character who strolled in front of the house to entice customers inside; but the story seems unlikely given Botsford's advertisement in the *Niagara Herald* in April 1830:

> FOR RENT on very easy terms, that well known stand situated in Niagara and known by the name of Promenade Tavern for one or more years; the principle object being to keep up the respectability of the House, sufficient testimony will be required to ensure the same ...

Niagara, 1846

Promenade Tavern, 55 Prideaux Street: in its heyday, *the* place to stay

Botsford had by this time expanded his horizons. He had just purchased the Ontario House in York and hoped that his two establishments might both benefit from reciprocal business. He often urged visitors at Niagara Falls to travel to the 'Capital of the Province, headquarters for the military, who have a superior band of music attached ...'

If the Promenade was not a 'house of ill repute,' that is not to say that there were no such places nearby. In 1836, the Court of Quarter Sessions at Niagara dealt with the case of innkeeper Eber Rice of Pelham Township. He was charged with 'keeping a disorderly house,' and although witnesses were reluctant to testify against him, they eventually did so, stating that at Rice's inn people were seen 'raffling with dice, for Money, Knives and handkerchiefs ... [and] playing at Skittles, or Nine pins.' But what really had the neighbours disturbed were the 'women of BAD CHARACTER from Buffalo' whose 'conduct was such by running about by day and by night that [witness David McAlpin] did not think them decent Girls. ... ' This was not, of course, the last time that 'girls from Buffalo' were to put in an appearance in the Niagara region.

From 1832 to 1843 the Promenade was owned by Colonel Philip Delatre, a British officer who had served in Ceylon. He lived at Lundy's Lane and undoubtedly leased the establishment to someone else, as did the next owner, Robert Melville. But the Promenade really came into its own when Richard Howard took over in 1845. On 2 July of that year the new owner proudly announced in the *Niagara Chronicle* the opening of Howard's Hotel.

The Angel Inn, Regent Street: doing a thriving business in 1826

HOWARD'S HOTEL

Richard Howard returns his sincere thanks to his friends and the public generally for the very liberal patronage afforded him during a period of more than twenty years. Finding the accommodation of his old stand, the 'Angel Inn' too limited, and at the suggestion of many influential friends, he has fitted up the house formerly called the Promenade House and is now prepared to receive visitors. Boarders will be accommodated liberally and satisfactorily.

R. Howard

Howard's became *the* place to stay during the middle years of the century, when Niagara was in its heyday. Richard Bonnycastle visited there in 1846, the year after Howard took over, and called it 'the most respectable [inn] in town.' He referred to the place as Howard's Inn, but by the following year its owner had adopted a more up-to-date title, calling it Howard's Hotel. Whatever its name, Howard's was a popular spot. It accommodated more people than its size today would indicate, for a rear wing once stretched along Regent Street. Howard lost his first wife, Sarah, the year after he purchased the Promenade, but he remarried when he was about fifty years old. His new wife, Elizabeth, presented him with a second family, two daughters being born to them in the late 1850s.

Richard Howard had started in business as the proprietor of the Angel Inn at 224 Regent Street, an establishment he had purchased after its owner, John Ross, advertised it for sale in the *Gleaner* of 19 June 1826. Ross described it as 'that excellent TAVERN and STAND known by the Sign of the Angel Inn ... at the corner of the Market square.' As Richard Howard was at that time only about nineteen years old, it seems likely that he leased the inn for a time before buying it. His name was connected with the Angel until he purchased the Promenade in 1845.

Howard sold the Angel Inn to John Fraser, a Scottish innkeeper who changed the name to the Mansion House and then to Fraser's Hotel. Today it is known once again as the Angel Inn, although its appearance is markedly different from what it once was. Many structural changes have been made, and the original siding has been covered with pebble-dash. In an age when so many frame inns came to a flaming end, somehow the Angel Inn managed to avoid that fate, so that it is one of the oldest buildings of its type still being used for its original purpose. The Angel has, over its many years, accommodated a library, church services, and an apothecary shop where a pioneer doctor performed blood-letting.

On the day before Christmas 1847, an advertisement in the *Niagara Herald* lured customers to Howard's new hotel, the former Promenade.

DAGUERREOTYPE LIKENESSES
Secure the Shadow 'ere the Substance fade.

Announcing that they had taken rooms at Howard's Hotel for this purpose, Howard Milne and Co. urged every man in town to preserve the likenesses of their loved ones, those 'who are so liable to be snatched away from his fond embrace' or of themselves 'as a solemn memento to his posterity, that he once lived, moved, walked and talked on this green earth.'

The business of benefiting posterity by catching daguerreotype likenesses of loved ones was only one of a host of wonderful and varied enterprises that took place in nineteenth-century hostelries. They were the catch-all for every new entrepreneurial adventure imaginable. At the same time that Milne and Co. were working at top speed before the loved one was snatched away, a doctor was treating patients, and travelling artists were displaying their works amid the comforts of Howard's Hotel. Travelling salesmen were welcome for the entertainment they provided while peddling their wares. All these people, of course, attracted customers to the inn.

Travelling players made halfway houses the first theatres in the province. Edward Ermatinger found himself almost on stage while staying at an inn in St Thomas in 1830. On returning to his room in the evening he discovered

> Mr Long's company in possession of my bedroom, which served them as the 'behind the scenes,' it being at the end of a long room and the end of the stage. Paid 12½ cents, or a York shilling, to see the performance, which consisted of slack-wire dancing, balancing tobacco pipes, sword, and plate, hatching chickens in a hat, the bull frogs and a sucking pig, tumbling etc.

Church services were held in inns and, in the case of the Black Horse Tavern in Albion Township, a burial ground was located there as well. The Black Horse Tavern cemetery was a Methodist burying-ground with forty-four interments dating from 1865. Fox hunts and local horse races had their headquarters at inns. Horses frequently visited inns in another capacity, as advertised to the public in the *Niagara Herald* of 2 May 1801 by G. Drake, a Yankee tavern-keeper who had just purchased the Lion Tavern in Niagara:

PRODIGAL
A Stout and Well Made horse, full 15 hands high
Will Stand at the Lion Tavern in Niagara every Thursday
... two dollars the Single Leap.

> Prodigal, if he cannot boast of a noble pedigree, possesses as many good qualities as any that pretend to trace back their ancestors to the horse that Alexander rode when he conquered the world, or that on which the Spartan general, Leonidas, sat during the never to be forgotten battle at the Straits of Thermopylae ...

The *Gleaner* of 19 August 1826 announced that A. Crysler, innkeeper, had procured one of the most popular of entertainments for his inn. The Royal Circus would be stopping there for a few evenings. Circuses nearly always set up their tents at an inn – good audiences were guaranteed, and the performers were assured of their comforts. The program sounded spectacular:

> The performance will commence with a Grand Military Cavalcade By six beautiful chargers which will lie down, sit up, and go through other manoeuvres.
>
> Horsemanship
>
> By Master Lesslie, the undaunted youth who will introduce a number of surprising feats never attempted by any person of his age, being only ten years old, in which he will go through the stirrup tricks and conclude with the arduous task of riding on his head.

Various other feats of vaulting were to take place, and then:

> The whole to conclude with the Hunted Tailor or Billy Buttons' Journey to Brentwood as performed for twenty nights in succession with unbounded applause.

Adam Crysler, the innkeeper who arranged this coup, had connections both with the Niagara Hotel of Alexander Rogers on Prideaux Street and the Niagara Coffee House of James Rogers on Queen Street. It is not certain at which of these establishments the circus took place – one of many tantalizing gaps in the history of the inns of Niagara and, in fact, of Ontario.

Innkeepers sometimes seemed to have one hand on the bottle and one eye on the hostelry down the street, ever ready to make a move to a more promising location. Niagara sprouted some twenty-eight taverns after the War of 1812, and their proximity to each other created a situation in which proprietors were virtually passing each other on the street as they moved to do business in that new and greener field. Often a change in proprietor meant a change in name, and this, coupled with the fact that there was a penchant for names that showed pride in the town, resulted in a plethora of such names as Niagara Hotel, Niagara Mansion House, Niagara Mansion House Hotel, Niagara Coffee House, and more. As well, some families were skilled at the business and had several members operating inns at the same time in the same town. The Niagara Hotel and the Niagara Coffee House are examples of the confusion.

Alexander Rogers's inn (no longer standing) did a brisk business for many years. It was located on Prideaux Street near Gate Street. It was also called the Niagara Hotel, and was run by Rogers and his wife, Agnes. The Rogerses owned the piece of property that spanned the block between Prideaux and Queen streets. On the Queen Street side of the property stood a Rogers house that became the Niagara Coffee House. Agnes Rogers, when widowed, was associated with both these houses. In later years Adam Crysler also worked at both stands. Also on Prideaux Street was the Niagara Mansion House, operated by John Brown. (Down the street, happily unique in its name, was the Promenade.)

In 1837, when Adam Crysler was proprietor of the Niagara Hotel on Prideaux

DANCING SCHOOL!

MR. B. KINGMAN having proposed to teach a *DANCING SCHOOL* respectfully informs those who wish to attend, that he will commence on Thursday next, the 4th of February at Mr. *A. Rogers'* Hotel.

Niagara, Jan. 28.

Niagara Spectator, 28 January 1819

James Rogers's Niagara Coffee House of many names and many owners

Street, David Wilkie, travelling to New York and Canada, wrote a spirited account of a night spent there. The Niagara Hotel, he recalled, was a rollicking place, with 'roaring and rumbling, smoking and tippling,' and when the host led Wilkie and his companion through two rooms to a third, they found it contained two double beds, one of which was already occupied. Worried about their valuables they placed these under their pillows and sank wearily onto their bed, but awakened abruptly within the hour to experience 'a most indescribable feeling of uncertainty and horror,' from 'a pair of long hands, fingering with utmost caution the bedclothing at our feet, and gradually creeping upwards, moving over our bodies with the circumspection of a pawing tiger.'

Front door, Niagara Coffee House

When the fingers reached his nose, a 'prominence with which no man or woman will ever allow undue liberties to be taken with impunity,' Wilkie grabbed the intruder with a shout and found that he was one of their room-mates, somewhat the worse for wear and searching on his hands and knees for the window. A swift kick from Wilkie's now angry friend sent the wanderer scurrying back to his bed.

Directly behind the Niagara Hotel, at 157 Queen Street, James Rogers established a business that started out in a circumspect manner as the Niagara Coffee House. He proudly announced its opening in the Niagara *Gleaner* of 4 July 1817:

> Niagara
> Coffee House
> James Rogers
> Respectfully informs the public that having completed his large and commodious House, on Queen Street in this town near the centre of the village, he is now prepared to entertain
> Genteel Company
> in handsome style and on reasonable terms; the utmost attention will be paid at all times to give satisfaction to those who may honour him with a call. His liquors will be pure and his table supplied with the best the market affords.
> Stabling good, and well attended.
> Niagara, July 4, 1817

Coffee houses were a product of the political and social scene in England. They were traditionally meeting places for the upper classes to gossip and discuss the events of the day. James Rogers called his establishment a coffee house in order to give it a more prestigious air but, hoping for the best of both worlds, he offered alcoholic refreshment as well.

The Rogers family were living in Niagara when the village was reduced to ashes during the War of 1812. They could have saved their house, since they were related to some of the retreating soldiers, but they were warned that they might be accused of sympathizing with the enemy if they took advantage of this relationship. So their home burned with the rest, and only a mantelpiece from it was saved, carried out by the intrepid Mrs Rogers as she fled the flames. This may have been the Baroque Germanic mantelpiece seen today in the coffee house that James Rogers built in 1817 to replace the original building. James Rogers lived only a short while after opening his establishment, but it remained in the family for many years, operated by a succession of proprietors, one of whom was Agnes Rogers, widow of Alexander Rogers. Papers remain to indicate that she presided over major additions to the building in 1823.

Charles Koune, the next proprietor, renamed it the Duke of Richmond Coffee House to commemorate the Duke's tragic death the previous year. By 1828, Robert Gray had taken over, and he, with a singular lack of originality, renamed the place Niagara House. The *Gleaner* of 30 June 1828 gave the change some modest praise:

> Mr Robert Gray is about opening an elegant house of entertainment in the House in Queen Street, formerly occupied by Mr Charles Koune. We do think that the establishment will be conducted by Mr Gray in a proper manner.

There are indications that a rear wing once provided additional space, and it seems likely that this wing had the galleries that allowed guests to view the countryside where, as Robert Gray boasted in an advertisement, 'the noble Niagara is seen emptying the waters of the great Western lakes into the bosom of Ontario.'

The house at 118–20 Johnson Street was built at least a dozen years before it became an inn, either by Peter McDougall, who owned the property until 1830, or by a hatter with the memorable name of Jared Stocking to whom McDougall sold. Stocking had a lucrative business by virtue of his hat stores in Niagara and St Catharines ('Beaver and Imitation Hats, Castor, Ror-

The Sign of the Crown: William Moffatt's inn, later a school

um & napt Mens' and Boys' Hats ... Ladies' Beaver Bonnets, Black and Drab assorted patterns'). In 1836 Stocking sold to William Moffatt, who named his inn 'The Sign of the Crown.' But in little more than a year Moffatt was moving on, according to the Niagara *Reporter* of 3 Oct 1837, which announced:

> To Be Sold or Let
>
> And possession given immediately – an excellent Tavern stand two storeys high, Sign of the Crown, situated in the Town of Niagara, belonging to Wm Moffatt ... consisting of eight Bed Rooms, two Dining Do., a kitchen and pantry – stabling for four span of horses, an excellent shed 18 feet by 32 together with a beautiful garden containing half an acre well stocked with the choicest of Fruit trees and Currant Bushes – Also an excellent well of Water within two or three yards of the door.

For whatever reason, Moffatt's hostelry didn't sell, and he leased the establishment to a schoolteacher, who announced in the *Niagara Chronicle* of 30 May 1838 that 'An evening Class will be opened on Monday the 28th inst. at Mr Platts house (formerly Wm Moffatt's Tavern) and instructions given in Writing, Arithmetic and the usual branches of English education. A French class will also be opened.'

The 1851 census showed that William Moffatt was still an innkeeper, and that one Richard Moffatt, who at forty-nine years of age was four years younger than William, also ran a hostelry in town. It, to confuse matters, was called Moffatt's Hotel, a substantial frame building at 60 Picton Street that Richard purchased in 1834.

The Whale Inn on King Street inspired poetry in its guests.

Possibly the two men were brothers. Richard Moffatt died during the 1850s, but his wife, Mary, continued to run the hotel for several years after his death.

The Whale Inn at 66 King Street had, by the middle of this century, fallen into a state of such disrepair that only a far-sighted and energetic optimist could envisage its possibilities. It was for years one of the town's most popular hostelries built, as were the Moffatts' hotels, in the mid-1830s. Niagara was a growing town with new industries, a busy shipyard, and a generally thriving economy. The full impact of William Merritt's newly opened Welland Canal (which bypassed Niagara and Niagara Falls) had yet to be felt.

Built originally to cater to sailors on Lake

Ontario – a body of water not particularly well known to whalers – the Whale Inn later was called the Elliot House after its owner, Walter Elliot. He, his wife, Mary (both from Scotland), and their son, Thomas, ran the inn, with Thomas carrying on after his father's death. Eventually two of Thomas Elliot's three daughters operated it as a summer hotel. An anonymous poet recalled those halcyon days and in later years penned a nostalgic poem that made up in sincerity for what it lacked in skill:

An Ancient Niagara Inn

No bumptious roar of bus or car
Disturbs my slumbers ever
And I am fain to love you more
Old Whale Inn by the river

Full nigh one hundred years have waned
And passed away since you
Built up with care and loving hand
And deft construction, grew ...

But time has changed all this anon;
Gone is the mast and sail,
Two gentle ladies carry on
The old Inn of the Whale.

Like the Moffatts' hotels, the Whale Inn has a five-bay front. Above the front door, an oval plaque showing clasped hands served as an identifying mark so that firefighters, who protected only their own customers, would know that the house was insured. To the left of the centre hall a taproom catered to visiting sailors, while the parlour on the right welcomed ladies, children, and overnight guests. The kitchen, a half flight down at the rear, was dominated by a huge fireplace.

An 1839 sketch of Niagara showed the Whale Inn at the foot of King Street. That same year Walter Elliot advertised a lottery for prizes worth six hundred and eighty-four dollars, including:

1 dun-coloured horse
1 grey mare
1 double-horse waggon
1 bay horse
1 double-barrelled Gun and case
1 milch cow

and various harnesses, sleighs, and saddles.

Inns were the natural places to advertise and conduct sales of all kinds – lotteries such as Elliot's, sales of Crown lands, and auctions were regularly held there. If someone died leaving no money for funeral expenses, the coroner would offer the deceased's meagre personal effects for public auction at the local inn, including every last handkerchief and nightcap.

Just south of the Whale Inn, at the corner of King and Prideaux, is one of the first buildings to be constructed after the fire of 1813. Local legend has it that it was made with stones from the foundations of buildings destroyed in that fire. Built as a residence, it was taken over prior to 1830 by James Miller who, after 'fitting it up in superior style for the reception of genteel company' called the place (what else?) the Niagara Coffee House. (James Rogers's Queen Street establishment of the same name had, by this time, been renamed several times.)

Over the years the building served as a store, a private school, a barracks, a public school, and then, in 1860, became home to the Masonic Lodge. Formed in 1793 as the Provincial Grand Lodge, its early membership consisted of virtually everyone who was anyone in Niagara. The brethren worked to assist the widows and orphans of deceased members, their operations veiled in the requisite secrecy.

In September 1826, however, the Freemasons were caught up in a scandal that soon had the town in an uproar. It began with the disappearance of Captain William Morgan, a man accused of writing a book that betrayed the secrets of Freemasonry. The river was dragged, to no avail, and Morgan's disappearance was never solved. The hubbub continued for a long time, with emotions at a fever pitch. 'We condemn as much as the abduction of

Store, barracks, school, and Masonic Lodge – James Miller's Coffee House

Morgan,' thundered the Niagara *Gleaner* of 24 September 1827,

> the machinations and contrivances of free masons. There is not a thinking man so lost to reason as not to know that the evil demon strides abroad on the earth and like a venomous serpent flings forth its poison. When these unholy bindings are snapped asunder, justice, as it should prevail will have free course, and jurymen unawed by the dread of death in darkness will do their duty.

Women, too, had their say. They met in groups to urge other women to have nothing to do with Freemasons and advocated that mothers tell their daughters not to marry them.

Of course the furore eventually died down, as it was bound to do, for many of the Freemasons were among the leading citizens of the community. As the incident occurred well before the move to the stone barracks in 1860, the Masonic meetings were being held in the only logical place – in the town's popular hostelries. After all, most of the innkeepers in town were Freemasons. At the time, the favourite taverns were the Niagara Hotel of Alexander Rogers, the Niagara Coffee House of James Rogers, Moffatt's Hotel, and the Angel Inn.

A mid-century fire destroyed some of the early records of the Masonic Lodge and, presumably, any references there might have been to the unfortunate Captain Morgan. A recent restoration has given renewed life to this elegant building that has played such a significant part in Niagara's history. Hand-painted Masonic symbols have been preserved, as has some of the furniture, including the deacon's benches where the loyal brethren once sat.

In 1842 the town of Niagara contained twenty-eight taverns, so it was understandable that a few temperance houses opened. They tried to offer alternative service, but with little success, and by and large they didn't last long. A Mr Eedson operated such an establishment in the pleasant frame house at 244 King Street, but it lasted for only a year, after which its Irish-born owner, Thomas Dority, had to look for another tenant.

Generally speaking those taverns serving the usual alcoholic refreshments were the ones to prosper. In the winter of 1825, one particularly enterprising individual built a temporary tavern on the frozen surface of the Niagara River, operating it until the spring thaw made it advisable to relocate.

Some tavern-keepers tried to make both tipplers and temperance advocates happy by offering, along with the usual liquor, an ale that, according to an advertisement by John Martindale in the *Gleaner* of 13 February 1830, 'may be drank freely by the most determined enemies of Intemperance without injuring either soul or body.' Nor were Martindale's customers the only ones to stray from the straight and narrow, for the Lundy's Lane Temperance Society reported in the same paper that its members were taking the term 'BODILY INFIRMITY' too literally.

Of all the early hotels in Niagara, the two best-known today are the Prince of Wales at the corner of King and Picton streets and the Oban Inn on Gate Street. Built as a private home in 1824, the Oban Inn did not become a hotel until 1870, when a second storey was added. Likewise the Prince of Wales, although it began business in the 1860s, bore little resemblance to the building seen today, an 1882 addition to the original.

As early as the 1790s, coaches were operating along the trail that led from Newark through Queenston to Niagara Falls, Chippawa, and Fort Erie. Queenston at this time was an unremarkable and quiet village of three hundred souls, but in October 1812 it found a place in Canadian history when the revered Major-General Sir Isaac Brock fell at Queenston Heights while leading his troops against an American battery. His tragic death brought grief and despair to Canadians and to the defending British forces.

Brock was not quickly forgotten. He was, in fact, honoured with a grand total of four funerals and four separate burials. The first funeral took place when Brock and Lieutenant-Colonel John Macdonell, who was also killed in the battle, were buried at Fort George near Niagara, three days after they died. A host of military and civic dignitaries were there to mourn their passing. Then, in 1824, a second funeral was held when the two men were reinterred in the base of a tall, impressive monument built in Brock's honour at Queenston Heights. Thousands of people, including Scots in Highland dress and John Brant with Indians of the Six Nations, formed a two-mile-long procession to the monument, with the bodies of Brock and Macdonell carried in a wagon drawn by four black horses.

A third funeral became necessary when, in the spring of 1840, Benjamin Lett, an Irish-Canadian rebel, destroyed the massive monument with a huge blast of gunpowder. Once again the bodies were disinterred and reburied in the nearby Hamilton family cemetery, where they stayed until 13 October 1853, the anniversary of the battle. The remains were then moved for the last time to the base of a lofty new monument. Thousands of people attended that event, too, including James B. Secord, a grandson of Laura Secord. (The occasion was particularly memorable for young Secord – he was inadvertently

Queenston's South Landing Inn, built following the War of 1812–14

locked in the tomb and not rescued until the next morning, having spent a terrifying night with only the heroes' remains for company.)

What with the four funerals for Isaac Brock and the thousands of people who in following years came to pay their respects at the battle site, the need for inns at Queenston was apparent. Even before the completion of the second monument, there were six taverns in the village, catering to visitors and locals alike.

Within a few blocks of where Brock fell stands an impressive two-storey frame inn, its wide verandahs offering a magnificent view of the Niagara River. Recently restored and once again a comfortable hostelry, it is now called the South Landing Inn.

The building may have been constructed shortly after the War of 1812. In any event, it was there in 1825 when an anonymous artist painted a picture of the village. During these years the property was owned by the influential Thomas Dickson, a successful merchant and Collector of Customs at Queenston. Dickson's first home, built before the war, stood close to the river, a somewhat hazardous location with the ever-threatening Yankees on the other side.

FOR SALE,
1600 *Gallons*
Rectified Whiskey,
AT
W. G. HEPBURNE & SON'S.
Queenston, April 1st, 1819.
5tf

Niagara Spectator, 29 July 1819

Dickson, one of ten children born into a distinguished family in Dumfries, Scotland, had come to Upper Canada as a boy and by the beginning of the nineteenth century had settled at Queenston. During the War of 1812 he served as a captain in the militia, earning a footnote in the history books for his courageous actions of 11 October 1812, when in the company of Lieutenant-Colonel Thomas Evans he crossed the Niagara River under a hail of musket balls to request an exchange of prisoners, a message the two men hoped to deliver to the American general, Stephen Van Rensselaer. Carrying a white flag of truce supplied by Dickson's wife, Archange, the two set forth in a canoe amidst, as Evans reported, 'an unsparing shower of shot which fell all around us.' So alarmed were the pair by their assessment of the Americans' strength that, when they returned to Queenston a few hours later, Dickson hurriedly moved his family from their unprotected home on the beach to a safer place away from the action.

Thomas Dickson died in 1825. The following year his widow, Archange, decided to sell their home, which she described as: 'a large and commodious dwelling house ... capable of containing two families.'

By 1830, the building was owned by Solomon Vrooman. His descendant, Jacob Vrooman, sold to Daniel Quackenbush in 1837, and from then until the mid-1860s the building was known as the Quackenbush Hotel. Queenston by this time had settled into comfortable obscurity. According to J. Caruthers, a traveller of the period, it had become 'a little, old, tumble-down village.'

In later years, the proprietor was James Wadsworth, a man well known for his smuggling proclivities. If indeed he was a smuggler, he was not alone. Smuggling was a way of life in those parts, and, according to one old-timer, 'no stigma in those times clung to the sobriquet of "smuggler" nor was it a crime to beat the customs officers.' Stones, he said, were piled at intervals along the road, to be used as ammunition when necessary during fights with these officials. One inn proudly announced on its sign that it was called the 'Smugglers' Home.' With the onset of prohibition in the United States, ambitious Canadians found a lucrative market in Buffalo. They were happy to meet the needs of thirsty Americans, and 'smuggling the filled barrels across the ice to Buffalo kept the smugglers in ready cash after the lake was frozen.'

A figure as towering as Isaac Brock attracts legends, and one such concerns an innkeeper in the St Catharines area who located on what is now Highway 8, lot 6, concession 5, Louth Township. His name was John McCarthy, and he, it was said, was the man who shot the man who shot Brock. McCarthy may or may not have been responsible for the deed, but the story was good for business.

The frame building known as McCarthy's Tavern was built in two stages. The stone part at the rear was built first and dates from the 1812 period when the land was owned by Richard Phillips. McCarthy bought the property in 1828 from James Crooks. Two years later he married Mary Price of Louth, built a frame addition at the front, and operated an inn and stage stop.

Smuggling stories were not confined to Queenston. They turn up time and time again near points of entry and wherever the US border beckoned enticingly to Canadians who harboured an entrepreneurial spirit, unencumbered by respect for the law. Nowhere have the stories been more numerous, imaginative, or long-lasting than in Fort Erie at the south end of the Niagara River, where Bertie Hall, a dramatic-looking structure at 657 Niagara Boulevard, is said to have been the home of smugglers and bootleggers as well as a 'station' on the underground railway. It was also, for a few years, a hotel.

William Forsyth, builder of Bertie Hall, was one of the more colourful characters to enliven the scene along the Niagara Frontier during the early years of the nineteenth century. The son of Loyalists who settled in

The Bertie Hall Hotel, home of William Forsyth

the area in 1783, Forsyth gained renown as landlord of the Pavilion Hotel at Niagara Falls, where, along with entertaining a steady stream of guests, he operated a tour boat, conducted sight-seeing tours, and for many years fought a government decision to remove the high fences that he had erected around his hotel. It was a losing battle. The wily Forsyth had attempted to monopolize the tourist trade at the falls by fencing off not only his own property but also the government's sixty-six-foot right-of-way on the river bank, thus ensuring that only his guests at the Pavilion could enjoy the view. Twice Lieutenant-Governor Sir Peregrine Maitland had the fences levelled while Forsyth engaged in lengthy and futile legal arguments.

In 1832 Forsyth gave up the struggle and moved with his family to Bertie Township and the village of Fort Erie. Within a few years he had completed construction of the stately Bertie Hall, its soaring Doric columns and classic splendour providing a startling contrast to the surrounding wilderness and the few unremarkable buildings that then constituted Fort Erie.

Bertie Hall was, of necessity, spacious, since the Forsyth family for whom it was built needed every bit of room it offered. Adam Fergusson, who met William Forsyth at about this time, described him as a shrewd man and well informed. His accomplishments were many. 'Mr Forsyth,' wrote Fergusson, 'may be said to have satisfactorily fulfilled one duty of a colonist, by no means unimportant. When I enquired of him, whether his family was numerous, "Why," says he, "Sir, I don't know what you call numerous; I've raised nineteen, ten by my first wife, and nine by my second."' An incomplete list of the Forsyth offspring mentions sixteen, some of whom died young: William, Nelson, Collingwood,

Sophronia, Samuel, Betsy, Melissa, Isaac Brock, Rodney, Wellington, Phebe, Matilda, Elizabeth, Hiram, Jane – and one called, simply, 'baby.'

The rooms at Bertie Hall, while spacious, are few in number. From the entrance hall, a beautifully proportioned staircase curves to the second floor providing added elegance to the interior. Fireplaces originally provided what heat there was. In time the properly proportioned cylindrical Doric columns on the front facade deteriorated and were sheathed in wood.

The Forsyth family retained possession of the house until it was purchased in the early 1870s by Stephen Jarvis of Toronto. Jarvis subdivided the property and, in 1875, sold the south-east corner, including the house, to John Crabbe. For several years afterwards Crabbe operated the Bertie Hall Hotel until, in the early 1890s, he lost it through default.

As recently as 1984, local history buffs claimed to have discovered at last the entrance to a tunnel leading from the high flagstone walls of the basement at Bertie Hall to the Niagara River, three hundred feet away. The existence of such a structure would authenticate one of the many rumours that still surround this intriguing building. Until funds are available, however, the tunnel will remain unexcavated, and the stories of the Forsyth family and their reputed smuggling activities will continue as part of the building's intriguing history.

Old William Forsyth may well have been on hand when, in the days he was running the Pavilion Hotel, the guests on one occasion included Tiger Dunlop and Adam Fergusson. The two were, not surprisingly, fast friends. Fergusson credited the Tiger with introducing him to a refreshing drink known as a shandygaff. 'I scarce recollect of anything more welcome,' wrote Fergusson,

> than a beverage with which my companion regaled me at Forsyth's, under some odd name, but which consisted of a bottle of good brown stout, turned into a quart of iced water, with a quant. suff. of ginger, cinnamon and sugar; truly it was a prescription worthy of being filed.

The Talbot Trail

JAMES FULTON.
Richmond Hill, Markham. Nov. 13th, 1829. 2873

Stray Ox and Steer.

Broke into the inclosure of the Subscriber, a LARGE OX, blind of the off eye, with seven wrinkles on his horn, a yellowish Red and White colour; also a RED STEER with him, nearly three years old; with a brindle face, and part white under his breast. The owner or owners are requested to prove property, pay charges, and take the animals away.

... indeed for cash, or if one half or one third of the purchase money is paid down. Immediate possession can be given, and, for further particulars apply to PHILIP CODY.
Toronto, Nov. 16th, 1829. 287z.

WHERE IS WILLIAM SUTHERLAND?

THE Subscriber is desirous of ascertaining the place of abode of Mr. William Sutherland and family. They lived in or near Glengarry, about the time of the last war, and were originally from the parish of Kildonan, Sutherlandshire. Address a letter to the Subscriber, at Niagara, care of Messrs. Chrysler, Merchants.
N. B. Mrs. Sutherland's maiden name was Catharine Macpherson.
DANIEL MACPHERSON.
Niagara, 17th Nov. 1829. 2873.

Boarding.

THE Subscriber can furnish Boarding, Lodging, &c. for six steady mechanics, reasonable, on Dundas Street, between Mr. Willmot's Tavern and four doors from Mr. Bird's Tavern, in the house lately occupied by Mr. George Hutchison, Plaisterer.
JAMES PARKER.
Nov. 18. 87.

STRAYED, on the 10th October last, into the premises of ANDREW BIGHAM, on lot No. 12, in the first concession of ETOBICOKE, A LIGHT IRON-GREY HORSE, rising five or six years of age.— The owner is requested to prove property, pay charges, and take him away.
Nov. 17. 873.

SAWYER & LABOURERS WANTED.

WANTED by the subscriber, a Sawyer who understands his business, and two men who understand Chopping; to whom liberal encouragement will be given. Apply to JAMES STEPHENS.

NEWMARKET MAIL STAGE.

WILLIAM GARBUTT, having taken the contract for carrying His Majesty's Mails between York and Newmarket, for the next four years, respectfully informs the public that THE MAIL STAGE will start from Joseph Bloor's Hotel, York, on Mondays and Thursdays, at 12 o'clock, noon, and arrive at nine o'clock, the same evening in Newmarket;—and will leave Mr. Barber's Tavern, Newmarket, for York, on Wednesdays and Saturdays, at ... in the morning, and arrive in York at 2 P. M. on the same days.

NEW ARRANGEMENT OF STAGES

Between York and the Carrying Place at the head of the Bay of Quintie.

The above arrangements are in connexion with the Steam Boats *Sir James Kempt* and *Toronto*, so that Travellers going the route will find a pleasant and speedy conveyance between Kingston and York, as the line is now fitted up in good order with good carriages, good horses and careful drivers.
Every attention will be given to render passengers comfortable while on the line, and the drivers instructed to stop at the best hotels on the route.
All baggage at the risk of the owners.
Extras furnished to any part of the country.
The Stage Books will be kept at Mr. Bradley's Steamboat Hotel.

CHAPTER ELEVEN

The Talbot Trail

SLEEPING ACCOMMODATION IN INNS

'The little fleas have lesser fleas
Upon their backs to bite 'em.
The lesser fleas have other fleas
And so ad infinitum.'

Anonymous

Tiger Dunlop was sure of a warm welcome when he paid an unexpected visit to his friend Colonel Thomas Talbot at his log home, Malahide Castle, high on a cliff overlooking Lake Erie. But, typically, Dunlop couldn't resist making a theatrical entrance. Turning his coat and bonnet inside out, he pounded on the door of Talbot's house with a hefty stick. He roared at the frightened servant who answered the door, telling the poor man to go to the devil and 'shake himself.' It was enough to send the servant scurrying up to his master. When Talbot looked out from the balcony over the door at the apparition below, he turned to the servant with instructions to let the visitor in. 'It's either Dunlop,' he said laconically, 'or the devil.'

The two men were fast friends. Both were known throughout Upper Canada. They were successful entrepreneurs in the business of promoting settlement and shared an abiding enthusiasm for their chosen country. Their life-styles and dress were eccentric. Anna Jameson called Talbot the sovereign of Lake Erie, and the same could have been said about Dunlop at Lake Huron. Although both men were 'to the manner born' and ably assumed positions of authority, they empathized with their settlers and managed to share with them their struggles for survival. No one who met either Dunlop or Talbot was likely to forget the experience. Even in an age of rugged individualists, they stood apart.

Thomas Talbot was the moving force behind the settlement of the south-western part of the province along the north shore of Lake Erie. During his lifetime, he settled twenty-nine townships with a population of more than thirty thousand. These communities were called the Talbot settlements. The road also bore his name. Then called Talbot Street, it roughly parallels today's Highway 3, stretching the 250-mile length of Lake Erie, from Fort Erie to Windsor, with a link from Port Talbot to St Thomas and London.

Born at Malahide, Ireland, in 1771, Thomas Talbot spent his early years in the army, receiving his first commission at the tender age of eleven. Talbot and Arthur Wellesley, the future Duke of Wellington, served together and became lifelong friends. When he was in his early twenties, Thomas Talbot arrived in Upper Canada as secretary to Lieutenant-Governor Simcoe. He returned to England in 1794, but six years later, at the age of thirty, sold his commission and returned to Canada,

Colonel Thomas Talbot's homestead, Malahide, on its lonely Lake Erie site

where he spent the rest of his long and lonely life. He died in 1853. During that fifty-year period the Crown granted him 700,000 acres of land in western Ontario. For every family he located there he received 200 acres, 50 for the settler and 150 for himself. (Talbot usually made 100 of his 150 acres available to the settler as well.)

Stories abound about Talbot's drinking bouts and his paternalistic approach, which by today's standards was highly autocratic. He insisted his settlers be persons of 'wholesome habits and moral character' in order to obtain a lease. Talbot, of course, was the sole judge of those attributes. But those who knew him well spoke of him warmly. Elizabeth Simcoe enjoyed his stimulating company and their wild horseback rides on Toronto Island during their days at York. Anna Jameson called him good-humoured and jovial. George Munro, an early settler who had known Talbot for many years, spoke of the Colonel as 'eccentric, laconic, and truly noble and honorable' and a man who unfailingly assisted those settlers who were sick or needy. In winter he enjoyed taking young people of the district on sleigh rides. 'No one,' said Munro, 'ever served him who did not love him sincerely and devotedly.' When he died he left his considerable estate to his servants.

Rarely does the name Thomas Talbot appear in Canadian histories without the adjective 'eccentric' tacked to it. Presumably he was. A lineal descendant of the kings of Ireland, he lived like a hermit. In 1803 Talbot located his isolated home west of what is now Port Stanley in a long stretch of unbroken forest between Long Point and Amherstburg. There were only male servants in Malahide Castle. Guests sometimes found their visit abruptly terminated when Talbot called for their horses in the middle of the meal, possibly because he suffered fools not at all. The Colonel milked his own cows and made his own bread. His clothing certainly caused comment. He chose to wear homespun garments like those of the settlers and in winter sported a bulky sheepskin coat that, given his short stature, tended to make him look not unlike a perambulating snowball.

While not technically an inn, the Colonel's home, Malahide Castle, housed many a travelling Britisher as well as Scottish, Welsh, and Irish immigrants who were selecting their land allotments and picking up supplies. To encourage settlement Talbot persuaded the government that a road was necessary along the north shore of Lake Erie. In 1809 a trail of sorts was begun, but it was years before it became passable. Prior to that the twelve families who were Talbot's only settlers relied on the Colonel for necessary supplies and shelter. The only source of food was Fort Erie at the eastern end of the lake, and supplies were transported to Malahide Castle by boat. Closer at hand but still sixty miles east of Talbot's was a fledgling community called Long Point.

About 1810 an Englishman arrived on the shore of Lake Erie at the mouth of Potter's Creek on Long Point Bay. He was John Mason, an ironmaster who had heard of the plentiful ore deposits in the area and decided to build an iron smelter. Mason died before his smelter was operative, and his widow was left with an untested operation to sell. In 1821, a partnership of enthusiastic Americans took up the challenge. They were Hiram Capron, founder of the town of Paris, and George Tillson and Joseph Van Norman, after whom Tillsonburg and Normandale were named.

In 1827 the brothers Joseph and Benjamin Van Norman bought out their partners' interests, formed Van Norman and Co., and founded Normandale on the north shore of Lake Erie, a village that before long became home to nearly 750 people. In the London district alone, one in every thirty people depended for a livelihood in one way or another on the Normandale furnace. Normandale was a progressive community, for the prospering Van Norman furnace required an ever-increasing number of workers to meet the demand for the iron products produced there. Their cook stoves were particularly popular.

The Union Hotel in Normandale was built in the 1830s by the Van Normans when the foundry was busy and the village was prospering. The traffic to and from Normandale made the building of an inn a necessity. Farmers were bringing huge quantities of wood required for charcoal; teamsters and ships carried ironware to markets as far away as Kingston and Chicago.

Van Norman's foundry had a short-lived heyday. After only twenty years the ore and charcoal needed for the furnace ran out. (The inn has outlasted Van Norman's iron foundry by more than 150 years.) After an ill-fated attempt to prosper with a foundry at Marmora, Van Norman and his family settled in Tillsonburg, where he became a manufacturer of bricks and shingles. After a long and difficult life (he and his wife, Roxilana Robinson, were predeceased by seven of their eleven children), Joseph Van Norman died on 14 June 1888, at the age of ninety-two. Highly respected, he was, according to a biographer, 'one of the most hospitable men that ever lived in these parts, his door standing open for fifty years for the entrance of the weary traveller ... the hungry he never turned empty away.'

The Van Normans sold the Union Hotel in 1842 and, after two brief changes of ownership, it was purchased by John Day Post the following year. Post had been raised in the inn. His father, a doctor, left Normandale after his wife's death and was persuaded to leave his son behind with Abraham Post, then employed by Van Norman as proprietor of the Union Hotel. John Day, considering himself abandoned by his family, took the Post name and eventually purchased the business. He ran it until 1859. Newspaper advertisements indicate that the hotel continued to be successful. James N. Spain, proprietor, announced in 1875 that:

> The subscriber has leased the above premises for a Term of years and having thoroughly refitted it is prepared to furnish the Public with first-class accommodation. The best

The Union Hotel, in once-bustling Normandale

brands of Liquors and Cigars kept constantly on hand. Good stabling and an attentive and careful Hostler always in attendance.

In 1813 five Quaker families from Pennsylvania, led by Jonathan Doan, founded the village of Sparta. It lay east of Thomas Talbot's home and south-east of St Thomas (which was so named in honour of the Colonel). Sparta's two-storey frame inn with its verandah overlooking the main intersection was the focal point of this lovely peaceful village. The recently restored inn stands today at the north-west corner of Highway 73 and Sparta Road.

For many years David Mills, son of an early Quaker settler, operated the local inn. He was one of three Quaker tavern-keepers in Sparta. The inn was called Sparta House, a fact announced on a sign swinging from a tall pole in front of the building. It was noted for its large kitchen and ballroom. Although it is believed locally that Mills built the inn, it seems probable that its first proprietor was John McDowell. Innkeeper McDowell was keeping tavern in Sparta in 1844, a fact that he advertised in the *True Teller* on 20 April of that year. A short-lived publication, the *True Teller* made up in charm what it lacked in professionalism. The only surviving issue is a unique document. Printed by hand, it reports a race held between two contestants, innkeeper John McDowell's 'chestnut sorrel Horse,

The old Sparta stage

Oregon, and Lowel Morton, Esq:'s Brown Mare Betsy.' The race

> came off about one mile out of the village of Sparta, on Saterday 13 inst, when after a Keen Race, the horse [McDowell's] was the winer by a very short distance, the stakes was honourably given up by the losing party ... afterwards, a shakepurse Race, took place when three horses started after a considerable jockeying, it was won by Mr Morton's Brown Mare, Betsy, who was rode by the celebrated Rider, Sir Isaac Moore, who on this occasion showed his admirable skill.

After Mills sold Sparta House it became a store and then a furniture and undertaking business. Today on the main floor a tearoom offers refreshment to travellers who, sometimes purely by chance, discover this almost untouched village, which, by good fortune remained in sleepy anonymity for the better part of a century and has therefore retained much of the flavour of the eighteen-hundreds.

Across the street from the Sparta House was the Elgin House, an establishment that John McDowell took over in 1853 after marrying the daughter of fellow Quaker (and equestrian) Isaac Moore, the previous owner. In 1908 an article in the London *Echo* reminisced about Sparta; the writer made no bones about his disapproval of the goings-on at the Elgin House. The hotel, he recalled was

> a rambling, low-blow and unkempt structure ... Modest women chose to walk in the roadway rather than challenge the attention of the soggy occupants of a row of chairs that stood up-tilted before its doors.

In due time the women had their day. Eighty local ladies formed the Sparta Public House Company, whose aims were 'promoting Social Purity [and the] increase of

The archetypal inn, the Sparta House graces the Quaker settlement of Sparta.

wholesome home influence.'

Wallowing through the isolated Talbot roads along Lake Erie or mired in the parallel Windsor-to-Chatham route, travellers encountered striking contrasts in accommodation. As the area became more settled, well-appointed hostelries became available. Four-posters, feather beds, and such amenities as looking-glasses and wash-stands were popular with the travelling public. At the other extreme were log huts in which a bed shared with a stranger was the best that could be expected. Anna Jameson, staying in one such hovel near Chatham, said 'To understand the full force of the scripture phrase "desolate as a lodge in a wilderness" you should come here!'

In Leamington, at the western end of the Talbot Road where it takes a swing northwest towards Windsor, Wigle's Tavern offered what English traveller W.H. Smith called 'the most comfortable quarters to be found between Amherstburg and Morpeth; a fair specimen of what industry and perseverance will accomplish in Canada,' And he was right. Leonard Wigle and his wife, Jane, were fine, hard-working people – the kind that our ancestors were purported to be. For thirty-eight years they operated their tavern by the Talbot Road, and so loved were they by everyone who knew them that they were generally referred to as Uncle Leonard and Aunt Jane. It was Jane Wigle who always made sure that a lighted candle was placed in the tavern window at sunset to guide travellers on the road.

Leonard Wigle, of German descent, was one of fifteen children of John and Susanna Wigle who settled in Essex County near the turn of the century. Jane was English-born but came to Canada as a girl; her family stopped briefly with Colonel Talbot while they waited for the land tickets that were necessary before they could settle on their property. In November 1824

F. St. A.

THE TRUE TELLER.

INDEPENDENT ON ALL SUBJECTS.

VOL I. SPARTA, [C.W.] SATURDAY, APRIL 20 1844, No 3

THE TRUE TELLER.

PUBLISHED EVERY SATURDAY.
S. PATCH. - - - - EDITOR.
TERMS. Three Dollars per Annum,
JOB Printing, Executed at this office, old ABBEY up Stairs.

BUSINESS DIRECTOR

L. LANSDELL.
Fashionable Tailor. Me. st.

J. McDOWELL
Sparta House. Me, St.

H. B. SMITH.
Merchant Tailor. Me, St.

J. A EAKINS'.
Dealer in Dry Goods &c. Me. St.

A. NELLIS.
Harness and Sadle Maker. Me. St.

C.D. NEWCOMBE.
Dealer in Dry Goods &c. Me. St.

E. GRAVES.
BOOT & SHOE MaKer, Me. St.

F. St AUGUSTINE.
Painter & Glazier &c. Me. St.

J. CHASE.
Manufacturer of Scythes. E. Me. St.

D. WILLSON.
Physician, Surgeon. Dentist. Me. St.
Post office Me. St.

H. CARTER.
Black SMITH'S Shop. Me. St.

L. TEEPLE.
BOOT & SHOE, MAKER. K. st.

J. J JOLLY.
Black SMITH, SHOP. Me. St.

Farm For Sale.

The subscriber offers for Sale, one of the Best Farms, in Canada, Lot No. 18. 5th concession Yarmouth consisting of 100 Acres. J. Steel,

A CARD.

Miss M. U. CHASE, Beg leave to inform the inhabitants of Sparta, that she is ready to execute all orders in her line of Buissness, as a Tailoress,

Pear Grove East Maine St.

Births

On the 17 Inst. the Wife of Isaac Mills Jun. Farmer South of Yarmouth of a Son.

Deaths.

On the 18th Instant after a short illness wife of E. Graves aged 31 years.

Enigma

I am a word of 21 Letters.
My 1.2.9.11.5.21. is a Kingdom in Europe
13.16.13.14.7.12. is one of the Months of the year
20.1.15.21.2 is a River in africa,
11.2.10.11 is a Lake in America,
15.2.21.21.3.21. is a celebrated country in the acient world
3.8.17, is a Domestic Animal.
And my whole is a celebrated character in Sparta.

An America paper says, in an obituary notice, that the deceased had been for several years a director of a bank, not withstanding which he cied a Christian.

True Teller, 20 April 1844

Leonard and Jane were married and, five years later, built the tavern that was to become, as the *Leamington Post* of 27 February 1878 reported, 'one of the most popular resorts for the travelling public in the west; ... thousands of business men from Quebec and intermediate towns to Sault St Marie ... spent pleasant days at that hotel.' Innkeeping was a family business for the Wigles. Two of Leonard's brothers, Michael and Wendle, also held tavern licences.

As well as their tavern, the Wigles ran a two-hundred-acre farm and in time became the parents of nine children, two of whom predeceased them. Leonard Wigle was by all accounts a gentle, generous man. When he died, on 27 February 1878, his funeral was the largest that had ever been held in nineteenth-century Essex County. At that funeral, according to his obituary, were forty Indians who 'wept like children who had lost a parent.' 'Intellectually,' it went on, he had been 'far above the average, and hence both in religion and politics he entertained none of the strong prejudices that mar the lives of numbers of our people ... He left not an enemy behind him.' Four years before his death, Leonard Wigle, a temperate man, closed the bar in his inn. This move, critics to the contrary, did not result in a loss of business, thanks to his personal popularity with the travelling public.

Wigle's Tavern stands today at 135 Talbot Street East. It is now a motor hotel. The brick has been painted and the enclosed verandah, a relatively recent addition, hides the front of the building. But its very presence testifies to the importance of Colonel Talbot's road and of the exemplary Jane and Leonard Wigle, who for more than half a century provided a clean and comfortable haven for travellers along that road's length.

Jane Wigle ran the tavern for a brief time after her husband's death. When she died three years later, the furnishings from their inn were divided among their children. Each son – Charles, John, Alexander, Leonard, and Robert – inherited 'one bedstead, bedding and clothing belonging thereto,' with Robert receiving as well stoves, cooking equipment, and a refectory table from the barroom. Two granddaughters each received a bed and bedding, as did Jane's two daughters, Susan and Mary. The daughters also shared the remaining beds, furniture, carpets, pictures, and picture frames from the 'Parlours and dining room.' The fact that there was enough good furniture for sons, daughters, and grandchildren to share indicates that the Wigles had a well-furnished establishment.

Travellers rarely bothered to describe in any detail the furnishing of the rooms they occupied. They saved their journalistic eloquence to outline the deficiencies of the hostelry. But it is possible, through descriptions such as those in Jane Wigle's will or more detailed inventories in other innkeepers' wills, to ascertain what were the basic requirements. One such inventory, made after the 1828 death of Kingston innkeeper John Scantlbury, listed fifteen bedrooms, all similarly furnished with:

1 Large 4 Post Walnut Bedstead with tester and chintz valence
1 straw Palliaf
1 Hair Mattras
1 Feather Bed Bolster and Pillow
1 White Cotten Counterpane
1 Feather Bed Bolster and Pillow
2 sheets cotten
1 Cotten Counterpane
1 Boudette
1 Cherry Washand Stand
1 White Ewer and Basin
1 Card table
1 Looking glass
1 Muslin Window Curtains
1 Bedside Carpet
2 Rushbottom Painted Chairs
1 Chamber Pot

It is probable that, try as they might, even Leonard and Jane Wigle, the most fastidious of innkeepers, had to deal with the three complaints about sleeping quarters

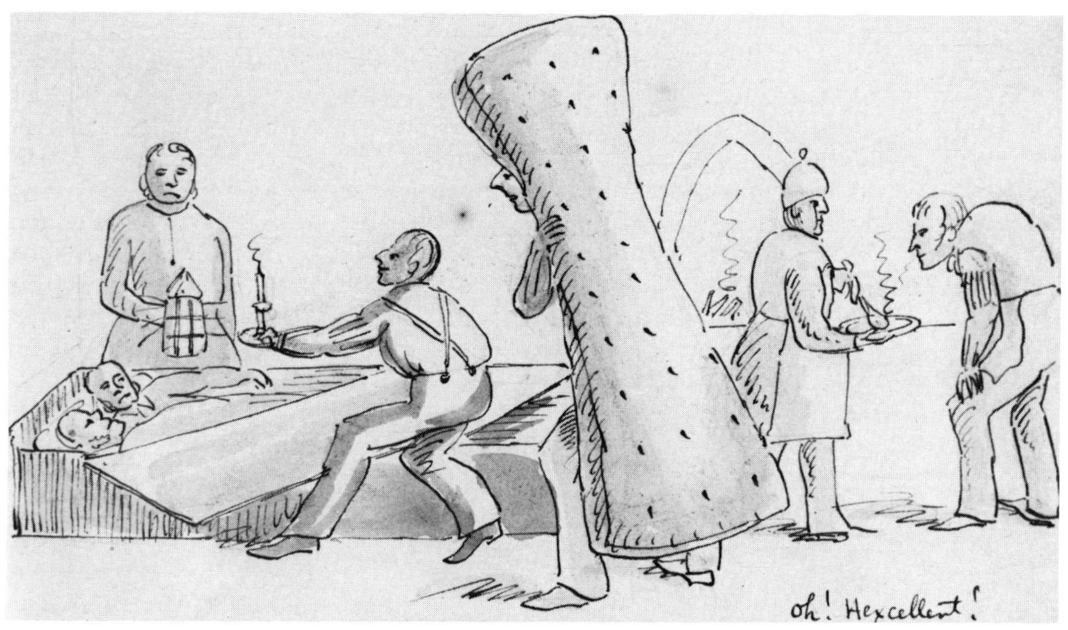

Sleeping accommodation was nothing if not ad hoc.

that run as a common thread through the jounals of suffering travellers: lack of privacy, proximity to the taproom, and, worst of all, fleas.

Fleas, the inhabitants of every hair mattress, feather bed, or counterpane, were called among other things 'those murderers of sleep.' Sir Richard Bonnycastle, who travelled across the province and thus became an authority on the subject, noted that fleas were found

> in every inn you stop at, even in the cities; for it appears ... that bugs are indigenous, native to the soil and breed in the bark of old trees; so that if you build a new house, you bring the enemy into your camp. Nothing but cleanliness and frequent whitewash, colouring, paint and soft soap, will get rid of them. If it were not for the strong smell of red cedar and its extreme bitterness, I would have my bedstead of that material; for even the iron bedsteads, in the soldiers' barracks, become infested with them if not painted often. Red cedar they happily eschew.

Captain Basil Hall, travelling the Talbot Road in 1828, found that a philosophical approach helped:

> For half the night I lay tossing, and growling, and ejaculating, in terms not fit to be printed. I tried to remedy matters by putting on a great-coat; then drew on gloves, stockings, drawers – all to no purpose! Got up, spread a sheet on the mud floor – still in vain! At last, about midnight, it occurred to me, that as the case was evidently hopeless, it would be best to lie still, grinning and bearing the torture as well as might be. So I lay revolving all the sweet and bitter thoughts I could muster, and at times almost managed to philosophize myself into the confession that even these annoyances were trifles in comparison with the varied, and boundless sort of interest, which was rising higher and higher at every step as the journey advanced.

The next problem was privacy – or lack of it. Since reservations were unheard of, innkeepers simply accommodated as many guests as they could until the house was full. The question was: when was it full? The answer: not until every inch of bed and floor space had been taken. The situation led to uncomfortable and unwelcome to-

A backwoods tavern by the Talbot Road where amenities were, at best, primitive

getherness. Even the best bedrooms often contained more than one bed – and that dormitory euphemistically called the ballroom accommodated several people in beds and more on the floor.

Samuel Thompson, author of *Reminiscences of a Canadian Pioneer,* had his first such experience at a small log inn near Barrie, where innkeeper David Root conducted Thompson to what he called his tavern:

It was a log building of a single apartment where presided 'the wife' – a smart, plump good-looking Irishwoman in a stuff gown and without shoes or stockings. They had been recently married [and] had selected this wild spot on a half-opened road ... with the resolute determination of 'keeping tavern' ... Bedtime drew near. A heap of odd-looking rugs and clean blankets was laid for accommodation and pronounced to be ready. But how to get into it? We ... had not accustomed ourselves to 'uncase' before company and hesitated to lie down in our clothes.

Fortunately the host set the example by simply 'uncasing' and taking to the couch, whereupon all followed suit, and the unruffled Mrs Root 'after hanging up a large coloured quilt between our lair and the couch occupied by her now snoring spouse,' disappeared for the night.

Pioneer settler Susanna Moodie expressed her feelings on the subject in tones bordering on hysteria:

In the bush all things are in common; you cannot even get a bed without having to share it in a public sleeping-room – men, women, and children ... Oh, ye gods! think of the snoring, squalling, grumbling, puffing; think of the kicking, elbowing, and crowding ...

David Sickelsteel's impressive inn near Chatham

Sharing a bed with the fleas and from one to five other occupants was bad enough, but it was worse still if you were located directly above the taproom, source of travellers' other main complaint. That was why W.H.G. Kingston endured a sleepless night in a Georgetown tavern in 1855:

> the affectionate feelings we had begun to entertain for the place ... were ... rudely dissipated, by the most terrific uproar which went on all night ... In vain the poor landlord endeavoured to put the offenders forth ... they fought and swore and shrieked, and threatened the lives of all or any who should dare to interfere with their rights ... we fully expected ... to find the ground covered with the corpses of the slain.

No sooner had the din subsided when, as it was nearly morning, the Toronto stage 'came wheezily trump-trumpeting through the village,' blowing a horn that sounded like 'an unhappy metal nose with a cold in it, blown against its will.'

The Talbot roads along Lake Erie and up to St Thomas were well travelled in the early 1800s; the parallel trail, west through Chatham to Windsor, developed later.

By the time Anna Jameson arrived there in 1837, Chatham was, she said, 'a beautiful little town.' She had anticipated staying at the well-known Freemans' Hotel but, finding that it was no longer in operation, she was forced to spend the night elsewhere. Freeman's, said to be one of the finest hostelries in the district, may have been named after its owner or, since Chatham was a principal terminus for the Underground Railroad, the name may also have had an anti-slavery connection. Founded by Lieutenant-Governor Simcoe as a military settlement, Chatham did not really develop until the 1830s. It became, prior to the American Civil War, a haven for fugitive slaves, descendants of whom are an integral part of the population today.

Benjamin Lundy, a Quaker anti-slavery activist, passed through Chatham in 1832. He mentioned a tavern and stage house there but made no further comment, so it seems unlikely that the splendid two-storey frame inn known as Sickelsteel's Tavern had yet been built. It stands today, moved back from its original site beside the road, just east of Chatham (on Longwoods Road, part of lot 9, concession 1). It is now a private home.

David Sickelsteel, who built the inn, was one of the first white children born in Kent County. His father, George, was Hessian, one of the German troops that served with the British during the American Revolutionary War when, as the Kent County Atlas put it, they became involved in 'the fruitless task of subduing the Americans.' Sickelsteel settled near Chatham before the turn of the century and received title to his land in 1802.

David Sickelsteel took out many mortgages on the property in the 1850s, but in all likelihood his inn had already been built by that time. It may well have been built in stages, as the traffic along the road from London to Windsor increased. All the siding is said to be tulip wood (commonly called whitewood), which is highly prized for woodworking and native to the southeastern United States. The taproom of the inn was entered from the rear of the house; according to legend, the door was large enough for a customer to ride his horse through, should he, for some reason, want to do so. The bar, it was said, was high enough to look over but too high for a horse to jump.

With the help of two wives, David Sickelsteel fathered a large family. His first wife, Nancy, died in the 1850s. By 1861 he had acquired a second wife, Margaret, and with her arrival switched his religious faith from the Church of England to the Free Church of Scotland. At some point in its history, the inn became known as the Caledonia Inn – possibly the change coincided with his marriage to the Scottish Margaret, Caledonia then being in common use as a synonym for Scotland.

As the family expanded its business interests, a small community grew up around the inn. By 1867, David Sickelsteel, Junior, calling himself a lumber merchant, was leasing some of his farm lands and operating a sawmill on the property. 'The large frame house used as a hotel' was still in business. Legal documents from that period mention fruit trees and other ornamental trees on the property – and so there are to this day. They enhance the singular beauty of this simple but well-proportioned building.

Windsor was a village first established by French settlers in the middle of the eighteenth century and later populated by English-speaking Loyalists. From earliest days, ferries crossed from Pierre St Armour's Inn at Windsor to Detroit, and hotels were built to handle the ever-increasing traffic along the Talbot Road. One, a modest two-storey frame structure, had the grandiose name of Windsor Castle; another, built where St Armour's Inn had stood, was the popular British American.

Smuggling, of course, became a way of life for people on both sides of the border. Then, as now, some people were better at it than others, but one woman had a particularly difficult time of it. According to a report in the Orangeville *Sun* of 8 October 1891,

> at Ferry Hill, Windsor, on Saturday morning ... a French woman had been over the river purchasing, and not wishing to bother the customs officials she carefully placed her purchases in her bustle. She did not tie it securely and got about half way up the hill when it took a tumble and enough goods to start a small general store rolled from under her dress. She gave a hurried glance back at the cus-

Salmoni House, Amherstburg: a 'station' on the Underground Railroad

toms office and then gathering the things up she vanished down the British American Hotel alley.

In Amherstburg, a few miles south, smugglers also found the Detroit River convenient for transporting goods when they didn't want to 'bother the customs officials.' But for many years the most important smuggling was that done with fugitive slaves who escaped to safety in Canada via the Underground Railroad. Slavery had been abolished in Canada since 1793.

Because of its location at the narrowest point in the Detroit River, Amherstburg was considered the major 'terminal' in the system. By 1860 there were eight hundred blacks living there and nearly that number in Windsor. Many settled in the Niagara peninsula as well. But the largest centre for black settlement was in Chatham where, by 1861, upwards of two thousand were living.

Taverns were an integral part of the Underground Railroad system. Some, such as the Life Henry Tavern in Simcoe, had an unsavoury reputation. Escaped slaves were pursued to Canada by 'Yankee sneaks' who were sent to recapture them. When caught, they were taken to the Life Henry, filled with liquor, and put on board ship at Port Dover to be returned to their owners in the United States.

Certainly there were enough escaped slaves in the Windsor–Chatham area to make it feasible for anti-slavery activist Harriet Beecher Stowe to visit Amherstburg. That is part of the legend that surrounds Salmoni House, an impressive three-storey brick building at 252 Dalhousie Street.

Records for the hotel no longer exist, so

there is no way of knowing whether Stowe ever actually stayed there. But since Josiah Henson, after whom Uncle Tom was supposedly modelled, lived nearby in Dresden, Stowe might well have interviewed him in Amherstburg around the time of the 1852 publication of her widely acclaimed novel, *Uncle Tom's Cabin.* Henson's life, in actuality, bore little resemblance to that of the fictional Uncle Tom.

Salmoni House was built in 1849 and was part of the scene when traveller and journalist W.H. Smith visited Amherstburg the following year. He described the town as having an old-fashioned look. The streets, he said, were narrow, with sidewalks paved with stones. 'Lately,' he continued, 'two or three spirited individuals have been erecting handsome, modern-looking brick houses, which appear to stare their more antiquated neighbours out of countenance.'

No doubt one of these spirited individuals was Thomas Salmoni, who had been operating a tavern for some time before building his big new hotel. Records of the Western District show that he had been licensed to run a tavern in 1840 and for the ensuing ten years, until the listing of licences was discontinued. Salmoni called his first tavern the White Horse, as did its next owner, Thomas Horsman, who took over when Salmoni moved to his new quarters. On 5 July 1851, the Amherstburg *Courier* announced the change:

THE WHITE HORSE

BY THOMAS HORSMAN

In the old stand formerly kept by Mr Salmoni, long known as a house of good entertainment for man and horse. To retain that good name the proprietor will spare no pain or expense to procure the best our market will afford ...

But by the time Mr Horsman was entertaining man and horse at his tavern, Thomas Salmoni was operating a competing establishment. He ran not only the hotel but also owned a forwarding business on

Thomas Salmoni,

KEEPS constantly on hand at the large brick store, at the head of Dalhousie Street,

DRY GOODS GROCERIES.

HARDWARE & CROCKERY;

and he hopes by strict attention and low prices to merit and receive a share of public patronage.

His Dry Goods consists in part of

Broadcloths and Casimeres,	School Books of all kinds,
Silk, Satin & worsted vestings,	Irish Linens,
Tweeds,	Mulls and Muslins,
Canada Grey Cloths,	Lisle Thread, Edgings & Laces,
Moleskins & Fustins,	Ribbons,
Red, White & Yellow Flannels,	Dress Hkfs,
Woolen Long & Sqr. Shawls,	Gloves,
Black Marino Shawls,	Fringe & Gimps,
Cotton Shawls,	Apron Checks,
Woolen Hkfs.	Worsted & Linen Table Spreads.
Worsted Embroidered Hkfs.,	Brown & Bleached Linen,
Black & Cold Alpacas,	Table Covers,
English Marinos	Towells & Diapers,
Mousline Delanes,	Crapes,
Gali Plaids,	Serges,
All Wool Plaids,	Blankets,
Ginghams,	Linen and Cotton Threads,
Blue & fancy Calicoes,	Sheetings & Shirting,
Bleached Cottons,	Canvass,
Silk & Cotton Hkfs.,	Padding,
Gents Cravatts,	Bagging,
Ladies Mufls,	Bed Ticking,
A large assortment of ready made clothing	Wadding,
Carpet Bags,	Candle Wick,
Fur & Cloth Caps,	Comforters,
Woolen & Worsted Yarn,	Drawers,
	And numerous other articles.

His Groceries consist of the following articles:

Tea, Green & Black,	Cinnamon,
Coffee,	Pickle Sauces,
Sugar—loaf, & muscovado,	Caster Oil,
Rice,	Sarsaparilla
Currants, & Raisens,	Soap,
Oat meal,	Salt by the Barrel.
Nutmegs, & Cloves,	Glass, 7X9 8X10 10X 12

His Hardware consists of:

Shovels,	Hinges of different kinds,
Spades,	Candle Sticks,
Scoop shovels,	Augers,
Rakes,	Axes,
Cut Nails,	Wagon Boxes,
Horse Nails,	Frying Pans,
Knives and Forks,	Trace chains,
Pocket Knives,	Brass Pans,
Spoons, Large & Small	And other articles too numerous to mention.
Locks of all kinds,	
Butts & Screws,	

His Crockery consists of:

Jugs,	Egg Cups,
Cups & Saucers,	Tumblers & Decanters
Bowls,	Mustard, Pepper and Vinegar Castors,
Tea Pots,	Salt Sellers,
Cream Jugs,	Looking Glasses,
Sugar Bowls,	And various other articles
Dishes,	
Jollin Bake Dishes,	

LIQUORS.

Brandy,	Peppermint,
Rum,	Gin in Cases,
Gin,	Also a hogshead of Hodge's London Gin
Wine,	Bottle Porter,
Port Sherry and Mederia	Bottle Ale,
Scotch Whiskey,	Also 75 barrels of Toronto Beer.
Canada do.	

THOS. SALMONI.

Amherstburg, Dec. 8th, 1851. 40

Amherstburg Courier, 5 July 1851

the Great Lakes, with goods stored at his warehouses and sold at the shop he operated from the hotel building. He sold everything and anything, from food and drink, shoes and shawls, boiled linseed oil and white lead, to 'Captain Bayfield's charts of Lake Huron.' Salmoni was also an agent for the Canada Western Insurance Company. On the third floor of his new building he provided a spacious ballroom, which also served on occasion as a meeting room for the Freemasons' Thistle Lodge, of which he was a loyal member. His hotel had forty bedrooms and seven fireplaces.

Salmoni was of English descent, his family having emigrated first to the United States. Legend has it that one family member, a prizefighter, had travelled to America to take part in a hotly contested boxing match. He lost. And because his family had bet heavily on him, they lost their money as well. They were unable to return to England, and so came to Canada, first to Montreal and then to Amherstburg.

Thomas Salmoni had only a few years to enjoy his prosperity. He died on 9 October 1858. For many years after his father's death, Mark Salmoni ran the family business, until his death in the spring of 1877 brought an end to the Salmoni enterprises in Amherstburg.

In 1979 Salmoni's impressive hotel was renovated, its interior gutted to the structural walls, and the interior wood trim salvaged and used in the reconstruction. The exterior remains unchanged, adding immeasurably to the historic atmosphere of the town. During restoration, part of a stone tunnel was uncovered, thereby adding one more item to the long list of tunnel stories that abound along the Canada–US border.

Because that border was so convenient, the owner of a hostelry across the street from Salmoni's had little difficulty in fleeing the country after he absconded with government funds. George Bullock, at the time of his hasty departure, was treasurer of the Western District. But before his appointment to that position in 1850, Bullock had been a tavern keeper, owner of an establishment at 269–71 Dalhousie Street. During the 1837 Rebellion, when Amherstburg was attacked four times by rebel supporters of William Lyon Mackenzie, Bullock's Tavern served as an officers' mess for the militia.

To control the unrest caused by the rebels, a British garrison was stationed at Amherstburg until 1851, by which time the population of the town numbered about two thousand. Taverns flourished. Bullock, possibly anticipating the withdrawal of the garrison, sold his tavern. The new owner announced the change and its new name in the *Courier* on 16 January 1850. It was to be called (unimaginatively) the British American Hotel, and it was being run by Thomas Hirons, Junior, who had 'taken the house heretofor kept by George Bullock.'

(Nothing is known of Bullock after he so hurriedly departed for the safety of the American side of the border, but David Botsford, an Amherstburg historian, writes that Bullock's son, Seth, 'became a noted frontier character in the American West and was a friend of Theodore Roosevelt ... he assisted Roosevelt in raising the Cavalry Regiment known as the "Rough Riders" for service in Cuba in the Spanish American War.')

In 1866, the British American was taken over by William Horsman, who renamed it (of course) the White Horse Tavern. His relationship to Thomas Horsman of the earlier White Horse Tavern is not known. Obviously Horsman could not resist using the name again. At the turn of the century after another change of ownership, the White Horse became Columbia House, until prohibition brought to an end its viability as a drinking establishment. Subsequent remodelling and 'modernizing' have effectively hidden any vestige of the original stone structure.

The discomforts of sleeping accommodations and the abdications of innkeepers notwithstanding, the stoic traveller continued to pen his nightly journal, recording his every impression.

Even Edward Talbot, nephew of the sovereign of Lake Erie, was helpless to control the vagaries of travel; it is difficult to know whether he was happy or displeased at the outcome of one night's adventure. Talbot had asked for a single bed but was given no assurance in that regard. 'I retired early,' he reported and,

> after contending a short time with my apprehensions of some ineligible bed-fellow, I dropped asleep. About midnight, I was awakened by the chattering of five buxom girls, who had just entered the room and were beginning to undress themselves. Perceiving that there were only four beds in the apartment, – a double-bedded room! – each of which was already occupied by one person, I set it down as certain that I should have one, if not two, of these ladies. Under this impression, I raised up my head, and desired to be informed which of them intended me the honour of her company. 'Don't be alarmed, Sir!' cried one of them. 'We shall not trouble you nor your bed. A look is quite sufficient!'

Talbot confided to his journal that this 'was the first time in my life that I owed the luxury of a single-bed or any other luxury, to my looks.'

Northern and North-western Ontario

Subscriber.

JAMES FULTON.
Richmond Hill, Markham, Nov. 13th, 1829. 2873

Stray Ox and Steer.

Broke into the inclosure of the Subscriber, a LARGE OX, blind of the off eye, with seven wrinkles on his horn, a yellowish Red and White colour; also a RED STEER with him, nearly three years old; with a brindle face, and part white under his breast. The owner or owners are requested to prove property, pay charges, and take the animals away.

...very low indeed for cash, or if one half or one third of the purchase money is paid down. Immediate possession can be given, and, for further particulars appply to

PHILIP CODY.
Toronto, Nov. 16th, 1829. 287z.

WHERE IS WILLIAM SUTHERLAND?

THE Subscriber is desirous of ascertaining the place of abode of Mr. William Sutherland and family. They lived in or near Glengarry, about the time of the last war, and were originally from the parish of Kindonan, Sutherlandshire. Address a letter to the Subscriber, at Niagara, care of Messrs. Chrysler, Merchants.

N. B. Mrs. Sutherland's maiden name was Catharine Macpherson.

DANIEL MACPHERSON.
Niagara, 17th Nov. 1829. 2873.

Boarding.

THE Subscriber can furnish Boarding, Lodging, &c. for six steady mechanics, reasonable, on Dundas Street, between Mr. Willmot's Tavern and four doors from Mr. Bird's Tavern, in the house lately occupied by Mr. George Hutchison, Plaisterer.

JAMES PARKER.
Nov. 18. 87.

STRAYED, on the 10th October last, into the premises of ANDREW BIGHAM, on lot No. 12, in the first concession of ETOBICOKE, A LIGHT IRON-GREY HORSE, rising five or six years of age.—The owner is requested to prove property, pay charges, and take him away.

Nov. 17. 873.

SAWYER & LABOURERS WANTED.

WANTED by the subscriber, a Sawyer who understands his business, and two men who understand Chopping; to whom liberal encouragement will be given.

Apply to

Also; TO LET, for one or more years, the SAW WORKS of the Subscriber.

For further particulars, apply to the subscriber, on the premises.

WILLIAM KENT.
Stoney Creek, Nov. 13, 1829. 87z

THE SUBSCRIBERS have just received direct from London, a general assortment of
Hosiery,
Black and Colored Gros-de-Naples,
Figured Norwich Crapes,
Black Silk and Cotton Velvets,
Sewing Silks,
Lace Thread Edgings,
Worked Insertions, and Scollop Muslins,
Reel and Ball Cotton,
Geo. the 4th Regulation Swords, Belts, and Sashes,
...ware and Cutlery,
...ral Stock of Saddlery: also an extensive ... of England Cloths, &c. &c.

J. C. GODWIN & Co.

...fine Mustard

... advantage to purchase it ... as it is commonly sold.

...rrels of ... WHISKEY.

J. C. GODWIN & Co.

NEWMARKET MAIL STAGE.

WILLIAM GARBUTT, having taken the contract for carrying His Majesty's Mails between York and Newmarket, for the next four years, respectfully informs the public that THE MAIL STAGE will start from Joseph Bloor's Hotel, York, on Mondays and Thursdays, at 12 o'clock, noon, and arrive at nine o'clock, the same evening in Newmarket;—and will leave Mr. Barber's Tavern, Newmarket, for York, on Wednesdays and Saturdays, at ... in the morning, and arrive in York at 2 P. M. on the same days.

Price for passengers conveyed between York and Newmarket, six shillings and three pence currency, and in proportion for shorter distances. Packages carried on the route at moderate rates.

Mr. BARBER will accommodate passengers arriving with the Mail Stage at Newmarket; and they may be comfortably conveyed to the Holland Landing, or in other directions if required.

York, March 30th, 1829. 254z.

NEW ARRANGEMENT OF STAGES

Between York and the Carrying Place at the head of the Bay of Quintie.

THE Public are respectfully informed that a Mail Stage will run regularly twice a week between York and the Carrying Place; leaving York every Monday and Thursday at 12 o'clock, noon, and arriving at the Carrying Place on Tuesdays and Fridays at 2 o'clock, P. M. Will leave the Carrying Place every Tuesday and Friday at ... o'clock A. M. and arrive at York on Wednesdays and Saturdays, at 12 o'clock noon. There will also a Stage leave Cobourg every Monday at 10 o'clock, A. M. and arrive at the Carrying Place the same day, and leave the Carrying Place every Saturday at 9 o'clock, A. M. and arrive at Cobourg the sameday.

The above arrangements are in connexion with the Steam Boats *Sir James Kempt* and *Toronto*, so that Travellers going the route will find a pleasant and speedy conveyance between Kingston and York, as the line is now fitted up in good order with good carriages, good horses and careful drivers.

Every attention will be given to render passengers comfortable while on the line, and the drivers instructed to stop at the best hotels on the route.

All baggage at the risk of the owners.

Extras furnished to any part of the country.

The Stage Books will be kept at Mr. Bradley's Steam boat Hotel.

SALT RHEUM.—This inveterate disease, which has long baffled the art of the most experienced physicians, has, at length, found a sovereign remedy in Dr. La Grange's genuine ointment. Few cutaneous diseases are met with more reluctance by the physician, which he is so adversely unsuccessful. This has stood the test of experience, and justly obtained unparalleled celebrity. It immediately removes ...

PETER PATERSON, Agent.

SWEDES IRON.

...nding from the Ship *General Wolfe*, direct from ...TENBURGH.

...NS ASSORTED SWEDES IRON.

WILLIAM BUDDEN,
Point a' Callieres.
August 18, 1829. 274-z

LOOKING GLASSES.

...eived by the subscriber, a large and elegant ...ent of Looking Glasses; German Plate; a variety, and the prices remarkably low.

J. R. ARMSTRONG.
...ept. 16th, 1829.

YORK FURNACE.

F. R. DUTCHER continues his FURNACE in complete operation, where can be had, at short notice,

Castings of any description from one to thirty cwt:

Also on hand a general assortment of STOVES, HOLLOW WARE, PLOUGH CASTINGS and PLOUGHS.

F. R. D. having erected a first rate Lathe for ..., is ready to complete any order at short notice.
...ept. 22.

THEODORE BURLEY,
SMITH AND *Brass Founder:*

Yonge Street, next door to Judge Macaulay.

...CASTINGS for Mill work, &c. &c. done on ...ortest notice.

...f White and Blacksmith's work done to order. ...highest prices, in CASH, will be paid for old ...er and tin.

CHAPTER TWELVE

Northern and North-western Ontario

INNS ON THE NEW FRONTIER

'I never have gone to the James Bay; I never go to it; I never shall. But somehow I'd feel lonely without it.'

Stephen Leacock, 'I'll Stay in Canada,' 1936

THE BUILDING of inns went hand in hand with the building of Ontario. Roads were cut through the wilderness and inns sprang up beside them 'like mushrooms in the night.' In southern Ontario roads meant corduroy pathways through the bush. But in northern Ontario the first roads were lakes and rivers and, later, the railway. Transportation was different, but the result was the same – innkeepers were the facilitators for the settlement of the province, whether at York, Kingston, and Niagara, or at Moosonee, near the shores of James Bay.

The St Mary's River is the 'road' that joins Lake Huron on the east with Lake Superior on the west. It was the road the Cree and Ojibway used as they moved from lake to lake early in the seventeenth century. Explorers, missionaries, and fur traders used it as a point of access to the western frontier, with its lakes to be charted, souls to be saved, and animals to be trapped. The North West Company of fur traders established a post on the St Mary's River canoe route in 1783 and built a canal past the rapids. The settlement there was called Sault Ste Marie (Rapids of the St Mary).

George Heriot, artist and deputy post master of British North America, saw the village in 1807 and noted:

> The factory of the company of merchants of Montreal [the North West Company] is situated at the foot of the cascades of Saint Mary, on the north side, and consists of storehouses, a saw-mill, and a bateaux-yard. The saw-mill supplies with plank, boards, and spars, all the posts on Lake Superior, and particularly Pine point, which is nine miles from thence, has a dock-yard for constructing vessels, and is the residence of a regular masterbuilder, with several artificers. At the factory there is a good canal, with a lock at its lower entrance, and a causeway for dragging up the bateaux and canoes. The vessels of Lake Superior approach close to the head of the canal, where there is a wharf; those of Lake Huron to the lower end of the cascades.

(The North West Company and the rival Hudson's Bay Company called their outposts 'factories' so as not to embarrass the original partners, who didn't want to appear associated with the retail trade.)

Across the river from the North West Company post, on the American side, lay Fort Michilimackinac. In July 1812, Charles Oakes Ermatinger, serving under a British commander, led a party of men in a successful attack on the American fort, an action designed to keep British control of the St Mary's River.

Ermatinger, son of a founder of the North West Company, had settled in Sault Ste Marie a few years before the battle, having moved there from Montreal. He was married to Charlotte, the daughter of Catawabeta, an Ojibway chief. In the summer of 1814 an American attack destroyed all the log buildings in the community. A traveller, Gabriel Franchere, arrived on July 31 and reported that 'the houses, stores and saw mills of the company were still smoking.' He 'found Mr Charles Ermatinger, who had a pretty establishment: he dwelt temporarily in a house that belonged to Nolin, but he was building another of stone, very elegant, and had just finished a grist mill.' This was the two-storey fieldstone house that dominated the town and served, first unofficially and later officially, as an inn.

The building, later known as the Stone House Hotel (831 Queen Street East), was built at the cost of two thousand pounds. Obtaining the materials needed for the elegant house that Charles Ermatinger wanted was not easy; the structure took almost ten years to complete. The walls of fieldstone and lime mortar are thirty inches thick. The heavy beams are cedar logs, hand-planed. The floor is tongue-and grooved cedar. Nine rooms housed the family and travellers. The family consisted of Charles and Charlotte Ermatinger and their thirteen children, only eight of whom lived to adulthood.

Thomas Douglas, fifth Earl of Selkirk, stayed at Ermatinger's in 1816. Lord Selkirk, humanitarian and colonist, had settled eight hundred Scottish Highlanders in Prince Edward Island in 1803 on land he purchased for them. His family then bought into the Hudson's Bay Company, a purchase that resulted in a large grant of land to Lord Selkirk, who used it to establish the Red River Colony in Manitoba. Charles Ermatinger was Selkirk's agent for handling supplies for the settlers. (Ermatinger's connection with both the Hudson's Bay Company, for which he was an agent, and the North West Company, of which his father was a founder, crossed the battle lines that existed between the two fur-trading giants.)

WEST END HOTEL.

THE SUBSCRIBER invites the attention of travellers and land hunters to the comfortable quarters provided for their accomodation at the above hotel, which commands a full view of the busy scenes on the river and at the canal. The table will be found to be bountifully provided with all that goes to make up a good square meal, and the preparation beyond a question of excellency. Board by the day, week or month. An "express waggon" for the conveyance of baggage meets every steamer.

THO'S. RICHARDSON

Sault Ste. Marie Dec. 7th 1883.

MANHOOD

HOW LOST, HOW RESTORED

We have recently published a new edition of Dr. Culverwell's Celebrated Essay on the radical and permanent cure (without medicine) of Nervous Debility, Mental and Physical Incapacity, Impediments to Marriage, etc., resulting from excesses.

☞ Price, in a sealed envelope, only 6 cents, or two postage stamps.

The celebrated author, in this admirable Essay, clearly demonstrates, from thirty years' successful practise, that alarming consequences may be radically cured without the dangerous use of internal medicines or the use of the knife; pointing out a mode of cure at once simple, certain and effectual, by means of which every sufferer, no matter what his condition may be, may cure himself cheaply, privately and radically.

☞ This lecture should be in the hands of every youth and every man in the land.

Address

CULVERWELL MEDICAL Co,

41 Ann St. New York.

PostOffice Box 450.

Algoma Pioneer, 24 April 1885

Home to fur trader Ermatinger, later the Stone House Hotel, Sault Ste Marie

When Lord Selkirk stopped at the stone house in 1816 he was on his way to the Red River Colony to assess its security in view of threats of attack by the North West Company. It was while at Ermatinger's that he learned of the death of Governor Semple and a number of his colonists at the hands of the Métis at Seven Oaks near the Red River Colony.

When MacDonnell [the messenger bearing news of the massacre] arrived at Ermatinger's, Selkirk was already asleep and Dr John Allan, having listened to the news, declined to wake him. As darkness covered the last remnant of the flaming sky ... the men sat talking of the news that must be broken in the morning.

Ermatinger was hospitable to all and constantly entertained travellers. In 1823 a Hudson's Bay Company clerk wrote that Ermatinger was still working on his house:

the inside work will take at least a couple of years more to finish at the rate it has gone on and the elegant way he is getting it done ... The death of one of his sons at Montreal last summer and two here last fall by the dysentry prevented the usual winter amusement further than a game of whist now and then.

Ethnologist Henry Rowe Schoolcraft wrote in the same year:

I made a party of sixteen, who dined with Mr. Ermatinger. I here tasted the flesh of the cariboo which is a fine flavoured venison. I do not recollect any wise or merry remark made during dinner which is worth recording.

Charles Ermatinger left Sault Ste Marie for Montreal in 1828 accompanied by Charlotte. Most of their children, however, stayed on in Sault Ste Marie, including a son, Charles, who later became an Ojibway chief through his mother.

In 1833 the Reverend William McMurray arrived in Sault Ste Marie to serve as a missionary to the Ojibway. The stone house became his home and chapel for nine years. McMurray had recently completed his studies in divinity when he received the posting to Sault Ste Marie. Neither John Strachan nor Lieutenant-Governor Sir John Colborne were certain where the place was, so they told McMurray to go to Detroit and ask the way. This he did, travelling by steamer, schooner, and canoe to his destination.

William McMurray, like Charles Ermatinger, was an unofficial innkeeper. During those early days, when all travellers were adventurers, any pioneer with a spare bed and sufficient food was likely to welcome their company. In 1837 William McMurray was host to Anna Jameson, an Englishwoman whose courage and consummate curiosity led to a journey that resulted in the popular *Winter Studies and Summer Rambles in Canada.* Anna was the wife of Robert Jameson and came to Canada when her husband accepted the position of Attorney-General of Upper Canada in 1833. Not one to sit in a parlour in Toronto with her embroidery, she set out to explore this new country. She fell in love with it. After meeting two Indian sisters, Mrs Schoolcraft and Mrs McMurray, during her travels and developing an immediate rapport with them, Anna Jameson proceeded on a long and hazardous journey to visit them.

Anna Jameson stayed with the McMurrays in the Ermatinger house. She met many Indians and grew to admire them. A born adventurer herself, Jameson was exhilarated by the thought of attempting something no European woman had done and so decided to shoot the rapids on the St Mary's River:

> The canoe being ready, I went up to the top of the portage, and we launched into the river. It was a small fishing canoe about ten feet long, quite new, and light and elegant and buoyant as a bird on the waters. I reclined on a mat at the bottom, Indian fashion, (there are no seats in a genuine Indian canoe;) in a minute we were within the verge of the rapids, and down we went with a whirl and a splash! – the white surge leaping around me – over me. The Indian with astonishing dexterity kept the head of the canoe to the breakers, and somehow or other we danced through them. I could see, as I looked over the edge of the canoe, that the passage between the rocks was sometimes not more than two feet in width, and we had to turn sharp angles – a touch of which would have sent us to destruction – all this I could see through the transparent eddying waters, but I can truly say, I had not even a momentary sensation of fear, but rather of giddy, breathless, delicious excitement.

William McMurray and his family left in

Anna Jameson, author and adventurer

1842 for his new parish in Dundas. After a few more occupants and a few years of neglect, David Pim took over the house, operating it as the Stone House Hotel from 1852–8.

One year after Irish innkeeper Pim had taken over as landlord, W.H.G. Kingston travelled north from the 'sweetly smiling village of Orillia' to Sault Ste Marie and stayed at Pim's Stone House, which he described as follows:

there also stands in the British territory a substantial stone-house, built by an enterprising gentleman some fifty years ago for the purpose of establishing a fur-trade with the Indians in opposition to the Hudson's Bay Company. He succeeded some time tolerably well, but ultimately that all monopolising body swamped him. The farm lay uncultivated, the fences decayed, the outhouses tumbled down, and the sturdy house itself remained unoccupied till it was taken by a worthy, industrious little Irishman, Pim by name, with a Canadian wife, who opened it as a hotel, and there we had been advised to take up our abode.

Kingston found that Pim provided

the most comfortable public room we have been in since we left England: ... a blazing fire in a neat little parlour, with all sorts of nick-nacks and books scattered about – sofas, armchairs, and footstools. A dinner of trout and whitefish was well served at the table.

After Pim's departure, the stone house was occupied by Richard Carney, first sheriff of Algoma. When Sault Ste Marie became the capital of the judicial district of Algoma, Judge John Prince's court was held there. In 1965 the City of Sault Ste Marie wisely purchased the old stone house, restored it, and opened it to the public.

Ermatinger's stone house was undoubtedly the most prestigious stopping place in town, but there were others. Captain Marryat, travelling in 1839, not long after Anna Jameson's visit, described his impression:

Sault St Marie. – Our landlord is a very strange being. It appears that he has been annoyed by some traveller, who has published a work in which he has found fault with the accommodations at Sault St Marie, and spoken very disrespectfully of our host's beds and bed-furniture. I have never read the work, but I am so well aware how frequently travellers fill up their pages with fleas, and 'such small gear,' that I presume the one in question was short of matter to furnish out his book; yet it was neither just nor liberal on his part to expect at Sault St Marie, where, perhaps, not five travellers arrive in the course of a year, the same accommodations as at New York. The bedsteads certainly were a little ricketty, but every thing was very clean and comfortable. The house was not an inn, nor, indeed, did it pretend to be one, but the fare was good and well cooked, and you were waited upon by the host's two pretty modest daughters – not only pretty, but well-informed girls; and, considering that this village is the Ultima Thule of this portion of America, I think that a traveller might have been very well content with things as they were. In two instances, I found in the log-houses of this village complete editions of Lord Byron's works.

Sault St Marie contains, perhaps, fifty houses, mostly built of logs, and has a palisade put up to repel any attack of the Indians.

The development roads that sliced through the bush to open northern Ontario were the long-trestled paths of the railways. The Ojibway, Cree, and Chippewa and the fur traders of the North West and Hudson's Bay companies traversed the area by canoe – and by instinct. The waterways were their roads. But as settlement gradually moved up from the Ottawa Valley and southern Ontario, the concept of a 'New Ontario' in the north emerged. Good farmland around Lake Timiskaming seemed particularly appealing.

The main line of the CPR went through in the 1880s heading west and north from North Bay. But this was a horizontal link with western Canada, while settlements like Haileybury and New Liskeard, at the

The lonely road from Swastika to Kirkland Lake

north-western end of Lake Timiskaming, required a north-south link with the rest of the province. In 1898 the government sent Duncan Anderson to do a study of Port Arthur (now Thunder Bay), the Wabigoon area, the Rainy River Valley, the Timiska-

The Lucky Cross Mine, Swastika

ming district, and the country around Sault Ste Marie. This intrepid man travelled 6,450 miles by rail, 525 miles by boat, 110 miles by buggy and buckboard, and 315 miles on foot and concluded that a railway should be built to 'Témiscamingue.'

Construction began on the Timiskaming and Northern Ontario Railway (later called the Ontario and Northland Railway). Even while this line was under construction, with New Liskeard as its terminus, a new frontier was luring surveyors farther north. James Bay beckoned, as did a link with the proposed National Transcontinental Railway, a dream that became reality when the link was made at Cochrane. But all that paled in comparison to what was happening south of New Liskeard in the vicinity of the town that came to be called Cobalt.

Legend has it that silver was discovered when a blacksmith one day threw his hammer at a fox, missed, hit a rock, and revealed the vein of silver that spawned the silver- and gold-mining industry in northern Ontario. However, a more prosaic claim that in 1903 two railway contractors made the discovery is closer to the truth. In any event, the result was the same. The railway became a road to riches, and hopes of silver and gold brought a steady stream of entrepreneurs, prospectors, miners, and suppliers. Among the first people to arrive, of course, were innkeepers and, in the rough and rowdy mining town of Swastika, a man with a note pad who asked endless questions of everyone. That man, it is believed locally, was Leon Trotsky.

Swastika, south-west of Kirkland Lake, is ninety miles north of New Liskeard. In 1906 the railway line was officially opened for half that distance, to the town of Englehart, but rail lines were laid well beyond that mid-point. During late 1906 and 1907 claims were staked on the site of Swastika. The claims staked by the Dusty brothers and Michael Steele became the Swastika Mining Company (1908) and the Lucky Cross Mine (1911). (Those mines and the town were named after a symbol that, although associated with the Nazi era, had an earlier significance for the ancient and modern world as a symbol of good luck and prosperity.)

In March 1911, prospector Sid Antram got off the train at Swastika to find work in the mine. He found only one railway

Train station at Swastika: it swarmed with prospectors in 1916.

platform and two log buildings. But within three months, the promise of gold created a boom town.

That summer the Cobalt *Daily Nugget* followed and reported on Swastika's spectacular growth:

26 June: Although practically only three months old, the Swastika camp is a very busy spot these days and a good-sized town is springing up over night ... The afternoon train going north now unloads many prospectors and business men from southern points.

27 June: Mr James Doig, general merchant of this place, has received the appointment as post master for the town which will be called Swastika ... What is needed now is a station for Swastika ... Between twenty and fifty passengers alight every day at the small platform which is now by courtesy called the station but it is all too inadequate to handle the crowd.

5 July: The spectacular free gold discovery made on the Miller claim a few days ago has been further opened up and continues to show large quantities of the precious metal. Some pieces taken out are estimated to be worth $50 a pound and very rich specimens are freely scattered about the town ... the president of the company now operating the Miller claim arrived in town a day or so ago and when shown his gold find immediately presented each of his employees with a brand new $100 United States gold certificate ... Many discoveries too numerous to mention have been made in the last few days and from 25 to 75 men are arriving every day. The hotel and rooming houses about town are very busy ...

10 July: The old log cabin, for the past two months occupied by James Doig as a general store ... was burned to the ground by a fire of unknown causes last night ... the residents of the town had some difficulty coping with the flames, which were fanned onto the new three storey hotel. They managed to form a lengthy bucket brigade and their work undoubtedly saved the hotel and other buildings on the townsite. The guests removed all their goods from the hotel.

That new hotel was the Swastika Inn. It opened for business 25 June 1911, just two months after prospector Antram had found only two log buildings and a platform in what swiftly became a lusty, brawling, boom town. The Swastika Inn was a plain, three-storey frame building with thirty-one rooms – not enough to meet the demand. Fifty or seventy-five men often slept in the halls on blankets. The proprietor of the Swastika Inn was Joseph Boisvert.

Boisvert was interviewed by the *Northern Daily News* on 1 February 1950. His story was the story of the north. Joseph Boisvert was then sixty-seven and had a lot to tell about the growth of Ontario's last frontier. He spoke proudly of his 'Victoria nugget which weighed 193 pounds over a ton and was nearly pure silver.'

I came up from New Glasgow, Quebec, to the Northern Area in 1898. After a few years I started, as some had already been found in the New Liskeard and Haileybury, staking the Cobalt area for silver. Together with some American mining promoters we formed the Cobalt Gem Mining Co. in 1906.

We worked our claims for a few years but nothing came of it. Then on May 6, 1909 one of my woodsmen, Arthur Phillip, went out for fun with a prospector's hammer, tapping the rocks and tearing up the moss in the likely spots ... and struck at what he thought was a boulder sticking out from beneath a tree. It happened. The hammer did not rebound from the hard surface of the rock as it should have done, but it gave a hard metallic sound.

Phillip tore away some of the moss and discovered that as far as he could strike, and as far as he could feel, it was metal, and that metal was silver pink with the cobalt bloom ... Soon we had the whole force tearing away at the subsoil, uprooting the two-foot tree that had wound its roots around it. At last we found we had a monster of a silver nugget, shaped like a gigantic wedge ... The Victoria nugget, when we finally got it out in one piece, was put on exhibition all over Canada and the border states of the United States. This served to bring more people into the area ... Try as we did, we never could find the mother lode, from which the nugget was broken off ... I settled down in the Swastika area and with the finding of a good vein of gold near the Timiskaming and Northern Ontario Railway track near Swastika we founded the Lucky Cross Mining Company. Later I decided I should build a hotel in the region.

Boisvert knew two prospectors whose claims brought them fabulous fortunes – Harry Oakes, whose Lake Shore Mining Company yielded over $265 million in gold, and William Wright whose Wright-Hargreaves Mine amassed the fortune that created the Toronto *Globe and Mail.* Joe Boisvert met Wright four months before he literally struck it rich.

I can remember once when I was coming back from an assaying trip in 1912 with a sled and a team of dogs, I decided to head for Bill's camp as it was close one evening. 'Just in time for dinner, Bill,' I remember telling him. His face went ashen, and he didn't say anything for a moment, then, 'Sorry Joe this is the wrong time, we haven't got a thing.' I unpacked the sled and we shared my grub. Bill and his partner, Bill McDougal, a former Australian sailor, really had it hard then – no tent, just rabbit skins to sleep in and a rabbit or the odd bird to eat, and nothing to smoke ... The same story can be told about Harry Oakes, who had a rough ride for years. Even when he found the Tough-Oakes mine they had a hard time digging up investors to keep it going ... Even when Harry found the rich vein at Lake Shore, you could buy the stock for 15 cents. I can remember when it went up to 50 cents and Harry advised me against buying into it, telling me the chances weren't good.

Harry Oakes later owned estates in England, Niagara Falls, Kirkland Lake, and the Bahamas, where he was murdered in 1943.

Wright, Oakes, and many who got rich from the north, left after they had what they wanted, but Joe Boisvert stayed on and ran the Swastika Inn. Early regulations did not permit him to sell beer or liquor because he was within five miles of an operating mine. His inn was used for court sessions, a schoolroom, and church services – Catholics in the morning and Methodists in the evening. A drug store and a butcher shop operated from the first floor. The top floor was removed in the 1970s. The Swastika Inn is located at the corner of Boisvert Street and Cameron Avenue.

Boisvert made a claim for his inn that is impossible to authenticate but that deserves consideration nevertheless – the claim that Leon Trotsky stayed at the Swastika in 1916.

Trotsky came to Swastika in the fall of 1916 from Timmins, asking for room and board for three weeks – When he arrived, he seemed to me just another fortune hunter attracted to this newly opened area ... Trotsky was a note-taker. Dressed as a business man in a hard collar and blue suit, he made notes from the time he got up until he went to bed ... Trotsky seemed out of his element in the booming hustle of sharks and prospectors wildly staking claims as near as possible to the fabulous finds of Bill Wright and of Harry Oakes ...

In answer to the question we all wanted to ask him – why was he making all these notes – he told one of the boys at an evening session in the hotel, within two years my friends and I are going to overthrow the Czar of Russia who has been crushing my people for centuries. But we have to know what type of government and social conditions we must aim for after the revolution of the people. How we laughed at him ... I can remember one of the boys kidding him for being slightly off his head, telling Trotsky he had about as much chance of upsetting the Czar as a man catching the moon with his teeth.

Although Boisvert's tale cannot be authenticated, Trotsky was in North America in 1916 and was detained in Halifax, Nova Scotia, in 1917.

Inns, hotels, and stopping places adopted the personality of their host and the spirit of the community. The diversity of both in northern Ontario led to extremes. Accommodation could be fifty cents for 'the soft side of three feet of plank' or, as in a hostelry in Thunder Bay, the privilege of pitching a tent in the lobby as protection against the wind that blew through the cracks in the walls. On the other hand, there were instant millionaires to accommodate, and so, naturally, one of those millionaires opened an inn. In Haileybury, Arthur Ferland, a millionaire by virtue of his luck with a silver claim, opened the Matabanick Hotel. He offered his wealthy clientele the best in gleaming silver, crisp linens, fine china, and vintage wines, so they might feel at home while they contemplated their wealth.

From late in the eighteenth century when the first primitive roads were cut through southern Ontario, to early in the twentieth century when rail lines opened the north to a later breed of adventurers, wayside inns were an integral part of the picture. As one Englishman wrote, inns were 'the busy man's recreation, the idle man's business, the melancholy man's sanctuary, the stranger's welcome, the scholar's kindness, and the citizen's country.'

To Ontario's pioneers the wayside inn was indispensable. Frequently it was the building that marked the beginning of a new settlement – only later were the settlers able to erect a church, and so, as travellers soon learned, the sight of a church steeple in the distance usually signalled the presence of a tavern as well. Both buildings met the needs of people struggling to survive in a harsh new land.

These old inns provided a traveller with the only comfort he was likely to receive in the course of a hard day's journey, and so stops for refreshment were pleasant interludes that made travel bearable. With luck, the tired traveller would be welcomed with a warm fire, a cheerful host, and an obliging ostler to care for his horse. A good meal might – or might not – be forthcoming.

Both travellers and the community depended on inns, and as settlement progressed, these buildings came to play an ever more important role in the social history of the province. Above all they provided settlers with a chance to be free, if only for a little while, of the loneliness and the hardships with which most of them coped. William Shenstone, an eighteenth-century English poet, said it best:

Whoe'er has travelled life's dull round,
Where'er his stages may have been,
May sigh to think how oft he found
The warmest welcome – at an inn.

Recipes

These old recipes are presented for interest only;
they should not be used.

DARK BRANDY

1 gal. Alcohol.
4 gals. Whiskey.
1 oz. Spirit of Nitre.
1 oz. Tincture of Catachue.
5 drops Essence of Almonds.
1 qt. best French dark brandy.
Colored with burnt Sugar.

BEST AMERICAN GIN

5 gals. best Proof Whiskey.
½ oz. Sweet Spirits of Nitre.
25 to 40 drops Oil of Juniper.
½ gal. Best Hollands Gin.
The Oil of Juniper to be mixed with 1 pint of Alcohol, the whole to be well shaken together.

5 GALLONS RUM

5 gals. Proof Spirit.
1 oz. Spirits of Nitre.
⅛ oz. Oil of Anise, in half pint Alcohol.
¼ lb. W. Sugar, dissolved in hot water.
1 qt. best Rum.
Colored with burnt Sugar.

BEST PALE BRANDY

5 gals. Proof Whiskey.
2 gals. Water.
2 gals. Alcohol.
1 oz. Tincture of Kino.
1 oz. Acetic Ether.
½ drachm Benzoic Acid.
½ gal. best Pale French Brandy.
Colored with burnt Sugar.

PORT WINE

28 gals. of Cider.
9 gals. of Whiskey.
4 oz. of ground Cinamon
4 oz. of ground Cloves
3 oz. of ground Orange Peel
} Boiled and Strained.
4 oz. of ground Cochineal, boiled and mixed with 2 oz. of Carbonate of Potash.
15 lbs. White Sugar, dissolved in hot water.
If it is necessary, 2 oz. Ground Alum.

CHERRY BRANDY

For 1 gal. Whiskey.
¾ lb. Sugar dissolved in hot water.
10 drops Oil of Bitter Almonds in 1 oz. Alcohol.
Colored with burnt Sugar.

GIN

For each gal. of Whiskey put 5 to 10 drops of Oil of Juniper in 1 oz. of Alcohol the day before used, and about 1 oz. of White Sugar dissolved in hot water.

5 GALLONS OF BRANDY

1½ gals. Alcohol.
3¼ gals. Whiskey.
½ oz. Spirit of Nitre.
½ oz. Acetic Ether.
1 oz. Tincture of Kino.
1 qt. best pale French Brandy.
Colored with burnt Sugar.

5 GALLONS OF LEMON SYRUP

10 lbs. White Sugar, dissolved in one gal. of Water.
¼ oz. Oil of Lemon, with ½ pint Alcohol and 4 oz. Tartaric Acid, then add 4 gal. hot water.

10 GALLONS OF PEPPERMINT

5 gals. Whiskey, 5 gals. Water.
5 lbs. Sugar boiling in 1 qt Water.
1 oz. Oil of Peppermint in qt. Alcohol.
10 drops of Oil for each Gallon.
Colored with burnt Sugar.

GINGER WINE

4 oz. good Ginger in 1 qt. of Alcohol, let stand for six days. Take 4 gals. water and 1 lb. White Sugar dissolved in hot water. Colored with Cochineal boiled.

Acknowledgments

WHEN WE BEGAN our research for *Tavern in the Town* in 1983 we realized that it was impossible for us to follow every old stage-coach route in Ontario. We therefore wrote to every historical society and LACAC (Local Architectural Conservation Advisory Committee) in the province asking for help in locating the early inns in their area. We were delighted with their enthusiastic replies and with their attitude that history is meant to be shared. For the leads that they gave us we thank them and hope that in return we have been able to provide them with added information about the inns to which they directed us.

Some areas of the province are better represented than others. There are reasons for this: sometimes the buildings we found were in poor condition or radically altered, bearing little resemblance to the original structure; in some places there were no early hostelries remaining; in some instances we received no reply to our queries; and occasionally we could learn little or nothing of the building's history. In the end, we simply had to make choices.

It is impossible to thank individually the more than two hundred people who wrote to us. We followed up all their suggestions and in the process found other inns as well. But there were a few people who spent a great deal of time with us and to whom we wish to give special thanks:

In Maitland we were fortunate to meet historian Richard Dumbrille. When he heard of our project he promptly offered to drive us through his inviting village and assist us in our research. He is co-author, with Stephen Otto, of *Maitland, A Very Neat Village Indeed.*

We heard from the knowledgeable John Dunn of Almonte, who explained the importance of 'stopping places' in the Ottawa Valley. When we visited the valley he gave us an extensive tour and talked of legends and lore. Author Brenda Lee-Whiting of Deep River also gave freely of her time.

In Ottawa we received invaluable help from architectural photographer Hellmut Schade, producer of an extensive slide catalogue, *A Gateway to Canadian Architecture.*

Joyce Sowby of Toronto gave us access to the research for her MA thesis on the subject of Sir John A. Macdonald. This was of particular help to us in Kingston and led us to Macdonald's friendship with the memorable innkeeper Eliza Grimason.

Teresa Miceli, a student at York University and author of a paper on Toronto's Wheat Sheaf Tavern, generously provided us with her year's research on that colourful establishment – which remains today one of the city's favourite 'watering holes.'

Our friend Russell Cooper, Administrator of Black Creek Pioneer Village, shared with us research on the village's Halfway House that once stood by the Kingston Road.

Peter John Stokes, one of Canada's leading restoration architects, has the happy faculty of almost total recall when it comes to Ontario's historic buildings. He met with us, talked in general terms about old stage-coach inns, and gave us many helpful leads.

And from the mining town of Swastika, in the Cobalt region, Carolyn O'Neil wrote (with understandable asperity) of the tendency of many writers to ignore the fascinating history of Ontario's vast and intriguing northland. As she pointed out, the settlement of the north, although it took place primarily in this century, is as deserving of attention as is that of the south. We thank her for her knowledgeable assistance.

There are many who espouse the cause of historic preservation but few who go to the lengths that Stratford's valiant Jim Anderson did in 1981, when the nearby Fryfogel's Tavern appeared doomed. Anderson, of the Perth County Historical Board, attracted nation-wide attention by staging a sit-in atop the city hall. He camped there for days, but his efforts, unfortunately, did not produce the desired results. This splendid building, one that played a vital part in the development of Ontario, remains abandoned, its future uncertain. Jim Anderson ably assisted us in our research on inns in western Ontario.

As with our previous three books, much of our research was done in the Provincial Archives of Ontario. We are grateful to the archivists and staff there for their assistance. In Ottawa, the staff of the Public Archives of Canada were equally supportive.

Early journals formed an essential part of our research. Sometimes they were difficult to date and attribute but, in all cases but one, we were able to verify the authors and dates of these journals. However, the source of the poem on page 191 in Chapter Ten eluded us. Perhaps an answer to this omission will be provided by a reader who is familiar with it.

On the publication of this our fourth book we would like to thank our good friend Ian Montagnes of the University of Toronto Press. Nearly twenty years ago he sensed a growing interest in Ontario's historic buildings and encouraged us in our first efforts. To him we will always be grateful.

Selected Bibliography

Adam, Graeme Mercer. *Prominent Men of Canada.* Toronto 1892

Anderson, James. 'Fryfogel's Tavern.' Unpublished paper. 1978

Armstrong, Frederick H. *Toronto: The Place of Meeting.* Toronto 1983

Arnott, G.R., ed. 'Glengarry Life,' *Glengarry Historical Society.* 1976

Arthur, Eric. *Toronto, No Mean City.* Toronto 1964

Barnes, Michael. *Link with a Lonely Land.* Erin 1985

Berchem, Frederick R. *The Yonge Street Story, 1793–1860.* Toronto 1977

Berton, Pierre. *Flames across the Border.* Toronto 1981

– *The Invasion of Canada.* Toronto 1980

Bigelow, Timothy. *Journal of a Tour to Niagara Falls.* Boston 1876

Bird, Isabella Lucy Bishop. *The Englishwoman in America.* London 1856

Bond, Courtney C.J. *The Ottawa Country.* Ottawa 1968

– *City on the Ottawa.* Ottawa 1964

Boyer, Robert J. *Early Exploration and Surveying of Muskoka District.* Bracebridge 1979

– *Footpaths to Freeways.* Toronto 1984

Brown, Ron. *Ghost Towns of Ontario.* Langley, B.C. 1978

Byers, Mary, and Margaret McBurney. *The Governor's Road.* Toronto 1982

Byers, Mary, Jan Kennedy, Margaret McBurney and the Junior League of Ontario. *Rural Roots.* Toronto 1976

The Canadian Biographical Dictionary and Portrait Gallery of Eminent and Self-Made Men, Ontario vol. Toronto 1880

Canadian Broadcasting Corporation. *Coaches and Inns.* Historic Road Series. 10 May – 28 June 1937

Caniff, William. *The Medical Profession in Upper Canada.* Toronto 1894

Careless, J.M.S., ed. *The Pre-Confederation Premiers: Government Leaders 1841–1867.* Toronto 1980

Careless, J.M.S. 'Letters from Thos. Talbot to J.B. Robinson.' *Ontario History,* vol. 49. 1957

Carnochan, Janet. *History of Niagara.* Toronto 1914

Chadwick, Edward M. *Ontarian Families.* Toronto 1894–8

Coleman, Thelma. *The Canada Company.* Supplement by James Anderson. County of Perth 1978

Coombe, Geraldine. *Muskoka Past and Present.* Toronto 1976

Crawford, Michael. *1837: Mackenzie.* Jackdaw No. 17. Toronto 1967

Cruickshank, Tom, and Peter John Stokes. *The Settler's Dream.* Picton 1984.

Daum, Elizabeth. 'Victorian Charm for Today's Illustrious Guests.' *Key to Kingston,* Oct. 1982

Davies, Blodwin. *Storied York: Toronto Old and New.* Toronto 1931

de Visser, John. *Upper Canada Village.* Toronto 1981

Dickens, Charles. *American Notes for General Circulation.* London 1842

Dufferin and Ava, Marchioness of. *My Canadian Journal.* London 1891
Dumbrille, Dorothy. *Braggart in My Step.* Toronto 1956
– *Up and Down the Glens.* Toronto 1954
Earle, Alice Morse. *Stage-Coach and Tavern Days.* New York 1901
Eff, Ellen H. *Hamlet on the Otter.* Tillsonburg 1964
Farewell, John E. *County of Ontario.* Whitby 1907
Fazakas, Ray. *The Donnelly Album.* Toronto 1977
Finnegan, Joan. *Giants of Canada's Ottawa Valley.* Burnstown 1981
– *Some of the Stories I Told You Were True.* Ottawa: Deneau 1981
Firth, Edith G. *The Town of York 1793–1815.* Toronto 1962
Fitzgerald, Doris M. *Thornhill 1793–1963: The History of an Ontario Village.* Thornhill 1964
Fraser, Alexander. *A History of Ontario.* Toronto 1907
– *The Last Laird of MacNab.* Toronto 1899
French, T.P. *Information for Intending Settlers on the Ottawa and Opeongo Road and Its Vicinity.* Ottawa 1857
Garland, M.A., and J.J. Talmane. 'Pioneer Drinking Habits, etc.' *Ontario Historical Society Papers and Records*, vol. 27. 1931
Gateman, Laura M. *The History of the Township of Brant.* Brant Township 1979
Gillham, Elizabeth McClure. *Early Settlements of King Township, Ontario.* King City 1975
Godfrey, Charles M. *Medicine for Ontario.* Belleville 1979
Gosse, Rose Gourlay. *I Remember Glengarry.* Glengarry 1978
Greenhill, Ralph, and Thomas D. Mahoney. *Niagara.* Toronto 1969
Greenhill, Ralph, Kenneth MacPherson, and Douglas Richardson. *Ontario Towns.* Toronto 1974
Greenwood, Michelle, and the North Pickering Community Development Project. *Historical Complexities of Pickering, Markham, Scarborough, Uxbridge.* Pickering 1973
Groves, Abraham. 'The First Elective Appendectomy?' *Canadian Journal of Surgery*, July. 1961
Guillet, Edwin C. *The Story of Canadian Roads.* Toronto 1966
– *Pioneer Life in the County of York.* Toronto 1946
– *Pioneer Inns and Taverns.* 5 vols. Toronto 1954–62
Gwyn, Sandra. *The Private Capital.* Toronto 1984
Haig, Robert. *City of the Big Ears.* Ottawa 1970
Harris, Edith Norine. *Stories of My Canadian Pioneers.* Vancouver 1979
Hart, Patricia. *Pioneering in North York.* Toronto 1968
Head, George. *Forest Scenes and Incidents in the Wilds of North America.* London 1829
Heriot, George. *Travels in the Canadas.* London 1807
Higgins, W.H. *The Life and Times of Joseph Gould.* Toronto 1972
Hinds, A. Leone. *Pioneer Inns and Taverns of Guelph.* Erin n.d.
History of Derby Township 1839–1972. Owen Sound 1972
Hykel, B., and C. Benn. *Thomas Montgomery: Portrait of a Nineteenth Century Businessman.* Etobicoke 1980
Jackes, Lyman B. *Tales of North Toronto.* Toronto 1948
James, C.C. *Early History of the Town of Amherstburg.* Amherstburg 1909
Jameson, Anna. *Winter Studies and Summer Rambles in Canada.* London 1838
Johnson, Dana H. *Reports on Selected Buildings in Kingston.* Ottawa 1977
Johnson, Leo A. *History of Guelph.* Guelph 1977
Kalman, Harold. *Exploring Ottawa.* Toronto 1983
Kennedy, Clyde C. *The Upper Ottawa Valley.* Pembroke 1970
Kingston, W.H.G. *Western Wanderings, or a Pleasure Tour through the Canadas.* London 1856
Lake, Ernest Lloyd. *Pioneer Reminiscences of the Upper Ottawa Valley.* Ottawa 1966
Lauraston, Victor. *Romantic Kent.* Chatham 1952
Leavitt, Thadeus William Henry. *The History of Leeds and Grenville.* Belleville 1972
Lee-Whiting, Brenda. 'Auction Sale at a Stopping Place.' *Canadian Collector.* vol. 16, no. 2, March / April 1981
– *Harvest of Stones.* Toronto 1985
– 'The Opeongo Road – an Early Colonization Scheme.' *Canadian Geographical Journal,*

March 1967
Legget, Robert Ferguson. *Rideau Waterway*. 2nd ed. Toronto 1986
Leitch, Adelaide. *Into the High Country*. Dufferin County 1975
Lett, William Pittman. *Recollections of Bytown and Its Old Inhabitants*. Ottawa 1874
Lizars, Robina, and Kathleen Lizars. *In the Days of the Canada Company*. Toronto 1896
Mactaggart, John. *Three Years in Canada*. London 1829
Marryat, Frederick. *A Diary in America, with Remarks on Its Institutions*. London 1839
Marsh, E.L. *A History of Grey County*. Owen Sound 1931
Martyn, Lucy Booth. *Aristocratic Toronto*. Toronto 1980
Mason, D.H.C. *Muskoka: The First Islanders and After*. Bracebridge 1974
Masters, Donald Campbell. *The Rise of Toronto, 1850–1890*. Toronto 1947
Mathews, Hazel C. *Oakville and the Sixteen*. Toronto 1953
McBurney, Margaret, and Mary Byers. *Homesteads*. Toronto 1979
McDonald, John. *Emigration to Canada: Narrative of a Voyage to Quebec*. Edinburgh 1823
McGill, Jean S. *A Pioneer History of the County of Lanark*. Bewdley 1968
McKay, William A. *The Pickering Story*. Pickering 1961
McKenzie, Ruth. *Leeds and Grenville: Their First 200 Years*. Toronto 1967
McLean, Mrs Erven, and Beatrice R. McLean. *Greenwood through the Years*. Greenwood 1960
Miceli, Teresa. 'The Wheat Sheaf Tavern.' Unpublished paper. 1987
Mika, Nick. *Mosaic of Kingston*. Belleville 1969
Mika, Nick, and Helma Mika. *Bytown: The Early Days of Ottawa*. Belleville 1982
– *Ontario of Yesterday*. Belleville 1971
Miller, Hanson Orlo. *Twenty Mortal Murders*. Toronto 1978
– *The Donnellys Must Die*. Toronto 1962
Miller, Robert A. *The Ontario Village of Brougham*. Brougham 1973
Mitchell, John. *The Settlement of York County*. Toronto 1952
Moodie, Susanna. *Roughing It in the Bush*. 1852. Reprint. Toronto 1962
Moore, F.H. *The Story of Uxbridge*. Uxbridge 1927
Morrison, Neil F. *Garden Gateway to Canada*. Toronto 1954
Mulvany, C. Pelham. *Toronto: Past and Present until 1882*. Toronto 1884
Murray, Florence B. *Muskoka and Haliburton, 1615–1875: A Collection of Documents*. Toronto 1963
Muskoka and Parry Sound. Toronto 1879
Myers, Jan. *The Great Canadian Road*. Toronto 1977
Nalon, John. *A History of Gananoque*. Gananoque 1985
National Capital Commission. *Lower Town Ottawa*. vol. 2, Ottawa 1981
– *The Mile of History*. Ottawa 1981
– *A Guide to Lowertown Ottawa*. Ottawa 1981
Need, Thomas. *Six Years in the Bush*. London 1838
O'Leary, Peter. *Travels and Experiences in Canada, the Red River Territory, and the United States*. London 1877
O'Neil, Carolyn. 'The Growth and Development of the Temiskaming and Northern Ontario Railway.' Unpublished paper. 1979
Ontario Department of Planning and Development. *Rouge, Dufferin, Highland and Petticoat Valley Conservation Report*. 1956
Otto, Stephen A., and Richard M. Dumbrille. *Maitland: 'A Very Neat Village Indeed.'* Erin 1985
Peacock, Suzanne, and David Peacock. *Old Oakville*. Willowdale 1979
Popham, Robert E., and the Addiction Research Foundation. *Working Papers on the Tavern*. Toronto 1976
Price, Mrs Carl, and Clyde C. Kennedy. *Notes on the History of Renfrew County*. Pembroke 1961
Reeve, Harold. *Former Taverns in the Township of Hope*. Port Hope 1962
Rhys, Horton. *A Theatrical Trip for a Wager! through Canada and the United States*. London 1861
Robertson, John Ross. *Landmarks of Toronto*. 6 vols. Toronto 1894–1914
Robertson, Norman. *History of the County of Bruce, 1845–1906*. Toronto 1906
Rolling, Gladys M. *East Gwillimbury in the 19th Century*. East Gwillimbury 1967

Rose, George. *The Great Country, or Impressions of America.* London 1868
Roy, James A. *Kingston: The King's Town.* Toronto 1952
Scadding, Henry. *Toronto of Old.* Toronto 1873
Scott, James. *The Settlement of Huron County.* Toronto 1966
Shanley, Walter, and Francis Shanley. *Daylight through the Mountain.* Montreal 1957
Shirreff, Patrick. *A Tour through North America.* Edinburgh 1835
Sinclair, David, and Germaine Warkentin, eds. *The New World Journal of Alexander Graham Dunlop.* Toronto 1976
Skelton, Isabel. *A Man Austere: William Bell, Parson and Pioneer.* Toronto 1947
Stewart, John W. *Heritage Kingston.* Kingston 1973
Stokes, Peter John. *Old Niagara on the Lake.* 1971. Reprint. Toronto 1977
– *Early Architecture of the Town and Township of Niagara.* Niagara Foundation 1967
Streetsville Historical Society. *Inns and Hotels in Streetsville.* 1977
Strickland, Samuel. *Twenty-Seven Years in Canada West.* 1853. Reprint. Edmonton 1970
Tatley, Richard S. *Industries and Industrialists of Merrickville.* Ottawa 1979
Thumm, Eileen, and Silver Wyatt. *Kingston Walking Book.* Kingston 1980
Todd, Eleanor. *Burrs and Blackberries from Goodwood.* Goodwood 1980
Trollope, Anthony. *North America.* New York 1862
Trollope, Frances. *Domestic Manners of the Americans.* London 1832
Tucker, Albert. *Steam into Wilderness.* Toronto 1978
'Upper Canada Village.' *Canadian Geographical Journal,* vol. 62, June 1961
Utting, Gerald. *Toronto the Good: An Album of Colonial Hogtown.* Toronto 1978
West, Bruce. *Toronto.* Toronto 1967
Wild, Roland. *MacNab: The Last Laird.* London 1938
Wilke, D. *Sketches of a Summer Trip to New York and the Canadas.* Edinburgh 1837
Winearls, Joan, and Isobel Ganton. *Mapping Toronto's First Century, 1787–1884.* Toronto 1984
Wood, William R. *Past Years in Pickering.* Toronto 1911
Woodhouse, T. Roy. *Ancaster's Heritage.* Ancaster 1973
Woods, Shirley E., Jr. *Ottawa: The Capital of Canada.* Toronto 1980
– *The Molson Saga.* Toronto 1983

Picture Credits

All photographs not specifically credited here are by Hugh Robertson.

5 London District Tavern Regulations. Archives of Ontario, J.M. Snyder Collection

7 St Andrew's Society. *Daily Union*, Ottawa, 27 November 1865

21 Phrenology. *Brockville Recorder*, 8 October 1846

24 Provincial House. Archives of Ontario, *Grand Trunk Railway Gazetteer*, 1862–3, p. 289

32 Lumbering Timber Raft. Picture Collection, Archives of Ontario

34 The MacNab, by Sir Henry Raeburn; mezzotint. C–11069, Public Archives of Canada

36 The Leckie Hotel, Burnstown. Joan Finnigan Collection

42 *Northern Advocate*, Parry Sound, 19 April 1870

46 Byward Market before the coming of the automobile. Picture Collection, Archives of Ontario

55 C–6225, Public Archives of Canada

61 *Upper Canada Herald*, 9 August 1825

75 *Cobourg Star*, 19 January 1853

77 *Colonial Advocate*, 16 July 1829

85 Half Way House. Picture Collection, City of Toronto Archives

90 Jordan's York Hotel. *Historical Prints of Old Toronto*, Fred W. Halls Paper Co. Ltd, copy from Metropolitan Toronto Library

91 Red Lion Hotel. Metropolitan Toronto Library

92 The Sun Tavern, J. Ross Robertson Collection, Metropolitan Toronto Library

93 C–98774, Public Archives of Canada

94 The Wellington Hotel. J. Ross Robertson Collection, Metropolitan Toronto Library

95 Russell's Hotel. J. Ross Robertson Collection, Metropolitan Toronto Library

96 City of Toronto Archives

106 (top) The Tecumseh Wigwam. Metropolitan Toronto Library

106 (bottom) O'Halloran's Hotel, pen and ink sketch by B. Gloster. Metropolitan Toronto Library

107 Lindsey's *Life of Mackenzie*, Adrian Sharp

108 Jolly Miller Tavern, pen and ink drawing by B. Gloster. Metropolitan Toronto Library

109 Golden Lion Hotel, pen and ink drawing by B. Gloster. Metropolitan Toronto Library

110 The Bird in Hand, pen and ink drawing by B. Gloster. Metropolitan Toronto Library

111 Stage Coach of John Thompson, Richmond Hill. Picture Collection, Archives of Ontario

135 *Gore Gazette*, 31 May 1828

137 Elgin House, Dundas. Picture Collection, Archives of Ontario

139 C–98836, Public Archives of Canada

142 Western Hotel, London. In UWO collection, London, Ontario; copy from Archives of Ontario

151 Chepstow Hotel. Picture Collection, Archives of Ontario

155 Commercial Hotel, Priceville. Picture Collection, Archives of Ontario

161 *Sun*, Orangeville, 15 February 1866

170 C–115040, Public Archives of Canada

176 Sketch of Tiger Dunlop. Picture Collection, Archives of Ontario

178 Colonel Samuel Strickland. Picture Collection, Archives of Ontario

183 Royal Livery Stable. *Huron County Directory*, 1869–70, Archives of Ontario

192 C–98756, Public Archives of Canada

193 C–23674, Public Archives of Canada

197 Dancing School. *Niagara Spectator*, 28 January 1819, Archives of Ontario

205 For Sale. *Niagara Spectator*, 29 July 1819, Archives of Ontario

212 The Talbot Homestead. Picture Collection, Archives of Ontario

215 Old Sparta Stage. Picture Collection, Archives of Ontario

217 *True Teller*. Archives of Ontario

219 "Oh! Hexellent!" C–98824, Public Archives of Canada

220 Campbell's Inn. Picture Collection, Archives of Ontario

224 *Amherstburg Courier*, 5 July 1851

230 *Algoma Pioneer*, 24 April 1885

232 Anna Jameson. Copy, Archives of Ontario

234 Road between Swastika and Kirkland Lake. Picture Collection, Archives of Ontario

235 Lucky Cross Mine, Swastika. Picture Collection, Archives of Ontario

236 Swastika: The Station. Picture Collection, Archives of Ontario

Index